Interviews in
Qualitative Research

Interviews in Qualitative Research

Nigel King
Christine Horrocks

Los Angeles | London | New Delhi
Singapore | Washington DC

First published 2010

SAGE Publications Ltd
1 Oliver's Yard
55 City Road
London EC1Y 1SP

SAGE Publications Inc.
2455 Teller Road
Thousand Oaks, California 91320

SAGE Publications India Pvt Ltd
B 1/I 1 Mohan Cooperative Industrial Area
Mathura Road, New Delhi 110 044
India

SAGE Publications Asia-Pacific Pte Ltd
33 Pekin Street #02-01
Far East Square
Singapore 048763

Library of Congress Control Number: 2009930311

British Library Cataloguing in Publication data

A catalogue record for this book is available from
the British Library

ISBN 978-1-4129-1256-3
ISBN 978-1-4129-1257-0

Typeset by C&M Digitals (P) Ltd, Chennai, India
Printed by MPG Books Group, Bodmin, Cornwall
Printed on paper from sustainable resources

Contents

Boxes, Figures and Tables

Boxes

Figures

Tables

ONE

Introduction

Defining the qualitative research interview

Turn on your television and flick through the channels; there is a good chance you will see someone being interviewed. It may be a politician facing a grilling from a tough political journalist, a celebrity answering flattering questions about her latest film, book or exercise DVD, a football manager explaining how his team let a two-goal lead slip. Perhaps it is a fictionalised representation of a canny detective extracting the truth from her prime suspect, or a psychiatrist diagnosing the nature of a patient's neurosis. And interviewing may well have impinged directly on your own life, be it in the form of a job interview, or someone with a clipboard questioning you on the street about your preferences for cosmetic products. It is no exaggeration to state that interviews have become a ubiquitous aspect of contemporary life, to such an extent that Gubrium and Holstein (2002) claim we are now members of an 'interview society'.

This book is about a particular form of the phenomenon: the qualitative research interview. Undoubtedly, interviewing is the most commonly used method of data collection in qualitative research, and this familiarity has advantages for us as researchers. As the first author has stated elsewhere (King, 2004a), when you tell a potential participant that you want to interview them, they will usually have a pretty good idea of the kind of encounter they are agreeing to. However, this familiarity also carries risks. The qualitative research interview differs in important ways from other forms to which people (including inexperienced researchers) will be more accustomed. Failure to recognise the special requirements of a qualitative research interview can result in the elicitation of data that have serious limitations for a study. For example, the interview may be shallow and superficial if the interviewer is too deferential to the interviewee, or the participant may clam up if she feels the interviewer is too aggressive. In this book we will spell out in considerable detail the distinctive characteristics of qualitative research interviews, also drawing attention to important variations within the method. To start you thinking about this, consider the comparison between qualitative research interviews and three other types of interview, shown in Table 1.1.

Of course, we have had to generalise in this table about qualitative research interviews (and indeed the other forms), but it does help to highlight key

Table 1.1 Characteristics of different types of interview

INTERVIEW CHARACTERISTICS	TYPE OF INTERVIEW			
	Investigative journalistic interview (e.g. with politician)	Celebrity interview	Job interview	Qualitative research interview
Style of questioning	Interrogative and confrontational	Deferential, with the interviewer aiming to coax the celebrity into sharing their experiences	May be challenging at times, but also seeks to enable interviewee to present their strengths effectively	Emphasises open-ended, non-leading questions, focuses on personal experience, seeks to build rapport with interviewee
Power dynamics	Potentially high stakes for interviewee in terms of personal and party reputation Especially in broadcast media, interviewer needs to demonstrate ability to get beyond the interviewee's defences	Interviewee likely to have high level of control; may even have given prior approval of questions Can be much at stake for interviewer in terms of keeping celebrity happy, so they may be cooperative in future	Power very much in hands of interviewers, bounded in its exercise by organisational policies and legislation (e.g. regarding equal opportunities)	As the person asking the questions, interviewer may be seen to be in the more powerful position. However, the balance is often complicated by factors such as age, gender and status of the two parties. Also, the interviewee has the explicit right to withdraw at any time with no further consequences for them Qualitative interviewers usually try to minimise any power imbalance between the parties
Visibility	Highly public and visible. Any word out of place could be in tomorrow's headlines	Also highly public – indeed, maintaining the celebrity's visibility is their key reason for participation	Details of what happens are confidential to the interview panel, but outcome (success or failure to get the job) will be public knowledge	High level of confidentiality and anonymity expected in great majority of cases

features of the method. We would suggest that the following are defining characteristics of the generic qualitative interview:

- It is flexible and open-ended in style.
- It tends to focus on people's actual experiences more than general beliefs and opinions.
- The relationship between interviewer and interviewee is crucial to the method.

Of course, how these characteristics translate into interview practice will differ in different types of qualitative study, as will their relative importance. We will discuss such differences in more detail in the rest of this book.

Aims and structure of this book

In this book we aim to provide you with comprehensive coverage of what you need to know to conduct a research study using qualitative interviews. Our emphasis is strongly practical; we will take you through the processes of designing and carrying out qualitative interview research in detail, using numerous examples based on our own and others' projects. At the same time, we believe that even the most applied research needs to have a strong theoretical and philosophical grounding, and we will cover these aspects of qualitative interviewing too. Each chapter ends with an annotated list of recommended reading. In terms of discipline, our focus is broad, drawing on literature from across the social sciences in such diverse topic areas as health, education, criminal justice, business and management, and others. As to level, we see this book as being particularly useful for postgraduate and advanced undergraduate students who may be carrying out substantial research projects utilising qualitative interviews. We also believe it should be helpful for more experienced researchers who are relatively new to qualitative interviewing, or who need updating in specific areas – for instance, the possibilities offered by online interviewing (see Chapter 6).

We have structured the book to take you sequentially through all steps involved in carrying out a qualitative interview study. The chapters are, though, relatively self-contained so you can dip into areas that especially interest you. Chapter 2 introduces the philosophical issues which should inform your choice of approach, to ensure you have a firm foundation to the methodological decisions you make in the course of developing a project. The next two chapters move on to the practicalities of designing and carrying out a qualitative interview study. Our goal here is to be as specific and concrete as possible in the advice we give, rather than staying at the level of general principles. We have done this by using real-world examples and also by considering in some depth aspects of the research process that are often addressed sketchily (if at all) in methodological textbooks. These include such things as the pros and cons of different ways of contacting potential participants, the choice and effective use of recording equipment, and issues around your self-presentation in varying interview settings.

The next two chapters address variations from the conventional format of the individual face-to-face interview. In Chapter 5 we look at the challenges involved in group interviews, concentrating mainly on focus groups, but also highlighting other less well-known forms. In Chapter 6 we consider the use of 'remote' interview techniques in qualitative research – telephone and online interviewing. The former are quite widely used and yet have received very little attention in the methodological literature. The latter is a burgeoning field that no examination of qualitative methods can afford to ignore. It includes both synchronous ('real time', such as Instant Messaging) and asynchronous (e.g. e-mail) forms and can be either one-to-one or group in design.

Next we move on to address two key areas that any qualitative project needs to consider: ethics (Chapter 7) and reflexivity (Chapter 8). Regarding ethics, we cover the philosophical bases of ethical thinking in relation to social scientific research, explain the role and function of ethical review boards, and offer guidance on how best to tackle specific ethical issues in the design and execution of qualitative interviews. Similarly, in the chapter on reflexivity, we combine an examination of the theory and philosophy underlying the concept with pragmatic suggestions for how to incorporate a reflexive approach into your own work. Considerations of ethics and reflexivity do not only apply to research design and data collection, they must also be borne in mind in relation to what you do with your data. While this book does not seek to be a comprehensive text on qualitative data analysis, in Chapter 9 we have provided a thorough introduction to the principles and practice of thematic analysis, particularly for those relatively new to the field. We also briefly cover some of the main variants to this style of analysis and provide pointers to further information on different analytic approaches.

Chapters 10 and 11 differ from earlier ones as each focuses on a particular philosophical and methodological tradition in some depth, and considers the place of interviewing within them: Chapter 10 covers *phenomenology* and Chapter 11 *narrative*. If you are new to these traditions, we would suggest you read the earlier chapters first. This should allow you to get a good grasp of some of the generic principles and practices in qualitative interviewing before getting to grips with how these apply and might be adapted when taking a specific theoretical approach. At the heart of each of these chapters is an examination of what it means to use a phenomenological or narrative interview method, but we also introduce the philosophical and theoretical backgrounds to each, and give an overview of some of the main ways of analysing interview data from these perspectives.

Over many years of conducting qualitative interviews in varied styles and settings, it has been our experience that it is a challenging but ultimately very rewarding way of doing research. Through close and sustained engagement with participants, not only can you gain insight into the topics you are studying, you can also learn about yourself. We hope this book helps you make the most of this endeavour.

Recommended reading

Gubrium, J.F. and Holstein, J.A. (2002) From the individual interview to the interview society, in J.F. Gubrium and J.A. Holstein (eds), *Handbook of Interview Research: Context and Methods.* Thousand Oaks, CA: Sage.
A critical examination of the rise of the interview in contemporary society. Gubrium and Holstein argue that the interview not only enables us to inquire about our social world, but it is actually a significant constituent of the kind of society we live in.

TWO

Philosophical Assumptions

Qualitative interviewing has become a prominent research method in the social sciences. Face-to-face conversation is an everyday occurrence and this has probably resulted in an assumption that interviewing is a preferred option because the researcher feels most at ease with this technique. In well-executed research, preferences are not the issue, rather the focus is on 'justification'. To what extent can the methodology and methods adopted be justified in relation to the purpose/rationale for the research? This question brings to the fore a host of issues that need to be carefully worked through, examining our philosophical assumptions about reality and associated theoretical perspective(s). With this in mind, this chapter will explore the epistemological and ontological thinking behind qualitative research and qualitative interviewing. We will concentrate on the following philosophical issues as they have direct relevance for qualitative interviewing:

- methodology and methods
- different approaches to research
- theoretical groundwork and making connections
- developing a rationale
- epistemology and qualitative interviewing

Methodology and methods

Having supervised numerous undergraduate and postgraduate student research projects, we can say with confidence that the issue of methodology and methods is always something that causes confusion. The two are not the same. Methods are easily explained; they are the techniques or procedures we use to collect and analyse data. In qualitative research, interviewing is one of the most frequently used methods when generating data. Other methods could include, for example, observation, diaries, the generation of visual images or other forms of text. In this book we will cover using qualitative interviewing as a 'method' – a means of collecting and analysing data. Having said this, we will also aim to make evident how methods are informed by *methodology*. Methodology, as the word suggests, relates to a process where the design of the research and choice of particular methods, and their justification in relation to the research project, are made evident. As such, methodology requires more from the researcher than just preference or intuitive appeal to justify the choice of particular techniques of data collection and analysis. It becomes necessary to outline the philosophical and theoretical positions informing the research process. Thus there is a requirement to outline assumptions embedded in the methodology adopted. Often you will find methodology explained as an 'approach' or 'perspective' that has within it implicit and explicit expectations about how research is undertaken.

Different approaches to research

Two paradigms: qualitative and quantitative

Holliday (2002) refers to two 'paradigms' in research, suggesting that the qualitative and quantitative paradigms represent very different ways of thinking about the world. It is not our intention to become overly embroiled in the qualitative *versus* quantitative debate. However, it is fairly standard to begin any conversation about qualitative research by saying what it is *not* in relation to quantitative research. While this seems a useful place to begin, it can create unhelpful prohibitions resulting in novice researchers feeling that they are required to 'choose' a side. You're either qualitative or quantitative. We are both psychologists and all too familiar with the assumption that because we employ qualitative methods in our research, and have developed a certain level of expertise, it is thought that we either disapprove of or see no merit in quantitative approaches. This assumption is inaccurate in that we have used, and will continue to use, some quantitative methods if this enables us a route to the required knowledge in a particular project.

Quantitative research is concerned with measurement, precisely and accurately capturing aspects of the social world that are then expressed in numbers – percentages, probability values, variance ratios, etc. Measurement, a term loosely employed here, is approached differently by qualitative researchers. The aim is still to capture aspects of the social world but this is done in numerous ways that do not rely on numbers as the unit of analysis. Using the term 'qualitative interviewing' situates the methodology and method deliberately within the qualitative domain where a broad and holistic approach is taken to the study of social phenomena.

Temptingly, Kvale (1996: 1) says that: 'If you want to know how people understand their world and their life, why not talk to them?' If only life were so simple when embarking on a research project. As Kvale suggests, in order to use the interview as a 'construction site of knowledge', the researcher is required to develop a rationale that is methodologically sound. Hence, we cannot emphasise enough the importance of this phase of the research. A newly appointed PhD student, who had recently been asked to read up on methodology, returned saying: 'This is the crux of everything, I can't progress until I understand more of this!' We would wholeheartedly agree with this evaluation. Thus, in this section, the differing paradigms of qualitative and quantitative research will be compared and discussed with a view to revealing a process that illuminates an often bewildering methodological journey.

Epistemology

A concise definition of epistemology is the philosophical theory of knowledge. Of major importance is the issue of what counts as knowledge and social scientists are often preoccupied with attempting to formulate sufficient criteria for evaluating knowledge statements – what it is we can claim to know. Unfortunately, differences between qualitative and quantitative research often become drawn as fervently oppositional rather than merely rooted in different understandings around what we *can know*, and what we might *want to know*, as researchers. If we take the idea of *knowing* as the basis for elaborating on the differences between qualitative and quantitative research, we can hopefully make clear the fundamental methodological issues that underpin the justification for a specific approach. Our rationale for the choice of methods becomes less idiosyncratic (something we will return to later) and more complex when we ask knowledge-based questions about specific issues and phenomena. This, then, promotes consideration of what might be a reliable route to such knowledge. Therefore *epistemology*, how we know what we know, a means of establishing what counts as knowledge, is central in any methodological approach. Marshall and Rossman (2006) use the term 'epistemological integrity' when referring to the connections between the nature of the research, overall strategy, research questions, design and methods. Developing such integrity is not always easy and involves thinking through the values and ideals, principles and rules by which the phenomena under investigation can be known.

Ontology

Ontology is likely to be an unfamiliar term to those new to social research and is seldom unproblematic for others who might consider themselves seasoned researchers. It should be said that ontological and epistemological issues often arise together, resulting in a somewhat confusing representation. Blaikie (1993: 6) offers a 'root definition' of ontology: the 'science or study of *being*' (our emphasis). We are not sure that this takes us much further in our endeavours to unravel methodological approaches. However, he goes on to say that ontology means 'the claims or assumptions that a particular approach to social enquiry makes about the nature of social reality' (1993: 6). There are those who would say that, strictly speaking, we should stay with ontology as the study of 'being' (e.g. see Crotty, 2006) where the emphasis is on the theory of existence. Nevertheless, for our purposes, Blaikie's pragmatic view provides us with a clear indication of why we need a philosophical perspective for our methodology. Without a perspective on the nature of social reality – how people might exist in the world – it would be impossible to consider what might count as relevant knowledge in the research process. For example, if we assume that people's behaviour – their way of being in the world – is brought about by their interactions in social situations, our view of social reality is very different from our belief that genetic inheritance explains behaviour. These are two very different ontological approaches regarding the theory of existence. One approach relates to social practices and people as social actors; the other is biological, suggesting that what 'drives' our being in the world is inherited and located within the individual.

Ontological positions are often described primarily as 'realist' or 'relativist'. Put somewhat simply, a *realist* ontology subscribes to the view that the real world is out there and exists independently from us. The world is made up of objects and structures that have identifiable cause and effect relationships. Indeed, the natural sciences (e.g. chemistry, physics, biology) are all broadly founded upon a realist ontology. Quantitative, experimental methods in social research are also based upon the belief that 'real' elements of our existence can be uncovered using appropriate methods of data collection and analysis. For example, social researchers have used twin studies to investigate criminal behaviour and the impact of genetic inheritance (Walters, 2006). *Relativist* ontology rejects such direct explanations, maintaining that the world is far more unstructured and diverse. Our understandings and experiences are relative to our specific cultural and social frames of reference, being open to a range of interpretations. Within relativism, society is not viewed as a pre-existent 'real' entity with objects and structures but rather is the product of people engaging with one another. Therefore relativism is more consistent with the social practices and interactive explanation of how people exist and live in their world. Existence is therefore explained differently within these two approaches and, as such, the data that would need to be collected to investigate these different versions of reality are not the same.

There are, however, variations that blur the somewhat crude realist/relativist distinction. Offering a version of experience and existence that only takes account of people as social actors (relativism) with no recognition of the constraining impact of social structures has been questioned (see Willig, 1999b). Similarly, conceiving the person as a mere automaton subject to social or biological mechanisms that then determine behaviour (naïve realism) has also been treated with sceptism (Bhaskar, 1991). *Critical realism* is a perspective that retains a core element of ontological realism, whereby behaviour and experience are seen to be 'generated by' underlying structures such as biological, economic or social structures. These structures or mechanisms do not directly determine people's actions; instead, structures have tendencies that may impact on our lives. For example, social structures can create inequalities that have the potential to influence our existence. Bill Jordan (2004: 3), when exploring the transformation of collective life in modern society, gives a very candid account of how structural inequality with regard to gender and education in the 1950s impacted upon his family life:

> My own marriage was to the daughter of close family friends, and the commitment to it made before I went to university. My wife subscribed to the new ethos of autonomy for women, but had none of the advantages of education or opportunities of

a profession. We had several children in quick succession, and she justifiably felt excluded from the exciting public life which I enjoyed. I became the inept partner to a resentful, highly competent person trapped in domesticity.

Social structures are seen to be located outside the individual's control; the sexual division (social structure) of labour inherent at the time had consequences that cannot be disregarded when trying to understand both Bill's and his wife's experience. A critical realist ontology would take account of such structures when attempting to make sense of social reality. Yet, while recognising the 'real' potentiality of mechanisms and structures, critical realism does not propose 'hard' determinism. People can transform their lives, having insight into their own contextually located existence.

Generally speaking, quantitative research subscribes to a realist ontology with qualitative research having its foundations in more critical realist and relativist approaches. Therefore epistemological questions around what represents knowledge within a particular ontological view expose the connectedness of research. By this we refer to how theory and philosophical understandings impact on what we believe can be known and these beliefs and understandings then influence how we gather and make sense of information. For example, if we believe that genetic inheritance determines behaviour, we would not use qualitative interviews to investigate this explanation. Conversations and words do not provide the kind of data that would be required to explore the genetic transmission of behaviour. However, if we subscribe to a social and interactive explanation for behaviour, then speaking with people in order to explore their social experiences would be consistent with our ontological position. Thus research is connected – our ontological beliefs and understandings impact upon what counts as knowledge. Ontology, epistemology and methodology and methods are all connected and cannot be viewed in isolation.

Theoretical groundwork and making connections

Supporting what we have already said, Williams (1998) makes the point, when discussing various methodologies, that the differences between quantitative and qualitative approaches are not wholly technical matters. Instead, he suggests that differences result from particular philosophical and theoretical traditions. Theory guides us in research; it can sometimes help to define the problem, offer insight and show us possible solutions. Just imagine, as a student, you ask one of your lecturers how to write a good essay. The lecturer could begin by explaining in detail the overarching learning outcomes of the course and how these link to pedagogical issues in higher education. This insight might enable you to understand the broad aims of the course and how these are exemplified in different forms of assessment that require certain strategies. You might argue that a simple set of pointers would have sufficed and taken much less time. Then again, you might think that now you know how things work, you have an understanding of how things fit together and can put this into practice. In research, this theoretical understanding of how things fit together is fundamental to the research process.

Interpretivism

Qualitative approaches are generally, but not always (see Holliday, 2002), founded upon theoretical perspectives rooted in *interpretivism* and are variously described as hermeneutics, phenomenology, ethnography, discursive, interactionist – to list only a few. Each of these approaches to qualitative research has distinct features, many of which we will expand upon in later chapters in relation to qualitative interviewing. The point being made here is that within the social sciences the term 'interpretative' is quite broad but can be encapsulated in concerns around how the social world is experienced and understood. Interpretative research is generally *idiographic*, which literally means describing aspects of the social world by offering a detailed account of specific social settings, processes or relationships. The focus for research might be to uncover how people feel about the world and make sense of their lives from their particular vantage points. Therefore, qualitative interviewing fits; actually conversing with people enables them to share their experiences and understandings. While this might appear a rather obvious comment to make, it is said with a degree of caution and is something to which we will continually return. In research it is all too easy to adopt such simplistic and seemingly rational viewpoints. As we shall see, interpretivism perceives experience and understanding as seldom straightforward; people participate in indeterminate lifeworlds, often attaching different interpretations and meanings to seemingly similar 'facts' and events. Alfred Schütz (1962: 5) explains that:

> All facts are from the outset facts selected from a universal context by the activities of our mind. They are, therefore, always interpreted facts, either facts looked at as detached from their context by an artificial abstraction or facts considered in their particular setting. In either case, they carry their interpretational inner and outer horizons. (also cited in Flick, 1998: 31)

The stance Schütz takes is that what we might see as 'facts' become open to levels of interpretation. The notion of searching for one overarching truth about the reality of how we live our lives is seen to be misplaced. Rather, we have 'multiple realities' or different interpretations.

Locating scientific methodology

Positivism
Interpretivism is usually seen as counter to 'scientific' approaches which are more accurately referred to as 'naturalist' approaches to research. The naturalist approach assumes an ontological view that human beings are part of

nature and can be studied in the same way as other objects in the physical world. This is a controversial and much contested viewpoint in the social sciences. The idea that human beings and human behaviour are reducible to variables that can be measured and subject to statistical analysis continues to be a major topic for debate. Even so, the theoretical approach within the natural sciences, and dominant also in the social sciences, is *positivism* (often viewed as akin to naïve realism). The positivist approach is *nomothetic* which means developing general laws or principles to explain particular phenomena.

The positivist position is situated within the epistemological tradition of *objectivism*, where objects in the world have meaning that exists independently from any subjective consciousness of them. Therefore, the underlying aim for research within this tradition is to provide objective knowledge – knowledge that is value-neutral, unbiased by the research/researcher process. Of vital importance for science is the belief in an objective reality that can be uncovered. This objective reality is more commonly referred to as 'truth' – a belief in the correspondence of knowledge with what can actually be proven to exist. Objectivism and the search for regularities, principles and laws underpin the quantification of scientific research. Aggregate data across large populations, statistical analysis, replication, generalisation and the reduction of intervening social variables are scientific strategies that claim to make known the 'real' aspects of existence.

The positivist ideal of objective knowledge existing independently is distinctly unlike the interpretivist view, where the activities of our mind select and give meaning to the world around us. Take, for example, the issue of climate change. Evidence exists that demonstrates changes in the earth's atmospheric conditions. Changes in air temperature, solar variation and weather conditions can all be measured and exist independently from our subjective viewpoints. What do we actually know from this evidence? There is continual disagreement among experts about causality and projected consequences. While this may infer that there is conflicting evidence, there are also the interpretations and investments of the researchers to consider. It may be possible to argue that subjective understandings are different from the scientifically established 'facts' inherent in objects, as with the climate change illustration. On the other hand, it remains hard to comprehend how such facts can effectively be distanced from any interpretation of them.

Banister et al. (1994) refer to a 'gap' between the object of study and the way it is represented. Interpretation is seen as the bridge between representations of particular phenomena – what we claim is occurring – and the actual world out there. How we represent data can be influenced by a host of factors, including the context in which the data were generated, moral and political concerns and researcher agendas. Pursuing objective knowledge, and indeed truth, becomes somewhat elusive if it forever pivots on interpretations and understandings which are open to the vagaries of human relations. It is fair to say that even those who operate within the confines of scientific method often acknowledge that preconceptions and suppositions can impact upon explanations. Yet it is these concerns that create the methodological and ideological chasm often exemplified by the qualitative/quantitative *divide*.

Empiricism

Central to the scientific approach is *empiricism* – the view that our knowledge of the world is gained from experience. No problem here, you might say, but what this means is that only the systematic collection of sense data via observation gives rise to the development of knowledge. Willig (2001) describes how nowadays few social scientists would subscribe to a pure form of empiricism, or indeed positivism. Such forms seem naïve when much of what passes as scientific research is founded upon pre-existing theory. What empiricists would claim is that the acquisition of knowledge depends upon the collection of observation data. Therefore, on the basis of multiple observations, researchers are able to develop general laws based upon the 'fact' that under particular conditions certain effects will always occur. This process and form of reasoning are called *induction*. The philosopher David Hume (1711–76) did not share such confidence, arguing that there could be no logical justification for such claims. Hume's position is that there can be no certainty as the seemingly logical connection between cause and effect is based upon expectations created by past experience. How can we claim that something will always have the same effect in the future? Experiences may change and therefore reasoning with regard to cause and effect changes. Karl Popper (1902–94) proposed the *hypothetico-deductive method* whereby theory claims are put to the test and are either rejected or retained for the time being. With this scientific method, the emphasis is not on conclusive verification – the establishment of a proposition as true for all time – but on *falsification* – facts are not unassailable; rather they are open to constant challenge.

Undoubtedly, the key issue is that science is 'based on facts … Based on what we can see, hear and touch rather than personal opinions or speculative imaginings' (Chalmers, 1999: 1). Interestingly, Kvale (1996) takes exception to the implication that qualitative interviews are necessarily 'unscientific', arguing that this depends on how science itself is defined. He offers the following definition of science: 'the methodological production of new, systematic knowledge' (1996: 60). Inherent within Kvale's argument is the view that scientific method based upon hypothesis testing, objective results and generalisability is one way of configuring science. Alternatively, scientific method could also include systematically produced 'intersubjective reducible data', such as those produced in qualitative interviews.

Verstehen and the issue of causality

While we might question aspects of the scientific process, the overarching principles of data generation, founded upon hypothesis testing, observation and measurement, are sacrosanct in that domain. Alternatively, interpretivism prioritises the interpretation and meaning of human experience over measurement, explanation and prediction. Personal opinions and imaginings are not framed as merely 'speculative', but rather they constitute what makes life intelligible. This differentiation is attributed to the thinking of Max Weber (1864–1920), who suggested that the human sciences should be concerned with understanding (*verstehen*). The following explanation from Strike (1972: 28) is certainly outdated in its gendered assumptions, but it appears to exemplify why the scientific process alone may not be sufficient:

> … the *verstehen* doctrine will claim that human beings can be understood in a manner that other objects of study cannot. Men have purposes and emotions, they make plans, construct cultures, and hold certain values, and their behaviour is influenced by such values, plans and purposes. In short, a human being lives in a world which has 'meaning' to him, and, because his behaviour has meaning, human actions are intelligible in ways that the behaviour of nonhuman objects is not.

This search to uncover *meaning* is then contrasted with an emphasis on explaining (*erklären*) and establishing causal relationships exemplified by the natural sciences. Demonstrating causality requires the researcher to show that an effect is due to a particular cause/variable. For example, we might undertake research to investigate a causal link between early parenthood and relationship breakdown. Causal explanations are usually in a linear form, stating cause and effect in a straight line – X causes Y. Yet if we accept the general import of *verstehen*, such uncomplicated linear explanations seem incomplete, even unsustainable. The reason(s) for relationship breakdown might be connected with a combination of numerous factors: changing aspirations, differing values in relation to gender roles, factors related to the child, social difficulties. Further, what counts as 'relationship breakdown' itself may be a matter for differing interpretations. To prove causality we would need to eliminate the possibility that an effect might be due to something other than the causal variable (e.g. early parenthood). It is the complex meanings that people give to their existence that are of interest in qualitative research, and thus tracking down linear causal relationships often become erroneous or unproductive and of little value in developing understanding. Wilhelm Dilthy (1833–1911) had earlier contrasted *verstehen* and *erklären*, proposing that natural reality and social reality are different kinds of reality and therefore require different methods of investigation. Maybe this is the point at which the researcher has to make some decisions. What kind of reality do we subscribe to and how does this impact upon our rationale for using qualitative interviewing?

Developing a rationale

While much is made of the differences that exist between qualitative and quantitative research, it is undeniable that both paradigms share a purpose. The purpose of research is to enhance knowledge, to in some way enable us to know more. When undertaking research it is standard practice to develop a research proposal outlining a clear rationale for the research – what is it that we want to know, what is the purpose of the research and how this might be achieved? This is often where those new to the use of qualitative research methods hit problems. Crotty (1998: 13) argues, when discussing the research process, that 'we need to be concerned about the process we have engaged in; we need to lay that process out for the scrutiny of the observer; we need to defend that process as a form of human inquiry that should be taken seriously'. Nonetheless, the philosophical underpinnings of quantitative research are often not outlined, remaining implicit within the methods use for generating data. For quantitative research, the status of 'facts' supported by measurement and observations seems enough to demonstrate that the work has epistemological integrity. However, as we will see in the following chapters, a more detailed account for qualitative research is needed. This is not done out of any inherent need to defend qualitative methods. Rather, when we acknowledge multiple realities and different ways of being, it is essential to elucidate which approach/version of reality is being used in order to make specific connections. It is at this point that there is a need to make appropriate connections between the nature of the research, overall strategy and how we will go about collecting and analysing data.

Box 2.1 outlines two different rationales for research looking at coercive treatment for drug misuse. Using this particular research project, where the second author was part of a research team commissioned by a local agency, we make visible the initial implications of these traditions. Evident are the ways in which theoretical frameworks rooted in specific philosophical positions produce differing rationales for what might need to be known, thus advocating particular research methodologies and methods. In using this example we do not intend to exemplify a full account of any methodological approach. Instead, we aim to present the main aspects of interpretivist and positivist traditions in a format that enables a comparative assessment.

Box 2.1   Developing a rationale underpinned by philosophical theoretical perspectives

Recent government initiatives on coercive treatment (alternatives to prison) for those convicted of offences linked to substance misuse have resulted in a need to know more about the treatment process and the impact this might have in terms of bringing about behaviour change. The figure below aims to make evident how different philosophical understandings impact upon the rationale we might develop when proposing research in this area. Also evident is how the rationale then impacts upon what kind of data we aim to generate.

(Continued)

(Continued)

Interpretivist	**Positivist**

Interpretivist perspective ⬇ Multiple versions of reality	Positivist perspective ⬇ One version of reality

Need to understand how offenders are engaging with treatment:

- How might offenders perceive the treatment providers?
- How do offenders engage with treatment services?
- What impact do they believe treatment will have on their alcohol misuse and offending?

Proposed method of data generation:

- Semi-structured interviews with offenders aiming to enable participants the opportunity to present their individual understandings and experiences.

Need to know the impact of coercive treatment on offending behaviour:

- How many offenders are receiving coercive treatment for alcohol misuse?
- How compliant are offenders with the treatment regime?
- What impact does coercive treatment have on overall rates of offending?

Proposed method of data generation:

- Access and collate a range of statistical information that will aim to investigate if any association can be made between coercive treatment and rates of offending before and after the introduction of treatment.

The interpretivist rationale focuses on *understanding* how individual offenders experience treatment services and what it *means* for them. The positivist rationale relies on more factual, statistical information where *cause and effect* can be investigated. Thus it is more interested in comparing rates of offending. Both rationales have the potential to enhance our knowledge base around coercive treatment. However, philosophical theoretical underpinnings result in different rationales – different perspectives on what we might need to know.

Epistemology and qualitative interviewing

Having explained some of the overarching philosophical tensions that exist in the research process, we now aim to situate issues raised within very specific epistemological traditions. A useful place to begin is to consider the status of conversation. It is all too easy to view conversation, within the qualitative interview situation, as an uncomplicated exchange of ideas and opinions. As Breakwell (1990: 81) states: 'The interview approach relies heavily upon respondents being able and willing to give accurate information.' The assumption here is that accurate information is there to be discovered and thus such knowledge is achievable. We do well to take time to consider how these ideals have been challenged by more critical approaches.

Rorty (1979) emphasised how we constitute knowledge through conversation and social practice. So rather than knowledge being conveyed in conversation, it is brought into being. This has resonance for qualitative interviewing as we become increasingly aware of the constructive nature of social interaction and the part played by active subjects in making sense of their experiences (Gubrium and Holstein, 2003b). Indeed, Shotter (1993: vi) describes how 'conversation is not just *one* of our many activities in *the* world. On the contrary, we constitute both ourselves and our worlds in our conversational activity' (original emphasis). Here we return to the idea that it is our personal imaginings that make life intelligible. Thus the idea of conversation as no more than observable verbal behaviour, or verbal exchange, where knowledge of an objective reality is described and discussed, is continually being extended and challenged. It becomes clear that what counts as knowledge, and how that knowledge is generated and understood, carry real implications for qualitative interviewing. Methods and methodology do not exist in a vacuum; rather, they are subject to new and extended ways of thinking about the world.

In later chapters we will locate qualitative interviewing within specific philosophical, theoretical perspectives, endeavouring to reveal how data are intricately associated with beliefs about reality and knowledge. In an attempt to make clear the implications embedded in such beliefs we explore three discrete epistemological positions: *realist, contextual* and *constructionist*. We are aware of now presenting realism as an epistemological position, knowing that previously we have discussed realism as an ontology – a way of understanding the nature of social reality (how people exist in the world). The term 'realism' is frequently used to denote both an ontological and epistemological position; ontological because it denotes a particular way of understanding our existence in the world and epistemological due to the emphasis on specific assumptions about the 'real' truth status of knowledge. This said, the epistemological positions we offer are by no means the only ones appropriate when using qualitative interviewing (see Reicher, 2000). We select these three epistemologies for two reasons. Primarily, we would argue that they do span the different approaches taken by researchers who utilise qualitative interviewing, drawing on both realist and relativist thinking. Equally, as our aim is to provide accessible information, it is helpful that each one is distinctly different, making it easier to show inconsistencies and divergences. Having decided to take this route, we would want to be clear in stating that there is a certain amount of overlap with these positions (see Madill et al., 2000).

Of value in this process of exploring these different epistemologies are three questions posited by Willig (2001: 12–13), which she suggests provide a framework for elaborating on assumptions that might underpin particular methodological approaches:

- What kinds of assumptions does the methodology make about the world?
- What kind of knowledge does the methodology aim to produce?
- How does the methodology conceptualise the role of the researcher in the research process?

These questions will be evident as we try to outline these differing epistemological traditions. It might also be the case that these questions prove useful for any researchers who are in the process of interrogating the integrity and coherence of their research. Table 2.1 gives a summary of each position using this framework.

Realist

Assumptions about the world

A realist epistemology would uphold the view that the individual is part of a material, real world where processes and relationships can be revealed. We have already discussed how realism underpins scientific method, maintaining that we have unmediated access to a real knowable world. There is, according to this theoretical position, an unproblematic relationship between our view of the world and the world that exists. Thus the knowledge produced in qualitative interviewing reflects the actual reality of people's experience in the world. For example, research with marginalised groups is frequently characterised by the notion of giving 'voice', enabling people to share their previously unheard understandings and meanings. It is often assumed that qualitative interviewing with such groups can provide the route to such 'real', previously inaccessible knowledge.

Knowledge produced

We said earlier that epistemology relates directly to a means of establishing what counts as knowledge. Those utilising realist thinking believe that by adopting particular methods we can describe and measure the world out there. Fundamental assumptions about objectivity and reliability, dominant within quantitative positivist research, prevail when using qualitative interviewing underpinned by a realist epistemology. Attention is given to representative sampling and generalisability so that even if studying a small number of cases, the aim is to be inclusive of those that represent the larger group or population under study. Often this prompts the perennial question of 'how many people should we interview?' Within a realist framework the answer might be lots! Indeed, one of the authors has a colleague who undertook almost 200 telephone interviews because the principal researcher operated within a realist epistemology. Even when, after 50 or so interviews, it became evident that interviewees were merely providing data that replicated what had already been generated, the research interviews continued. This was necessary because the criteria upon which the results would be judged, what counted as knowledge, was set within a scientific realist framework where responses needed to be coded, categorised and counted. While this may be an extreme example, many researchers using qualitative interviewing will look towards such established criteria.

Role of the researcher

When engaging in qualitative interviewing within a realist epistemology the objectivity of the data is seen to be commensurate with the detachment of the researcher. The telephone interviews referred to earlier required the researcher to endeavour to ask set questions in the same format and with the same level of interpersonal engagement each time in order to produce data that had not been impacted upon by subjective researcher bias. The data were coded by a team of researchers who calculated inter-rater reliability in order to avoid error. Generally, qualitative research does not claim to produce objectively defined knowledge, as subjective interpretation is a philosophical keystone and value-neutrality a highly questionable notion. However, it should be noted that a modified version of positivism – 'post-positivism' – does exist. Here researchers maintain some positivist elements, such as being highly systematised and concerned with quantification and causal factors, while at the same time incorporating interpretivist concerns around subjectivity and meaning (see Seale, 1999). Grounded theory is often cited as a *post-positivist* method. Similar to scientific process, grounded theory, when first developed, relied on a process of inductive theory-building based on the observation of the data. Accordingly, Denzin and Lincoln (1994) say that grounded theory is a form of qualitative research that is systematised and fits well with a 'modern', rational social science. Nevertheless, some have argued that grounded theory displaces the false precision of positivism, offering *relevance* in its place (Guba and Lincoln, 1994). However, there is very little acknowledgement of the personal qualities of the researcher or the relationship between the researcher and researched. Therefore similar to aspects of the scientific, objectivist approach, the researcher role remains distant, unmarked. As we will see in later chapters, this is in stark contrast to other qualitative approaches to interviewing, such as phenomenology and narrative inquiry, where such relationships are made evident.

Contextual

Assumptions about the world

The basic assumptions of contextualism are that everyday life is set in a particular time, consisting of a myriad of factors, relations and activities and is in a state of incessant change. From this position 'facts' cannot be commensurate with, or reducible to, a decontextualised view of human nature (Jaeger and Rosnow, 1988). The context of a historical, cultural and social milieu is integral

Table 2.1   Summary of epistemological positions

Epistemological positions	Realist	Contextual	Constructionist
Assumptions about the world	There exists unmediated access to a 'real' world where processes and relationships can be revealed	Context is integral to understanding how people experience their lives	Social reality is constructed through language which produces particular versions of events
Knowledge produced	Seeks to produce objective data which is reliable and representative of the wider population from which the interview sample is drawn	Data is inclusive of context aiming to add to the 'completeness' of the analysis by making visible cultural and historical meaning systems	Does not adhere to traditional conventions Knowledge brought into being through verbal exchange
Role of the researcher	The researcher aims to avoid bias, remaining objective and detached	The subjectivity of the researcher is an integral part of the process The researcher is active in data generation and analysis	The researcher is 'co-producer' of knowledge and therefore required to be reflexive and critically aware of language

to how we live, understand and experience our lives. The realist, scientific linear process of cause and effect, where directly observable facts are the arbiter of what counts as knowledge, becomes just one of many explanations set within its own historical context (Feyerabend, 1993). This means that all knowledge produced is dependent upon the context, including the perspective or standpoint taken when formulating the research. Hence, contextualism is founded on the belief that all knowledge is local, provisional and situation dependent (Madill et al., 2000). Yet, we can see that acknowledging the impact of context suggests a critical realist position with particular social mechanisms (practices) having potentiality with regard to both exploring and understanding individual lives.

Knowledge produced

In the qualitative research interview there is often, but by no means always, a face-to-face verbal interchange where one person (the interviewer) attempts to obtain information or expressions of opinion or belief from another person or persons. It would therefore be important to know as much as possible about the context of a particular encounter in order to produce knowledge that acknowledges and understands situated perspectives. Despite this, the decontextualisation of experiences is often a feature of studies using qualitative interviews. Rightly, Pidgeon and Henwood (1997: 250) identify specific dimensions that play a role in the way that knowledge is produced. The four dimensions are: (1) participants' own understandings; (2) researchers' interpretations; (3) cultural meaning systems which inform both participants' and researchers' understandings; and (4) acts of judging particular interpretations as valid by scientific communities. All of these dimensions would appear to have relevance, showing context as a web of interrelations that has the potential to build a more complete picture.

Role of the researcher

Within contextualism, researcher influence within the qualitative interview is not treated as a source of 'bias' threatening to undermine the validity and reliability of results. When undertaking qualitative interviews the assorted context of people's lives becomes relevant data and all accounts are understood to be infused with subjectivity. Rather than remaining neutral, as in the realist approach, the researcher is required to communicate the perspective(s) from which they approach their work. Gender, age, ethnicity, social status are all factors that might reverberate in the research process and, as such, it becomes necessary to reveal the situatedness of the researcher so that the audience can appreciate the position from which they write. Importantly, objectivism and the naïve scientific position it supports, where knowledge claims are value-free and universal, are seen from this perspective to be unsustainable. Rather, the knowledge research generates will vary in a multiplicity of ways according to the context in which the data were collected and analysed. This may inescapably lead to findings that are very context-specific and therefore of relevance to a limited constituency. On the other hand, limitations are mediated by the opportunity to potentially retain original and fresh perspectives that may have been inaccessible within a more standardised approach. In later chapters we will explore the different ways in which contextualism is incorporated into qualitative interviewing, often providing insight into how people make sense of their unique lives.

Constructionist

Assumptions about the world

Any epistemology with its roots in constructionism begins by emphasising the role of language. The belief that language is referential, merely representing reality 'out there', is overwhelmingly brought into question within this relativist approach. Rather than objects having meaning in the world that exists independently from our conscious interpretations of them, our interpretations/representations construct objects. These are by no means immediately accessible ideas as they are counter-intuitive to more normative ways of thinking. Language does things. For example, Clarke and Cochrane (1998) trace how 'natural' forms of childcare rooted in biological drives can actually be understood as embedded in discourse. Discourse refers to the way that images, stories, statements, ways of talking can produce a particular version of events.

Let's use Hall's (2001: 72) quote to outline further what is meant by the term 'discourse':

> Discourse ... constructs the topic. It defines and produces objects of our knowledge. It governs the way a topic can be meaningfully talked about and reasoned about. It also influences how ideas are put into practice and used to regulate the conduct of others.

So, rather than claiming that mothering is a 'natural', biologically located instinctual drive, Clark and Cochrane make visible the way in which language effectively constructs a host of expectations and obligations that suggest, rather than prove, that forms of mothering are 'natural'. Therefore, language is conceptualised as being productive. This means that language has the potential to construct particular versions of reality. This contrasts dramatically with positivism, where the one 'true' knowledge of the world is accessible through observation. It is hardly surprising that the rise of social constructionism and related critical approaches has to some extent challenged the foundations of existing knowledge, necessitating a radical rethink of what we consider knowledge to be.

Knowledge produced

Social constructionism produces knowledge that does not adhere to traditional conventions. Objectivity and value-neutrality are seen as discursive devices employed by a positivist science to uphold its powerful grip on knowledge production. The idea that human beings can somehow remove themselves from the process of active engagement in knowledge production is viewed with a level of incredulity. As Burr (1995: 152) expressively states: 'No human being can step outside of their humanity and view the world from no position at all, which is what the idea of objectivity suggests, and this is just as true for scientists as for everyone else.' Also rejected is the view that there is an objective truth waiting to be discovered. What we have is meaning that comes into existence out of our engagement with the social world. Meaning is not out there waiting to be discovered; rather it is brought into being in the process of social exchange. Consequentially, social constructionism is relativist, seeing knowledge as historically and culturally located. At different times and places there will be different and often contradictory interpretations of the same phenomena.

Role of the researcher

Burr (1995) asserts that social constructionists call for the democratisation of research relationships, with research being necessarily a 'co-production' between the researcher and the researched. *Reflexivity* (covered in far more detail in Chapter 8) is seen as particularly relevant to a social constructionist epistemology as it requires researchers to consider their contribution to the construction of meaning. Willig (2001) identifies two kinds of reflexivity:

epistemological reflexivity and personal reflexivity. Epistemological reflexivity advocates that the researcher reflects upon assumptions about the world that have been made in the course of the research. This could include how the research questions have been defined, interview schedules structured and the method of analysis undertaken. Personal reflexivity involves giving consideration to the ways in which our beliefs, interests, experiences and identities might have impacted upon the research. Clearly, much of this echoes aspects outlined for a contextualist epistemology. However, Willig goes on to raise the issue of *critical language awareness* as a form of reflexivity. If the words we use are seen to construct meaning, then it would seem obligatory to reflect on the categories and labels the researcher might use in the research process, acknowledging how these might shape research findings.

Conclusion

Qualitative research, including qualitative interviewing, requires a great deal of effort, with researchers having to explore how they conceive the world. In this chapter we have made evident some of the philosophical and theoretical issues that prevail when engaged in qualitative interviewing. By showing that methods and methodology are distinct aspects of social research, we have sought to make accessible some of the more difficult features of qualitative research. We have covered several of the tensions that exist between qualitative and quantitative approaches, outlining theoretical differences and presenting particular epistemological positions that we believe have relevance for qualitative interviewing. In the following chapters, as we examine the process of carrying out qualitative interview research, we will endeavour to show in more detail the ontological and epistemological thinking inherent in particular approaches. Such detail aims to equip researchers with the tools to ensure that they have the insight and information needed to give credence to their work, moving beyond mere description to present theoretically-driven and coherent qualitative research.

Recommended reading

Layder, D. (1998) The reality of social domains: implications for theory and method, in T. May and M. Williams (eds), *Knowing the Social World*. Buckingham: Open University Press. pp. 87–102.
This chapter thoughtfully considers how social reality cannot be considered as a unitary whole with one explanatory principle. The implications of such complexity are given a methodological focus.

Pidgeon, N. and Henwood, K. (1997) Using grounded theory in psychological research, in N. Hayes (ed.), *Doing Qualitative Analysis in Psychology*. Hove: Psychology Press.

In this chapter, science, epistemology and qualitative methods are discussed with examples of how this impacts upon research that uses a grounded theory approach.

Ramazanoğlu, C., with Holland, J. (2002) *Feminist Methodology: Challenges and Choices.* London: Sage.
The first chapter in this book provides an accessible yet detailed account of 'what is methodology in social research'. While this account is clearly situated within feminist methodology, the outline offered is useful for other methodological approaches.

Tuffin, K. (2005) *Understanding Critical Social Psychology.* London: Sage.
The first three chapters of this book examine the ways in which researchers have attempted to understand the social world. Experimentation, science and social constructionism are all covered in some detail.

THREE

Designing an Interview Study

In this chapter we will outline the typical stages you are likely to pass through in designing a research study based on qualitative interviewing. In the light of the discussion in the previous chapter, concerning a variety of positions within qualitative research, it should come as no surprise that there cannot be a single universal protocol to follow for developing a qualitative interview study. In the latter part of this book, some of the distinctive features of particular methodological approaches are examined. Nevertheless, we would argue that there is sufficient commonality among many traditions of qualitative research to make a generic account of the project development process at least a useful starting point.

The chapter is organised around the following main tasks in the development of a qualitative research study:

- framing your research question
- choosing the type of interview to use
- defining your sample and recruiting participants
- developing an interview guide

Framing your research question

In framing a research question that is appropriate to a qualitative study, there are several issues that you need to take into account. The first is the *type* of question you should use. By this we mean the kind of knowledge that the researcher seeks to produce from analysis of interview data. The second is the *scope* of the question – how broad or narrow a range of experience is the study seeking to examine? A third issue is the need to avoid presuppositions in the question that might distort the research process. Finally, you need to consider the extent to which the research question itself might change in the process of carrying out a qualitative study.

Type of research question

One of the most common and potentially damaging mistakes made by novice qualitative researchers is to frame their research question in a manner requiring a type of 'answer' that qualitative research cannot provide.

This includes questions that ask about causal relationships. To give a real example, a student approached one of us for supervision, saying that they want to use qualitative interviews to find out 'What causes young women to develop eating disorders?' If you think this is a legitimate kind of question to ask (and see Chapter 2 for discussion of the problems many qualitative researchers have with conventional notions of causality), you need to address it using quantitative methods within the hypothetico-deductive tradition. You could, for instance, carry out an analysis of epidemiological data, or utilise a survey design, but qualitative interviews would never enable you to answer a question like this.

Another mistake that can be made in the type of the research question is to seek to establish general trends in the phenomenon under consideration. To extend the previous example, you might ask 'Are women more strongly influenced than men by media representations of body image?' While this question is not seeking to uncover underlying causes of behaviour, it *is* trying to produce a highly generalised understanding of the differences between two very wide categories of person ('young women' and 'young men'). Qualitative researchers differ in the extent to which they permit any attempt to generalise, or 'transfer', understanding from a specific study to a wider context (Murphy et al., 1998; Williams, 2002), but even those who argue for some degree of transferability would not see this as an appropriate question for a qualitative study.

The research question for a qualitative interview study should not, therefore, focus on establishing causal relationships or generalised patterns of behaviour. What it should focus on is *meaning* and *experience*, with reference to a particular group of participants. So, for example, you might ask, 'How do young women view the presentation of body image ideals in magazines and newspapers?' And while qualitative research questions should not seek to establish causality, they may very well focus on *perceptions* of causality from the perspective of research participants: 'How do people diagnosed with anorexia make sense of why they have developed the condition?'

Scope of the research question

Even when a qualitative research question has the right kind of focus, it may still be inappropriate in terms of its scope. Questions that are very broad in scope are problematic because of the emphasis in qualitative research on understanding people's lives in context. If a study tries to encompass experiences from too wide a set of social contexts, the findings are likely to present a scattering of unrelated snapshots, from which it is impossible to draw any kind of conclusion. The revised research question on body image, stated in the previous paragraph, would be likely to suffer this weakness, as the category 'young women' is almost certainly too broad. The researcher here would be best advised to narrow the scope somewhat, perhaps in terms of characteristics such as specific age groups, class, occupation, and so on.

While research questions that are too broad may in effect prove 'unanswerable', those that are too narrow are likely to produce findings that are simply not very interesting or useful. Qualitative research is interested in how people differ in relation to a particular phenomenon, as much as it is in what they have in common. A very narrow research question can result in a highly homogeneous sample that does not enable diversity of meaning and experience to be revealed. Also, such a question may generate findings so localised in their relevance that they cannot contribute to the intellectual debate around the topic in question.

When deciding on the scope of your research question, a key factor to bear in mind is the level of resource available to you. On the whole, broader questions will require larger-scale studies to address them effectively. Researchers who are new to qualitative approaches may be prone to over-reaching themselves in terms of scope, feeling uncertain about the value of narrower questions. If this describes your situation, remind yourself that qualitative research is fundamentally concerned with the particular rather than the general; on that basis we would advise that if in doubt, err on the side of narrowing the scope of your research question.

Avoiding presuppositions

Texts on qualitative interviewing stress the importance of avoiding leading questions in interviews, and offer various tips as to how this may be done. The present volume is no exception, as you will see in Chapter 4. However, it is important to note that it is possible for the research question in itself to be leading, such that it may blinker the way in which you go about exploring your topic with your participants. Take the following question: 'What are the perceived benefits to the victims of street crime of a self-help website?' The question seems suitably focused on meaning and experience (here in the form of 'perceptions') and realistic in scope. But there is an in-built presupposition that the website does have benefits for victims, which may lead you to neglect probing properly for any negative experiences associated with its use. A better form of phrasing would be to refer to 'perceived benefits and costs', but even this may tend to encourage you to seek a clear dichotomy of good and bad that may not correspond to the way participants see things. Better still would be: 'What experiences do users have of a self-help website for victims of street crime?'

The shifting research question

In qualitative studies it is not uncommon for the researcher to feel that the research question is shifting as the study progresses. While this would be a cause for great concern in a positivistic quantitative study, it is not necessarily a problem in a qualitative one. Qualitative research always has (to some degree) an exploratory character, and as such it is inevitable that sometimes a project will move in directions that are of relevance to the research topic but outside the scope of the original research question(s). If we return to the study of street crime victims, the researcher might find that participants consistently want to comment on their experiences of a help-line accompanying the website rather than just on the website itself. In deciding whether to allow this kind of redefinition to the research question, any researcher would need to consider a number of conceptual and practical issues for their project. These include the following:

- *Would the change to the research question undermine the coherence of the study as a whole?* In our example, we might feel that to examine the help-line as well would not substantially alter the underlying concern of the study with experiences of using self-help resources for victims. In contrast, we would be reluctant to extend the study to look in detail at victims' experiences of individual psychotherapy, as this represents a very different kind of resource from the website and help-line.
- *Would the change stretch the resources of the project to an unmanageable degree?* In our example, incorporating a detailed exploration of responses to help-line use might extend the interviews by 20 minutes or so. This will have a knock-on effect on time taken to transcribe and analyse interviews that the researcher would need to take into account.
- *Are key stakeholders in the project happy with the change?* Significant decisions about changes to a research project are rarely just the concern of the individual researcher. In a Masters or doctoral thesis, the student's supervisor will want to be sure that any change does not undermine the intellectual quality of the work, and that it will not result in unacceptable delays to completion. In externally commissioned research, funders are also likely to be concerned with completion times, and there may be political or ethical considerations as well.

Choosing the type of interview to use

In some cases, it is apparent from the start that a particular form of qualitative interviewing is the most appropriate, because of the nature of the topic to be studied and/or the requirements of the methodological and theoretical stance to be taken. For instance, if you wanted to follow a life story approach within the narrative tradition (see Chapter 11), you would of necessity use individual interviews. Very often, though, there are several types of interview that can be employed. You may, for instance, weigh the pros and cons of individual and group interviews. You may consider whether it is essential that you use face-to-face interviews, or whether telephone or internet interviews offer a viable alternative (see Chapter 6). Subsequent chapters of this book will, we hope, tell you enough about these different forms of interview to enable you to make an informed choice for your research. At this point, we simply want to urge you to bear in mind that when designing your study, you think about the different ways that qualitative interviews can be conducted, rather than automatically taking the 'default' option of the individual, face-to-face format.

Defining your sample and recruiting participants

Defining your sample

In quantitative studies, and especially surveys, recruiting a sample that is statistically representative of the population to be studied is of central importance because of the need to establish the generalisability of the conclusions drawn from research. For example, if a researcher wanted to test the hypothesis that attitudes to risk-taking in men's driving behaviour were associated with attitudes towards their own masculinity, he would require a sample that was representative of the male driving population as a whole. Qualitative research, in contrast, does not seek to make this kind of generalisation and therefore does not normally use sampling strategies aimed at producing statistical representativeness. However, as we saw in Chapter 2, qualitative research very often is concerned to achieve different forms of generalisability or transferability. As Mason (1996) and May (2002) point out, this means that a purely *ad hoc*, opportunistic sampling strategy is not appropriate; rather, the sample needs to relate in some systematic manner to the social world and phenomena that a study seeks to throw light upon.

The criterion most commonly proposed for sampling in qualitative studies is diversity. Researchers seek to recruit participants who represent a variety of positions in relation to the research topic, of a kind that might be expected to throw light on meaningful differences in experience. To continue the example from the previous paragraph, if we wanted to carry out a qualitative study of how men perceive risk-taking in driving, we might consider that age, years of driving experience and family status may be important, and therefore seek to recruit participants who vary on these aspects. (This kind of targeted sampling is often referred to as 'purposive'.) Of course, the effectiveness of such a sampling strategy will depend on the choice of aspects (dimensions or categories) from which to select participants. This choice will in most cases draw upon a mixture of the researcher's knowledge of the academic literature, personal knowledge and anecdotal information from those who have some involvement with the topic.

It is important to bear in mind the practical constraints on sampling arising from the scale of most qualitative interview studies. If your planned Masters dissertation research is likely to involve around 20 interviews, it would clearly be unwise to try to select a sample on the basis of differences in ten different aspects. It is generally best to 'fix' one or two key aspects that define the group you are looking at, and then seek diversity in other aspects. Gerson and Horowitz (2002: 205) argue that:

> By choosing a sample that controls for one consequential aspect of lived experience (e.g. age or generation), but varies on others deemed important in the theoretical literature (e.g. gender, race, class), the aim is to discover how similar social changes are experienced by different social groups.

In qualitative research, sampling and recruiting participants may occur at several stages in the course of a project. Thus an initial sample may be recruited and interviewed, and on the basis of preliminary analysis of their data, a further sample defined to address particular emerging issues. This kind of strategy is probably best known in grounded theory (e.g. Corbin and Strauss, 2008), in the form of 'theoretical sampling', although it may be used in other approaches too. In a recent study by the first author and Anne Little, we examined the users' experiences of a Community Gym in a highly deprived, predominantly South Asian area of a large northern English town. For our initial interviews, we recruited a sample that varied in age and gender. Our initial analysis suggested that a particular subgroup – women over 50 – were especially interesting in relation to the issues our funders were concerned with. We therefore recruited an additional sample just from this group (King and Little, 2007).

Recruiting participants

In this section we will look at some of the challenges that arise in the process of recruiting participants once you have defined your sample. We will consider how you may go about gaining access to potential participants, and the kind of information you need to provide for them, in order that they may make a decision about participation. Inevitably, this discussion will raise ethical issues, such as the need to avoid coercion and to ensure proper informed consent. Some of the practical consequences of these matters will be considered here, but a much fuller examination of the ethics of qualitative interviewing will be found in Chapter 7.

Gaining access

The precise nature of the tasks involved in gaining access to participants can vary enormously from study to study. In some, the main challenge may be that the kind of experience you are interested in is a very uncommon one, for example, winning a major lottery prize. In others, you may face the difficulty that your topic is a painful or emotive one, which people may be reluctant to talk to a stranger about, such as the experience of sexual assault within marriage. Alternatively, access may be problematic because it requires the approval of several 'gatekeepers' in a large and complex organisation, perhaps with political sensitivities to contend with too. The UK National Health Service (NHS) is a classic example of this kind of setting. These are only a few of the more common challenges regarding access that you may face. It is impossible to offer advice for every eventuality, so we will concentrate here on a set of issues that, in our experience, are quite commonly encountered in relation to gaining access for a piece of qualitative research: working with gatekeepers, using insiders to assist with recruitment, and advertising for participants.

Working with gatekeepers

In many research studies, potential participants must be reached through one or more gatekeepers. We are defining a 'gatekeeper' here as someone who has the authority to grant or deny permission to access potential participants and/or the ability to facilitate such access. Examples could include health professionals for access to patients, senior managers for access to their employees, headteachers for access to schoolchildren, and so on. Sometimes different people will play different gatekeeping roles for your project. You may need to acquire the overall permission for access from the managing director of a company, but have to negotiate the details of recruitment with one or more departmental head(s). Sometimes, while it may not be obligatory to go through a gatekeeper, there may be advantages in so doing – both in terms of identifying and facilitating contact with participants, and reassuring them as to your credibility and trustworthiness.

The first step in working with a gatekeeper to recruit participants is to be sure you have actually identified the appropriate person. This may sound self-evident, but it is possible to go awry by assuming, for instance, that because someone holds a particular position in an organisation,[1] they are automatically the correct person to help you with access. You need to be sure you have a good working knowledge about how the organisation is structured and how it functions before you begin working in detail on recruitment. In planning your research, you should budget for time to explore how the organisation works – especially where it is relatively unfamiliar to you.

You will normally need to provide gatekeepers with a range of information to enable them to grant you permission for access. They will require an overview of the project, summarising its aims, methods, anticipated outcomes, and clearly stating the time commitments required from participants. While you may provide this verbally, it is best also to have a written version available, using language that avoids jargon as far as possible. You should provide them with copies of any written information that is going to be given to potential participants, including the consent form (where one is to be used). Gatekeepers need to know the level of anonymity that is being promised – for instance, is the organisation as a whole to be anonymised, and will particular subsections of it be identifiable? It is important that they recognise your ethical obligations to individual participants, above all the need to maintain participants' confidentiality in relation to other members of the organisation (including the gatekeeper).

'Insider' assistance with recruitment

In some studies, researchers not only gain access through a gatekeeper within the organisation, they also use one or more insiders to actively assist in recruiting participants. Such a person might identify organisational members who meet the sampling criteria of the study, pass project information sheets and letters requesting participation to them, and forward queries to the research team. This kind of insider assistance can have real advantages. Where an organisation is located at a considerable distance from the researcher (or research team) it may not be possible within time and budgetary constraints to visit in person to deal with the nitty-gritty of recruitment. In these circumstances, you are much more likely to be successful with recruitment if an insider is actively helping you, than if you merely send information and requests to individual members. Also, if the request is coming through a known and trusted colleague, people are more likely to give it proper consideration than if it had arrived from a stranger, where it might be seen as just another form of junk mail (this may be especially likely to happen with 'cold' requests received via e-mail).

Alongside these advantages there are some significant risks associated with using insiders to help with recruitment. It is possible they may be overtly biased, consciously choosing participants likely to hold (or *not* hold) certain views. Perhaps a greater threat is that there will be an unintentional distortion stemming from reliance on personal networks within the organisation. There is also an ethical danger that insiders may exert pressure on people to participate that would deny them genuine, free informed consent. In balancing these risks and advantages, the following guidelines may help you to determine whether and how to use insider assistance with recruitment:

- Select insider assistant(s) carefully – consider whether they may have axes to grind on the topic, and whether they are likely to be seen as trustworthy by those you seek to recruit. This generally means spending some time getting to know potential assistants before you ask them for their help.
- Make sure insider assistants are briefed thoroughly about the study.
- Keep in regular contact during the recruitment process. This will allow you to discuss how best to deal with any problems in recruitment as they occur, and to determine whether there is anything you can do to facilitate the process – for example, providing clarification or additional information to potential participants.
- When potential participants have received their invitation to take part in the study, where possible they should respond directly to the research team, not via the insider assistant. This will enable their participation to be kept confidential if they so wish.

Box 3.1 provides an example of the process of gaining access through organisational gatekeepers and insider assistants.

Box 3.1   Accessing participants through gatekeepers

In a recent study led by the first author, we examined experiences of allotment gardening among allotment plot-holders (sometimes known as 'allotmenteers') on three sites in a northern English town. The sites had received development support from a local charity, which employed an allotment development worker (Hassan). We sought to recruit a cross-section of users in terms of age, gender and gardening experience. The process of gaining access is shown in the flow-chart overleaf:

Healthy living partnership manager

Overall permission for study

Access to allotment development worker

↓

Allotment development worker

Access to allotment site secretaries (one plot-holder at each site responsible for administration and liaison with Local Authority which owns the site)

↓

Allotment site secretaries

Provided names and information about potential participants in the light of our selection criteria, including in some cases personal introductions for the researchers

---

Note that in relation to the allotment site secretaries, the roles of 'gatekeeper' and 'insider assistant' are blurred. It would have been possible to recruit participants without going through the secretaries, and it was not an ethical, legal or administrative necessity to do so. However, not only did they have the most up-to-date knowledge about who held plots and was actively working them, they also had personal acquaintance with the other allotmenteers on their site. This meant they could give considerable help in suggesting people to approach in order to collect the kind of diverse sample we sought. Furthermore, they were also participants themselves and were interviewed early in the project, and thus able to reassure others about the research process.

Two main issues arose from using the site secretaries in the recruitment process. First, it was important that they did not exert any pressure on others to take part. We did not feel that this was a problem in reality because their role did not place them in any substantial position of power over other allotmenteers. (It should be noted that some allotment sites do operate in quite an hierarchical manner, but these three were strongly egalitarian in ethos.) Second, there was a danger that site secretaries might select those to approach whom they expected to take particular positions. We can be less certain that this did not occur, although by emphasising the need for a diverse sample we hoped that such bias might be minimised. Certainly the interviews themselves did not suggest participants taking any kind of 'party line'.

Snowball sampling

In snowball sampling, the researcher uses the initial few interviewees (often recruited opportunistically) to recommend other potential participants who fit the inclusion criteria for the study. They in turn will be asked to suggest further contacts, and so the sample builds up. This strategy inevitably introduces a form of bias into the sample. Participants may, for example, tend to recommend people who share their view of the phenomenon under investigation. If one is concerned with some degree of generalisability or transferability, then snowballing would not be the preferred option (Gerson and Horowitz, 2002). Certainly, where snowballing is used simply as a convenient way of recruiting participants, it is really no more than a form of convenience sampling.

There are circumstances, however, where snowballing may be an appropriate strategy – namely where the population to be sampled from is especially hard to access and quite tightly defined. Langdridge (2004) and Howitt and Cramer (2005) give examples such as drug addicts, street gangs, and even banjo players! A current doctoral student of the first author (Emma Turley) is investigating the lifeworlds of bondage/sado-masochism practitioners and is using snowballing in her recruitment as a way into a relatively self-enclosed community. Where snowballing needs to be used with these kinds of groups, some of the biasing effects may be reduced by giving very clear instructions about the characteristics sought. For instance, a researcher may ask a participant to recommend others of a particular age, gender or with other specified characteristics in order to enhance the diversity of the sample.

Advertising for participants

An alternative to contacting potential participants through organisational gatekeepers or insider assistants is to use some form of public advertising. This could include notices in public places (universities, doctors' surgeries, community centres, and so on), adverts in newspapers or magazines, or messages to internet discussion groups. There are a number of issues to bear in mind if you are considering using such strategies.

- Be sure to get proper permission before you put up notices in a public place. This includes permission to use an online discussion group for recruitment purposes.
- Effectively target the population from which you wish to recruit. If you were looking for sufferers from a rare chronic illness, it would not be very efficient just to plaster the corridors of your university with posters. In such a case, finding a relevant internet discussion group would be more sensible, or alternately identifying a self-help group who might be willing to distribute flyers to its members.
- Think carefully about the design of your advert. You need to provide enough information to let people know what the research is about, who you are, and what kind of commitment is required of them, but not so much that they might feel overwhelmed or intimidated. You need to use lay language, without being condescending. For material such as posters or flyers, you must think about the visual impact – font size and style, the use of colour and graphics.

- When recruiting through public advertisement, you will be accessing people who in most cases will be complete strangers to you, and will not even have come to you through someone else's recommendation (unlike all the other methods described above). You therefore need to be especially mindful of your own safety when meeting them. We discuss the issue of researcher safety in more detail in Chapter 7.

Methodologically, the major pitfall of recruiting participants through advertising is that the sample is highly self-selecting. This may mean that you do not get the balance of participants that you would ideally have liked. One way to mitigate this effect is to use a purposive sampling frame to select the sample you need from all those who respond positively. For example, you might have 20 people coming forward in response to the advert, of whom 15 are female and five male. If your sampling frame stipulated up to five participants of each gender you would pick all the men and five of the women. Of course, this relies on you getting substantially more positive responses than you need. If you do use this strategy, you should reply to those you are not going to interview, thanking them for making the effort to contact you and briefly explaining why you could not include all respondents. This process does reduce some of the biases that may be inherent in a volunteer sample; however, there may still be the difficulty that some subsets of the population are particularly unlikely to respond and therefore will not be represented.

Developing an interview guide

Flexibility is a key requirement of qualitative interviewing. The interviewer must be able to respond to issues that emerge in the course of the interview in order to explore the perspective of the participant on the topics under investigation. This means that the traditional interview schedule used in quantitative survey research – with fixed questions in a predetermined order – is inappropriate. Instead, qualitative interviews use an 'interview guide' that outlines the main topics the researcher would like to cover, but is flexible regarding the phrasing of questions and the order in which they are asked, and allows the participant to lead the interaction in unanticipated directions. The precise format of interview guides varies enormously, reflecting the needs of different methodological traditions in qualitative research as well as the personal preferences of individual researchers. Below we address some of the key questions you will need to consider when deciding on the form and content of your own interview guide.

Upon what do I base my guide?

We would suggest that there are three main sources you can draw on to identify topics to include in your guide. First, you can think about your own personal experience of the research area, both first-hand experience and stories and anecdotes told by people you know. For example, if you are studying responses to the experience of being burgled and have yourself been a victim of this crime, you could reflect upon your own responses. You could also think about accounts you have heard from family, friends and colleagues of being burgled. Second, you may consult the research literature on the subject, to see what previous research suggests. (Note, though, that there are some methodologies that discourage you from reviewing the literature before doing your inter-views, to minimise presuppositions that might distort your research – grounded theory (Charmaz, 2006; Corbin and Strauss, 2008) is the best known example of this.) Third, you may carry out some informal preliminary work to focus your thinking about the area. Thus, in the research the first author carried out on the psychological and social impact of allotment gardening, he spoke to several colleagues and family members about their experiences as well as to some of those involved in initiating the allotment development scheme that was being evaluated. This last point highlights the necessity to bear in mind the requirements of external funders when deciding upon the scope of your interview guide.

How comprehensive should I be in covering topics relevant to my research area?

When you have drawn on the sources noted above, you will probably have an extensive list of topics that you could cover in your guide. It is important to think now about whether you want to comprehensively cover most or all of the potentially relevant topics, or whether you are going to be more selective – perhaps choosing three or four broad areas that you are sure you will want to address in the interview. (Of course, you can choose to adopt a strategy anywhere between these two extremes.) This is really a question about the extent to which you as a researcher want (or need) to lead the direction of the interview. If you have a comprehensive interview guide, there will be a danger that you do not allow sufficient opportunity for the participants to bring up perspectives that may be unanticipated but actually of real interest to your research. If you go for a minimalistic interview guide, you may fail to address important issues, should the participant lead you into lengthy digressions from your research focus. In deciding how comprehensive to make your interview guide, you must reflect on the aims of your study and your methodological position. A realist evaluation study, for example, is likely to use quite a comprehensive guide to ensure that key aspects of the programme or intervention being evaluated are covered. A narrative study, seeking to elicit life stories from a particular group of participants, would use a much more minimalistic guide.

What types of question should I ask?

Patton (1990) argues that there are six types of question that can be asked in a qualitative research interview, each seeking to elicit a particular kind of infor-mation from the participant. In reality, these categories may not always be as distinct as he describes, and we would certainly not suggest that you take a mechanistic approach to including a certain number of each type in every topic guide. Nevertheless, they can be a helpful way to think about the different kinds of response you need within the course of an interview and about how you can best facilitate them.

- *Background/demographic questions*: These are straightforward descriptive questions about the personal characteristics of the participant that you might need to be aware of in your analysis – for instance, about their age, gender, occupation, and so on. It sometimes makes sense to collect at least some of this information on a simple form at the same time as obtaining written consent.
- *Experience/behaviour questions*: These questions focus on specific and overt actions that you could have observed were you yourself present at the time. Examples could be: 'What did you do when the doctor told you the diagnosis?'; 'What happened when you cautioned the suspect?'; 'What did you and the other candidates do while you were waiting for your interviews?'
- *Opinion/values questions*: These are questions that ask about what the participant thinks about the topic at hand, and/or how their thoughts relate to their values, goals and intentions. They might ask such things as: 'What did you hope to achieve by doing that?'; 'What do you think is the best way to deal with that kind of situation?'
- *Feeling questions*: These questions focus on participants' emotional experiences. Patton warns that they often get confused with the previous category because we habitually use the question 'how did you feel about …?' in a very loose way that can mean 'what is your opinion about …' as well as 'how did you respond emotionally to …?'. If you particularly want to explore emotional responses, you must phrase your question in a way that makes this clear to the interviewee. 'What feelings did this provoke in you?' would be a better formulation than 'How did you feel about it?'
- *Knowledge questions*: This category relates to questions about factual information the participant holds. The distinction between knowledge and opinions/values is a difficult one. The important thing to remember is that you are concerned here with what the participant believes to be a 'fact' and not with whether it is actually true in any objective sense. Knowledge questions might be formulated in such terms as: 'What do you know about the systems for referring students for pastoral support?' or 'How well did you know this patient's history?'
- *Sensory questions*: These are questions about sensory aspects of experience – what the participant saw, heard, touched, tasted or smelled in any given situation. While conceptually they might be seen as a subset of experience questions, they tend to be quite distinctive in form, asking the participant to recollect a very specific sensory impression in a specific setting. They are particularly important in studies where embodied aspects of experience are of central important (see Chapter 10 for further discussion of embodiment in interview studies).

Can I change my interview guide in the course of my study?

Not only is it permissible to change your guide in the course of your study, it is generally advisable. Remember, the aim of a qualitative interview is to elicit participants' accounts of aspects of their experience, rather than to collate answers to specific questions as if they were variables in a survey. As such, any insights you gain in the process of carrying out your first few interviews should inform subsequent ones. For instance, you may note a probe question that worked particularly well or recognise that an aspect of participants' lives you had overlooked initially may be important to the phenomenon you are studying. So long as you remain aware of the way your interviewing practice developed over the course of the project, you should be able to avoid such changes distorting the analysis of the data.

How should I format the questions or topic areas on the guide?

Interview guides vary in how they lay out the questions to be asked. One style is to formulate full questions, written in proper sentence form. The opposite approach is to just include short phrases or single words as reminders of the topics to try to cover – perhaps in bullet points or similar. Box 3.2 shows two different styles of interview guide for the same study. There are pros and cons to both styles of interview guide. The advantage of using full questions is that it forces the researcher to think carefully about question formulation – to avoid the leading question, endorsement of participant opinions and so on that can happen if the interview drifts into a style that is too conversational (Willig, 2008). The disadvantage is that with full questions stated on the guide, the interviewer may tend not to use it as flexibly as they should. The pros and cons of the topic heading format are, of course, the mirror image of those just stated – it encourages flexibility but does not help guard against inappropriate phrasing of questions.

Box 3.2   Examples of different styles of interview guide

Below is a extract from a recent study involving one of the authors, looking at user perceptions of a Community Gym set up in a highly deprived predominantly South Asian urban area. It is presented in two different formats: 'full questions' and 'key points'.

Extract from Interview Guide for Community Gym Users – Full Question Format

1. STARTING AT THE COMMUNITY GYM

How did you first hear about the Community Gym?
When did you start attending?
Why did you start attending the Community Gym?
Had you used a gym before?
Do you go to any other gyms now?
    If 'yes': Which? How does it compare to the CG?
    If 'no': Why not?
Do you take part in any other regular sport or exercise now?
    If 'yes': What do you do? When did you start this?
    If 'no': Why not?

8. Overview

What (if anything) has been the best thing about attending the Community Gym for you?

What (if any) changes or improvements would you like to see made to the Community Gym?

Would you recommend the Community Gym to a friend?

> **If 'yes':** Why?
> **If 'no':** Why not?

If the Community Gym closed, what (if anything) else would you do instead?

Extract from Interview Guide for Community Gym Users – Key Point Format

1. STARTING AT THE COMMUNITY GYM

- How heard about it?
- When?
- Why?
- Used a gym before?
- Other gyms now?

> **If 'yes':** Which? Compare to CG?
> **If 'no':** Why not?

- Other regular sport/exercise?

> **If 'yes':** What? When started?
> **If 'no':** Why not?

8. Overview

- Best things about attending CG?
- Desired changes or improvements?
- Recommend to a friend?

> **If 'yes':** Why?
> **If 'no':** Why not?

- Alternatives, if CG closed?

As can be seen, the 'key point' format is much more succinct; it would be very easy to glance at momentarily to remind yourself what you want to cover during an interview. However, there are several places where having the full question before you might help you to avoid an inappropriate formulation of questions. For instance, in the 'Overview' section, the first question asks 'What (if anything) has been the best thing about attending the Community Gym for you?' The parentheses here seek to remind the interviewer not to take it for granted that the participant thought there was any 'best thing' about the Gym. A similar formulation is used for other questions in this section, for the same reason – to avoid implicit leading of the participant. Using the 'key points' format, an interviewer – especially an inexperienced one – might fail to recognise this danger.

Two factors may be useful to consider when choosing how to format the guide. First, the experience of the interviewer is relevant. On the whole, we would recommend that relatively inexperienced qualitative interviewers opt for the full question format, as the skill of phrasing questions appropriately in the interview generally takes some time to acquire. Second, the methodological approach you are using may influence your choice. As we noted above in relation to the comprehensiveness of the guide, a key issue is the extent to which the methodology requires the researcher to take a directive role in the interview. Those approaches that seek to minimise interviewer directiveness – such as most narrative approaches – may be better served by the topic heading style of guide.

What are probes and prompts and how do I include them on my interview guide?

Sometimes you may see these two terms used interchangeably, but we feel it is useful to make a distinction here. We take probes to be follow-up questions that encourage a participant to expand on an initial answer in order to obtain more depth in their response. In contrast, we take prompts to be interventions that seek to clarify for the interviewee the kind of information a question is seeking to gather, usually used where the interviewee has expressed uncertainty or incomprehension about the initial question.

You will need to formulate many probes and prompts in the course of an interview, as you seek to obtain the fullest account possible from an individual interviewee. However, it is often reasonable to anticipate that certain probes or prompts are likely to be needed at a specific point in an interview, and in such cases it makes sense to include them on the interview guide. This may be done at the outset, when designing the guide, and probes and prompts may also be added in the light of experience as the study progresses. For example, returning to the topic guide in Box 3.2, we may anticipate the need for probes and prompts to follow up the question asking why the participant started attending the Community Gym. For instance, we may want to be sure that they reflect on a variety of possible reasons for joining, and find out whether there had been a particular 'trigger' to their decision. However, we may be concerned that the notion of a 'trigger' may need some clarification. This part of the topic guide might therefore be laid out as below:

Why did you start attending the Community Gym?

   Probe: Health, fitness, social reasons?
   Probe: Any specific 'triggers' to starting?
   (**Prompt**: e.g. following advice from a health professional, influence of friends or family, an incident that made you concerned about your fitness or health?)

Care must be taken in the way probes and prompts are formulated, so as to avoid them 'leading' participants such that they feel a particular answer is required. We will discuss this issue in detail in Chapter 4.

Conclusion

The success of a qualitative interview study is not just based on how well you ask questions and how skilfully you analyse the data. Rather, the decisions that you make at the very start of the research process, when you are designing your study, can have a major impact on its outcomes. In this chapter we have provided advice on each of the main steps on the journey, from framing your research question to deciding on the areas to include in your interview guide. We would stress again that doing all this effectively requires you both to be aware of your theoretical position and its underlying philosophical assumptions and to be pragmatic about what you can achieve within the resources available to you.

Note

1 Note that we use the word 'organisation' in a very wide sense, to include small, informal groupings such as self-help groups, clubs and interest groups as well as larger, more formal bodies.

Recommended reading

Patton, M.Q. (1990) *Qualitative Evaluation and Research Methods* (2nd edition). Newbury Park, CA: Sage.
An accessible and highly practical overview of all the main stages of designing and carrying out qualitative projects. Strongly focused on evaluation studies.

Robson, C. (2002) *Real World Research* (2nd edition). Oxford: Blackwell.
Covers all the main issues in designing research projects in real-world settings, including much of relevance to qualitative interview studies.

FOUR

Carrying Out Qualitative Interviews

Producing a good research project based on qualitative interviewing relies on much more than just 'interviewing skills', as we stressed in the previous chapter. Nevertheless, however thoroughly you understand your methodological position, and however well you design your study, what happens in the interviews themselves is crucial. This chapter therefore focuses on the process of actually carrying out a qualitative interview. It provides guidance on the following areas:

- the interview setting
- recording
- building rapport
- how (not) to ask questions
- probing
- starting and finishing interviews
- managing 'difficult' interviews

The interview setting

The physical space in which an interview is located can have a strong influence on how it proceeds. Three aspects of the physical environment are especially important: comfort, privacy and quiet. We will look at how you might achieve each of these in turn, and then in the light of this consider the pros and cons of the types of location you are most likely to use for your interviews.

The physical environment

The first requirement of the interview environment is that it should be as comfortable as possible, for the interviewee and for you. This means not only physical comfort but also (perhaps more significantly) psychological comfort. If participants feel tense and unsettled, it may be reflected in stilted and under-developed answers to your questions. Avoid sitting so that you face the interviewee over a desk or table; this can feel too formal and may remind the participant of a job interview – not an association you want to raise for them. Sitting around the corner of a desk is a better option, or you may be able to arrange two easy chairs with perhaps a small table between them – again at an angle that encourages informality. Ensure you are close enough to hear them clearly and read non-verbal communication, but not so close that you are intruding on their personal space.

Privacy for the interview setting is vital. You want to avoid as far as is practical any danger of being overlooked or interrupted during the interview. If you are using a room in the participant's or your own organisation, you should try to have phones switched off or diverted, and a note on the door asking people not to disturb you. Also, if you are booking a room, make sure you book it for longer than you anticipate you will need for the interview, to allow for introductions and briefing, and breaks the participant might want to take, and so on. We would suggest that you allow at least an hour and a half for what you would expect to be a 45-minute to one-hour interview.

In some circumstances, participants may not want others to know that they are taking part in your research. Perhaps they may fear censure from their organisation, their family or others because of the nature of the interview topic. Where you anticipate that this could be the case, you should have an option available to locate the interview where there is minimal danger of their participation being discovered by those they wish to conceal it from. This may often mean holding it on 'your' territory, such as a room in your university.

Try to use a location that is relatively quiet. This will not only help make the environment relaxing, but will also reduce the likelihood of problems with the audibility of recordings. Human attentional capacity means that we can quite easily filter out background noise when listening to someone talking in close proximity to us. Recording equipment does not have the same ability – indeed, background noises often sound surprisingly loud on tape. We have both had instances where recordings have been rendered almost inaudible by such things as traffic noise (even through a closed window), office machinery and in one instance birdsong! Even where you can avoid background noise, you need to consider the acoustics of the room you plan to use. Large, high-ceilinged rooms – especially if fairly empty – can produce an echo to the voice that seriously impedes comprehension.

Choosing the interview location

It is generally good practice to ask participants where they would like the interview to be held, and more often than not they will select somewhere on 'their' territory – such as their workplace or home. This of course limits your ability to arrange the physical space in an optimal manner, but you can at least let participants know what is required of the space in terms of comfort, privacy and quiet. If you are carrying out a series of interviews in an organisation over one or more day(s), it may be possible to negotiate access to a room that you can have control over for the duration of the data collection, and thus have more opportunity to arrange as you wish.

Where you are carrying out interviews in participants' homes, the presence of other family members or friends can create difficulties. You need to think in advance about whether you are happy to allow another person to sit in on the interview, as it is not uncommon for a family member to request this (and occasionally to insist on it). If the presence of another person is completely unacceptable for your research, you need to make this very clear to participants in advance, and reiterate it at the start of the interview. Equally, if you would be willing to allow another person to be present, you need to explain to them the level of participation permissible. In some projects it may be a positive benefit to have a joint interview, in others it may be vital that the second person contributes minimally to the interaction. When interviewing in participants' homes, your own safety is something you must think seriously about, and discuss with supervisors or colleagues. (We will address this issue in more depth in Chapter 7.)

Sometimes participants may prefer to be interviewed away from their home or workplace – perhaps because of concerns about privacy, as noted above. In these cases, your best choice is likely to be to find a suitable room in your university or other workplace, enabling you to organise the space yourself to suit the requirements of the interview situation. Another option could be a public space (indoor or outdoor). Public spaces can have the advantage of being comfortable and relaxing, and their neutrality may be an advantage. With indoor spaces such as cafés, the possibility of being overheard needs to be borne in mind, and you should let owners or managers know what you are doing to avoid suspicion. A park or similar outdoor space can also be a comfortable environment and one with less danger of being overheard. The major drawback is likely to be a practical one – it can be hard to obtain a good recording of a conversation in the open. At the very least, you need to try out your equipment *in situ* before agreeing to use a particular outdoor location. (If you live in a climate such as ours in the north of England, the weather is also a factor you will have to consider.)

Recording

In most qualitative research traditions it is strongly preferable, if not essential, to have a full record of each interview. Usually, this means utilising some form of audio-recording, although in a small proportion of studies video-recording is used. Keeping a detailed handwritten record can be necessary – for instance, when a participant refuses consent to be recorded or where there is a technical failure with equipment. In this section we will examine how to use each of these recording media optimally.

Before we consider the practicalities of recording, however, it is worth considering how the presence of an audio- or video-recorder may impact on the interview process. As Warren (2002) states, recording equipment inevitably has meaning for the interviewee; furthermore, it is likely to have different meanings for different people. For example, to a young offender it may be a reminder of procedures in the criminal justice system, and evoke suspicion or hostility. For others it may be seen as a sign of the 'serious' nature of the project, and encourage them to make an effort to provide the interviewer with 'what she wants'. While you can never be certain in advance how any one person will react to being recorded, you can often anticipate likely responses and seek to take action to alleviate potential problems. Where you might reasonably expect suspicion, you need to make a particular effort to emphasise the confidentiality of their participation and explain how that is going to be achieved – where tapes will be stored, who will have access to them, how transcripts will be anonymised, and so on. In contrast, when participants seem overly concerned to provide you with the 'right' answers for your needs, you should explain clearly that they can best help you by giving as full an account as possible of their own views and experiences.

Sometimes the inhibiting effect of recording only becomes apparent when you switch the machine off and the interviewee immediately opens up with some highly relevant material. One option here is to ask the interviewee whether they would be willing to repeat the comment on tape. If they are not, or the circumstances are such that you do not feel comfortable asking them, you can still keep a written record of they key points they have said, but you should check first whether they are happy for you to use the material or whether it is to be entirely 'off the record'. We discuss how to deal with 'off the record' comments in more detail in Chapter 7.

Audio-recording

The range of technologies for audio-recording interviews has broadened considerably in recent years. Where once almost all qualitative researchers used analog tape recorders (with standard, mini- or micro-tapes), today there are several digital options, including mini-disc and solid state recorders. In choosing between these, there are a number of factors to think about, including price, recording quality and convenience of use. Analog tape recorders are generally cheaper than mini-disc and solid state recorders, and within the former category the better quality recording tends to come from those using standard size tape. Cheap dictaphones – usually using micro-tapes – are almost always not up to the task of producing a good recording of an interview. Digital equipment can produce excellent recording quality, and audio files can be downloaded directly to a computer enabling the use of specialist transcription software. Market trends suggest that solid state recorders are increasingly popular and there is a danger that buying a mini-disc recorder could be an investment in a technology that becomes redundant fairly quickly. Using a solid state recorder is a little more complex than a conventional analog tape recorder, and may require software to download the files and to enable you to transcribe directly on to the computer.

Whichever technology you use, you must make sure you are thoroughly familiar with how it operates before you begin interviewing. If at all possible, you should test out the equipment in the room you will be using, to see whether there is a problem with acoustics and work out exactly where you will place the recorder and external microphone(s) if using them. Even though you should have made it clear on recruiting participants that you wish to record the interview, and must obtain consent so to do, people commonly feel uncomfortable about being recorded. We would suggest that one way to address this is to switch the recorder on as early as possible – for instance, when you start explaining the interview procedure to them. Our experience suggests that once participants get talking about a topic that matters to them, most quite quickly become less self-conscious about being recorded than they were at the start – so the longer they have to get used to the machine the better. During the interview avoid the temptation to constantly check that the machine is functioning correctly. Where possible, place it in such a way that you can clearly see the 'record' light illuminated.

One disadvantage of analog tape recorders is that you may need to turn the tape over during the interview. This means that you may miss something in the process, and the act of stopping the recorder and turning the tape over might draw the participant's attention to the recording process in a way that increases self-consciousness. The longest tapes generally available last one hour a side, but it is worth bearing in mind that these are more likely to snap or tangle than shorter tapes because greater length is achieved by making the tape itself thinner. A strategy to avoid losing any of the interview as one side of a tape ends is to have two recorders in use, one of which is started up five minutes after the other. The second recorder is thus still recording while you turn the tape over on the first. Naturally, digital recorders avoid this problem.

Video-recording

Video is more often used to capture 'naturalistic' interaction in approaches such as conversation analysis and discourse analysis (Heath, 1997) than for recording formal research interviews. However, there are occasions where you may find it worthwhile. A video-recording can be very useful in focus groups (see Chapter 5), to help you identify speakers and to enable non-verbal interaction among participants to be drawn upon in the analysis. Equally, any study which has a strong emphasis on the bodily aspects of experience may benefit from the availability of a visual record of the interview.

Inevitably, video-recording places more constraints on where you carry out your interviews than audio-recording. In order to obtain good data from both parties in the interview (which you would usually want to do), you may well need two cameras and ideally expert technical help with setting them up in the most effective possible positions. This means that it is usually preferable to carry out video-recorded interviews in a setting such as a university, where equipment and technical support will be available. You may also need technical help in preparing video tapes for transcription – for instance, digitising them (unless of course you can use digital video). Transcribing video so that you can match non-verbal with verbal interaction is an extremely arduous process, even where you are not seeking the level of detail required in conversation analysis and similar traditions.

As with audio-recording, you must let participants know from the start that you wish to video the interview, and must obtain their explicit consent to do so. Again, we would advise that you set the video recorder(s) going early in the proceedings, to enable participants to get used to the fact that they are being filmed. Note, though, that participants are not necessarily more self-conscious about videoing than audio-recording. Murray (2008) argues that interviewees quickly become accustomed to filming, so long as they have an interesting and meaningful topic to talk about.

Note-taking

It is always preferable in qualitative research to obtain an audio- (or video-) recording of the interview, and for some methods it is absolutely essential. You could not, for example, carry out conversation analysis or discourse analysis without a full, accurate record of what the participant said, and it is hard to see how a phenomenological or narrative analysis could be completed without a verbatim transcript. Nevertheless, there are circumstances where you may be forced to rely on written notes, and where such notes can be of value in the absence of a recording. You may also find it useful to take some notes to accompany audio-recording. Whatever the circumstances, we would always suggest you explain to participants why you need to take notes.

One situation in which note-taking becomes essential is where a participant refuses to allow audio-recording at the start of the interview. This is often due to suspicion about what may be done with recordings and who may have access to them, so if a participant declines to be recorded, it is worth checking that they have fully understood your arrangements to preserve confidentiality – though of course you should not exert any pressure on them to change their mind. If they persist with the refusal, but are still happy to continue with the interview, you will have to rely on the notes you take, and it is as well to be prepared for such an eventuality. The challenge is to balance the need to attend to what is being said and to framing your questions in response, and the need to keep the interview flowing reasonable smoothly. Unless you are an expert in shorthand, you should accept that you can only keep notes indicating the main points covered. Do not constantly ask the participants to repeat themselves but rather at key junctures, you might ask them to sum up their preceding points. Only when they make a comment that immediately strikes you as especially important might you ask them to repeat it again – and you should keep such requests to a minimum. We have found it a useful technique to leave plenty of space around the notes you have made. Then, as soon as possible after the interview, add in as much further detail as you can recall. Incidentally, where you have used audio-recording, always check that the machine has recorded properly; if it has not, you can use immediate post-interview notes to replace a failed recording, or to assist in the transcription of one that proves to be of poor quality.

Note-taking during an audio-recorded interview may serve either of two main purposes. First, you can provide yourself with brief written reminders to follow up issues raised by the participant at a later point, instead of interrupting them in mid-flow. Second, you can keep a written record of non-verbal behaviours where these may be essential to a full and accurate transcription. For instance, you may want to note gestures or facial expressions that suggest strong emotions. Of course, you cannot possibly keep a running commentary on the participant's non-verbal communication throughout the interview. The aim, rather, is to pick out those incidents where it appears particularly powerful in conveying meaning. When you take notes during an audio-recorded interview, it is often useful to do so on a copy of the interview guide itself, as this can help you subsequently to locate the notes within the course of the interview.

Building rapport

Building rapport with your participant is widely seen as a key ingredient in successful qualitative interviewing. It is important, though, to be clear what we do and do not mean by 'rapport'. Starting with the negative, building rapport is *not* about ingratiating yourself with your participant. If you try too hard to be liked by them, you may find yourself reinforcing their opinions in a way that can become leading. Rapport is essentially about trust – enabling the participant to feel comfortable in opening up to you. There are no guaranteed recipes for rapport, but there are things you can do to encourage a positive relationship that enables trust to develop. Much of the advice in the rest of this chapter is relevant to this goal – for instance, the sections on how to formulate questions and how to manage difficulties in the interviewer–interviewee relationship – but here we want to concentrate on how you present the research project and yourself to your participants. Getting these wrong can undermine anything else you do to build rapport.

Introducing your project

In the process of recruiting participants (see Chapter 3), you will have provided them with information about your project, most commonly in the form of a written information sheet. You may well have had more personal contact with them, via e-mail or a telephone call, for instance. Such communication is not merely an administrative process to ensure you have someone to interview, who is able to give informed consent to their participation in your research. It also serves to set up expectations in the participant-to-be that can impact on the way your relationship with them develops over the interview.

Institutional ethics review bodies will generally insist that information provided prior to interview is clear and comprehensible to the intended participant group, and provides an honest account of why the study is being undertaken and how data from it will be used. However, it is dangerous to assume that just because people have been given an 'approved' information sheet and are willing to sign a consent form, they share your understanding of the purpose of the research and the nature of the interview process. As Warren (2002: 89) states:

… there are many indications in the literature on qualitative interviewing that the [participant's] understanding may not match the interviewer's from the start, may shift over time, or may be 'confused'.

If this is not recognised and responded to, it can harm the rapport-building between interviewer and interviewee. It is therefore vital that you do not assume that because the participant has 'been told' what the research is for and has signed a consent form, no further explanation is needed on your part. Always take time before you start the interview proper to check that the participant has an adequate understanding of what is about to happen and why, and if necessary revisit this during the interview.

Self-presentation

In addition to what you tell participants about your project (in writing and verbally), how you present yourself will impact on your relationship with a participant. Self-presentation includes what you wear, your use of non-verbal communication, and the kind of vocabulary you use. These aspects do not just convey something of your personal qualities, such as whether you are warm and friendly or cold and distant, but perhaps more importantly provide the participant with information about your identity. For example, a PhD student of the first author was conducting group interviews with community nurses about some important and contentious organisational changes that were happening. At her first group, she found that participants were rather guarded and suspicious towards her, despite her reassurances about confidentiality and her independent status. On reflection she wondered whether the fact she had dressed rather formally for the interview might have aligned her in participants' minds with management. For subsequent interviews she dressed more casually and emphasised her student status more clearly: this did seem to contribute towards a more open and trusting atmosphere in the groups (Ross, 2005).

How (not) to ask questions

In this section we will focus on the process of actually asking questions in an interview. Our main concern will be with how questions are formulated, but we will also address the issue of managing your non-verbal communication in the interview setting.

Formulating questions: treating words carefully

We have seen in earlier chapters that interviewing can be seen as a special form of conversation. It differs from ordinary spontaneous conversation not only in that one party does most of the questioning and the other most of the answering, but also in that the former (the interviewer) has to be very careful about the way in which her questions are formulated. Adding to the challenge for the interviewer, her need to take care in her choice of words is coupled with the need to appear relaxed and comfortable in order to put the interviewee at their ease (see the section on 'Building rapport', above).

In order to clarify what constitutes good practice in questioning, it can be helpful to examine the opposite. Look at the interview extract in Box 4.1, in which a researcher is asking a teacher about his experience of dealing with disruptive behaviour in the classroom.

Box 4.1   Interview extract for 'How (not) to ask questions'

The extract below illustrates some of the pitfalls that can occur when asking questions in an interview. See the section 'How (not) to ask questions' for a discussion of these.

1   I: So can you give me an example of a recent incident where a pupil was
2   disruptive in your lesson?
3
4   T: Well, there was this lad – I'll call him 'Jack' – who's always…well, you,
5   know, at best he's just disinterested but very often he's messing about,
6   disturbing the kids next to him and all that. Anyways, yesterday he was up to
7   his usual tricks – leaning back on his chair to talk to his mate behind him,
8   throwing stuff at the girls in front, nothing REALLY awful, just constant low-
9   level disruption. I told him to stop two or three times, got nowhere, so I made
10   him move over to the isolation desk – out on the front beside me on his own.
11   He's not been there more than five minutes when the whole class starts
12   laughing and I spin round to catch him pulling a daft face at me!
13
14   I: Didn't that make you furious?
15
16   T: Well, to be honest it was a mixture – a mixture really – I WAS annoyed but
17   also I kinda saw the funny side.
18
19   I: Really? I would have been mad as hell.
20
21   T: Thing is, he's not at all a nasty lad, just not very academic and a bit of a
22   joker. Hmmm [pause] perhaps I should have been angrier. But anyway, I
23   sent him out into the corridor, told him to calm down there for ten minutes and
24   if I heard so much as a peep out of him he'd be at the Head's office before his
25   feet could touch the ground.
26
27   I: What did the Head say to him?
28

29 T: No, I didn't actually have to send him there in the end. He quietened down –
30 came back for last quarter of an hour and actually seemed to get a bit of
31 work done.

32

33 I: OK. Let's imagine though that he had carried on messing around, or if he –
34 or another pupil – had behaved in a more seriously disruptive way – at least
35 what YOU would see as more serious – in that case, what might be the sort of
36 tipping point that would have you taking the next step, whether that was the
37 Head's office or whatever?

38

39 T: Sorry, you lost me a bit there. Are we still talking about that specific
40 incident or what I might do in general?

41

42 I: Er, that incident I think. What kind of thing might have led you to sending
43 him the Headmistress? And what, other than the Head, might have been the
44 next escalation if you like in punishment?

45

46 T: Well, the choice could be between the Head and putting him on report. I
47 guess I thought sending him to Mrs Whitlow might be a kind of short, sharp
48 shock. And to be honest, it doesn't involve all the admin that going on report
49 entails.

This extract illustrates several of the kinds of mistake that can all too easily be made when formulating questions in a qualitative interview. Specifically, it includes instances of leading questions, over-complex and multiple questions, judgemental responses and a failure to listen to the interviewee.

Leading questions

A question is leading when its wording suggests to the interviewee the kind of response that is anticipated. In Box 4.1, the interviewer's question 'Didn't that make you furious?' (line 14) is leading. It suggests to the interviewee that anger is the appropriate response to the situation he has described. The danger is that the interviewee may feel some degree of pressure to conform to what appears to be expected by the interviewer. This does not mean that people are likely to give a knowingly false response; rather they may play up the extent of their conformity or play down aspects of their experience that go against the perceived expectations. Equally, they may just have the direction of their account sidetracked from that which it might otherwise have taken.

Over-complex and multiple questions

The wording of questions should be kept as simple, clear and direct as possible. The question that begins 'OK. Let's imagine...' (lines 33–37) shows what can happen when an interviewer fails to do this. A rather long and convoluted hypothetical question results in the participant losing the thread and having to ask for clarification. If this kind of questioning style persists, the smooth flow of the interview can break down, with an impact on the quality of the data obtained.

In this instance, the interviewer follows up with another example of a poorly formed question – namely a multiple question. This is where the interviewer asks two or more questions in combination, which can be confusing for the participant. The result is often that only one part of the question is addressed, as happens in our example – the interviewee fails to answer the part of the question asking about the circumstances that might have led to him sending the pupil to the Headmistress (lines 42–44).

Judgemental responses

The interviewer should try to avoid responding to what the interviewee says in a way that suggests she is making a judgement about their position. Judgemental comments are problematic for two reasons. First, they may have the same effect as a leading question, in that they signify the kind of answer that will be deemed appropriate. Second, they may harm rapport, by putting the interviewee on the defensive. In our example, the interviewer's comment that the example of pupil misbehaviour would have made her 'mad as hell' (line 19) is somewhat judgemental, suggesting that the teacher's own more ambiguous response might not be normal. The latter's subsequent remark ('…perhaps I should have been angrier') shows he is beginning to question the appropriateness of the response he gave previously. While a single mildly judgemental comment such as this is unlikely to derail the whole interview, if the interviewer persisted in the same tone it could well begin to have a deleterious effect.

Failure to listen

Failing to listen to the participant's response can lead to inappropriate questioning, potentially leaving him or her frustrated or irritated at the interviewer. Our interviewer demonstrates this on line 27, where she has missed the fact that the participant has just told her that he only threatened to send the pupil to the Headmistress. In reality, it is almost inevitable that in the course of a long interview your attention may lapse occasionally – especially as you are having to listen to what is being said and think about the overall progress of the interview. If you realise that you have missed something, you may ask the interviewee to repeat or clarify their last point, particularly if you seem to be at an important place in the interview. However, if you repeatedly have to make such requests, the interviewee may conclude that you are not really very interested in what they have to say.

One way to minimise the danger of lapses in attention is not to overburden yourself with your schedule of interviews. Carrying out three or four interviews back-to-back is tiring and demanding. If the practicalities of your project mean you do need to carry out multiple interviews on a single day (e.g. because of access issues), try to take substantial breaks between them.

Non-verbal communication

If you appear tense and nervous, the interviewee is unlikely to feel at ease either. Most of us have our own personal forms of non-verbal 'leakage' that can reveal any tension or anxiety we may be feeling – persistent foot-tapping, fiddling with jewellery, biting nails, and so on. Reflect on your own non-verbal 'habits' and try to be conscious of them in order to minimise them during interviews. It can be useful to carry out a mock interview with a friend or colleague and either video-tape it or ask a third party to observe and note any non-verbal behaviours that could be distracting for a participant.

Probing

We defined 'probes' as a specific type of question in Chapter 3, in relation to their inclusion in your interview guide. However, although you can sometimes anticipate and prepare useful probes, in most cases the majority will need to be devised in the course of the interview. In general terms, probing seeks to add depth to interview data. In reaching this goal, it is possible to identify a range of specific roles that probes can play. Drawing on Patton (1990) and Rubin and Rubin (1995), we would suggest three main types of probe. *Elaboration* probes encourage the participant to keep talking in order to gather more detail on the topic at hand. *Clarification* probes seek explanation – either of specific words and phrases or of more substantial sections of the account that the interviewer has not fully understood. *Completion* probes ask the interviewee to finish a story or explanation that seems to the interviewer to have broken off before its 'natural' end. Box 4.2 provides examples of the three types of probe, and considers how they might be combined.

Box 4.2   Types of probe

Tom has been interviewing a youth sports coach (Sarah) about how she tries to motivate teenagers to maintain commitment to their sport activities. Tom has just asked her what she does if she feels a member of the club is losing motivation. She replies as follows:

Sarah: Well, let me think. If it's someone who's been here a while, normally a good performer – actually I can think of an example like that. What I did with this girl, I thought she needed more of a challenge, so basically I got her aiming at Regionals.

(Continued)

(Continued)

Following this response, Tom could use each of the three types of probe. To encourage Sarah to say more on this topic he could use an elaboration probe – either a non-verbal/paralinguistic cue or an actual question:

Tom: Aha (nodding head)

or

Tom: And what if the person losing motivation was a less competent performer?

To make sure he understands what Sarah has told him, he could use a clarification probe:

Tom: Could you just briefly explain to me what 'Regionals' are?

If Tom is interested in the specific story Sarah has brought in as an example, he might use a completion probe:

Tom: And was that successful for this girl?

In this example, ideally Tom would use all three types of probe to maximise the depth of data obtained, but of course he could not use them all at once or we would have the problem of multiple questions. He therefore needs to think about the order in which to use the different probes. There is no absolute right and wrong in this, but the goal of facilitating the easy flow of the interview should guide his choice. In this case, we would start with the clarification probe, as knowing what 'Regionals' are might guide his subsequent questioning. Also, it is likely to produce a fairly simple response in the form of a definition and not lead the interview off on a tangent. We would then tend to favour using the completion probe in order to keep this particular story going. Finally, we could use the elaboration (question) probe, to get Sarah to discuss other strategies for motivating the young people in her charge. This part of the interview would then look as follows:

Tom: So what do you do if you think one of the kids is losing interest in what they do at the club, losing motivation?

Sarah: Well, let me think. If it's someone who's been here a while, normally a good performer – actually I can think of an example like that. What I did with this girl, I thought she needed more of a challenge, so basically I got her aiming at Regionals.

Tom: Could you just explain to me what the 'Regionals' are? **[clarification]**

Sarah: Sorry – just took it for granted…we have regular official competitions for all the sports we do, but Jenna's an athlete so I was thinking of athletics. In athletics its very structured – District, Regional, National. I thought she probably had the ability to get through to the Regionals in sprinting or long jump.

> *Tom:* And what happened? Was she enthused by this? **[completion]**
>
> *Sarah:* Yes! One of my success stories – probably why Jenna came to mind! She got through to the Finals of the 200m at Region, came fifth which is a real achievement, and she's determined to improve on it next year. She just might.
>
> *Tom:* That's great. What about kids who are less able than Jenna, who you don't feel have the talent to compete at the higher levels? What strategies might you use with one of them who was beginning to lose motivation? **[elaboration]**

Good use of probes requires good listening skills, in line with our comments in the previous section ('How (not) to ask questions'). We would reiterate the point that not over-burdening yourself with numerous interviews in succession should help you to remain alert and sensitive to opportunities for effective probing. Where a participant's response invites a number of different probes from you – as happens quite commonly – you may find it useful, once you have decided which to use first, to jot down reminders so you can return later to others. This is particularly the case where the answer to your initial probe invites further probing, perhaps resulting in three or four 'layers' of probe and response on a specific topic.

While probing is essential to obtaining real depth in interview data, you can do it too much. One example would be where you probe in enormous detail on an area of the interview that is of limited relevance to your research question, resulting in restricted time to spend on more crucial areas. Another is where you spend a great deal of time seeking clarifications of unfamiliar terms – technical language, professional jargon, slang words or whatever. As Patton (1990) points out, if you appear too ignorant of the participant's world and the topic at hand, he may simply decide that it is not worth his while making an effort to describe it in detail to you. In such circumstances, try to identify the terms that you absolutely must clarify in order to make any progress with the interview and concentrate your clarification probes on these. You may get a chance to ask for further clarifications later, and if (as is likely) you are audio-recording the interview, you should be able to inquire about others after transcription.

Starting and finishing interviews

You need to give special forethought to how you are going to start and finish your interviews. The way you start can have a significant impact on how your rapport (or lack of it) with the interviewee develops. It is normally seen as good practice to start with relatively unthreatening and simple questions, such as asking for descriptive information about the participant in relation to the topic under investigation. For instance, in a study of teacher experiences of classroom discipline of the kind used in Box 4.1, you might start by requesting an outline of their career history and continue by asking them about school policies regarding discipline. Neither of these areas requires self-disclosure on sensitive topics, but the sequence does ease the participant into the main focus of the interview.

As we have noted, it is commonplace as an interview develops to move into more difficult – perhaps emotionally-charged – areas of questioning. This can create a problem in terms of how you bring an interview to a conclusion, as you do not want to say your goodbyes and leave immediately after the participant has reached the most sensitive part of their account. Just as it is usually good practice to ease the participant into the interview, you should plan a strategy for easing them out. Try to plan closing questions that move away from self-disclosure and hand as much control as possible to the participant. One form that is often helpful is a question focusing on desired future changes or developments. Thus we could ask our hypothetical teacher what their top priority would be if they could influence government policy on discipline in schools. To close, it is generally good practice to ask the participant if there is anything else they want to tell you, and invite them to ask any questions they may have about the research project and/or their part in it. Unless the participant asks you to turn it off, leave your recording equipment running until the very end of the interview, as it is not uncommon for interviewees to mention something of interest and significance at this stage. Should this happen, do not miss the opportunity to reopen more detailed questioning, so long as the participant is happy to continue.

Managing 'difficult' interviews

Any qualitative interview can lead you in unexpected directions to face unexpected challenges, so that no amount of experience or preparation can provide you with a 'stock' response to every circumstance. Nevertheless, there are certain types of interview situation where you can reasonably anticipate particular difficulties and with some forethought at least be forearmed to face them. We will consider four such situations here: interviews where there are significant status issues, interviewer role conflicts, interviews on emotionally sensitive topics, and dealing with under- and over-communicative interviewees.

Status issues

If an interviewee perceives an interviewer to be of markedly higher or lower status than herself, this can have an impact on the quality of the interview. In the qualitative research literature, there tends to be more consideration of situations where the interviewer is perceived to be of higher status than the interviewee than vice versa. This is often in the context of discussions about power in the interview, and the desire to equalise this between the parties (Briggs, 2002; McKie, 2002). However, for postgraduate students in particular, perceived status differences are just as likely to be in the opposite direction. Status differences can deleteriously effect the course of an interview in two ways: directly, by inhibiting interviewees from discussing particular topics (e.g. for fear of appearing ignorant or losing face), and indirectly, by preventing the building of rapport between interviewer and interviewee.

Interviewees may see themselves as lower in status than the interviewer because of differences in social class, educational level, occupation, age, and so on. Sometimes such differences may be compounded by interviewer role conflicts – for instance, where a qualified nurse undertaking a Masters degree programme is interviewing an unqualified healthcare assistant. We will look more closely at the role conflict issue shortly. In general terms, where you anticipate perceived status differences in this direction, you should seek to minimise them through the way you present yourself and your research. How you do this must always take into account the specific context, although avoiding jargon and overly-academic language is always likely to be especially important. Inviting participants to attend the interview at a university or similar site should probably be avoided, and if your participants may be unable or unwilling to be interviewed at home, you should try to identify alternative settings that will be familiar and comfortable for them.

High status participants may be difficult to interview because they are used to being in control in their interactions with others – to asking rather than answering questions. This can result in the kind of situation we discuss below in relation to 'the over-communicative interviewee'. Rarely, more serious problems can develop where the interviewee experiences the reversal of roles as threatening, and seeks to assert his normal authority by undermining the confidence of the interviewer. He may do this by trying to show up the researcher's lack of knowledge of the topic under investigation ('Did you *really* not know that?'), by questioning the validity of her methods ('You can't learn anything from just chatting with people'), or the credibility of her discipline ('Of course, Psychology is not a proper science').

To reduce the likelihood of problems like these when interviewing high-status participants, you should avoid challenging their authority in their own field, but remain sure of your own expertise in yours. After all, it is most unlikely they know more about qualitative methods than you do. Make sure you have done some background research into your area of study, so you are at least as knowledgeable as a well-informed layperson might be expected to be. For instance, if you were interviewing school headteachers (principals) about discipline, you should ensure you have a grounding in the key points of relevant recent legislation. If you are unlucky enough to face an interviewee who is intent on belittling your role, your best option is to calmly and politely acknowledge your difference of opinion with them, but not get pulled into an argument, and try to move the interview forward.

Interviewer role conflicts

In some cases researchers can face a potential conflict between their role as an interviewer and other roles they may have (or be perceived as having) in relation to the interviewee. Probably the most common example of this is where the researcher is also a practising health or social care professional and is interviewing members of the service user group they work with in their professional life. If you are in such a position, the key requirement is to draw a clear boundary between your researcher and professional roles from the start. Tell participants explicitly that you are not in a position to deal personally with any health or social care problems they may talk about in their interviews as you are there only in the capacity of a researcher. You can, however, bring with you a range of contact information for services you may anticipate as being relevant to your participants, which you can offer if necessary at the end of the interview. Some professionals may be bound by professional codes of conduct that legally override other ethical commitments – for instance, responsibility to report cases where there are strong suspicions of child abuse or where serious professional malpractice may have occurred. Again, it is important that you make any such responsibilities clear to participants before the interview commences.

The other circumstance in which you might face role conflicts is where you are carrying out interviews with close friends and/or family members. We would advise that if you are doing this, you need to think very carefully beforehand about any issues that could emerge that might create problems in your relationship with the participant beyond the interview situation. After that, it is generally a good idea to have an informal discussion with the person so that they are sure about what the interview is going to cover, and can think in advance about what they are and are not happy to discuss. You should take special care in protecting confidentiality and anonymity in interviews like this, as whatever you publish may be read by other family or friendship-group members, to whom the interviewee could be easily identifiable (see Chapter 7 for more on this issue).

Dealing with sensitive topics

Any qualitative interview can raise issues that the interviewee finds upsetting, although of course some topics are more likely than others to evoke strong feelings from participants: serious illness, bereavement, conflict or harassment at work, criminal victimisation, and so on. You need to think ahead about how you will deal with situations in which a participant becomes distressed. What you should certainly not do is decide to immediately terminate the interview without consulting the participant. This may simply give the message that you cannot cope with their feelings. In any case, the fact that a participant becomes distressed does not necessarily mean that they are finding the interview experience a negative one. Especially where they have consented to take part in research on a sensitive topic (of the kind listed above), participants often report that they appreciate the chance to discuss a difficult subject with a sympathetic listener. In most cases, your best response if a participant becomes distressed is to calmly and gently offer them a range of options about how to proceed. For instance, you might say: 'I can see you're finding this difficult. If you want to move on to a different topic or take a break, that's fine. Or if you want to end the interview now, that's entirely up to you.' We will return to the issue of your responsibilities regarding the psychological well-being of participants when we discuss research ethics in Chapter 7.

Under- and over-communicative interviewees

Some interviews can be difficult because the interviewee says too little or too much. Given the aim in qualitative interviewing to explore experiences in depth, the former is generally more of a problem than the latter. If you have a participant whose responses rarely go much beyond the monosyllabic, you must consider what might be holding them back. One possibility is that despite everything you have told them before the interview, they are still con-cerned about confidentiality and/or anonymity. If you have the impression that this may be the case, it could be fruitful to reiterate what you will be doing with the data and how you will protect their identity. Sometimes people may feel they are helping you by getting the interview over with quickly. You can try to counter this by using frequent probes that encourage them to 'tell me more'. Of course, you don't want to do this so much that it feels like you are harassing the participant, so it can be particularly effective to use silence to coax a response. When the interviewee gives a very short, superficial response, just refrain from responding yourself for a few seconds. Often this will serve as a cue to the participant that it is still their 'turn' to talk, and they may then expand on their answer without the need for you to say anything.

Taking the other extreme, the fact that a participant has a great deal to say is not in itself a problem – quite the opposite! Similarly, if someone seems to go off on a tangent, it is usually best to let them run with it for a while – they may bring you to perspectives on your research topic that you had not considered before. But if they are spending a great deal of time on matters of minimal significance to your research, you will need to try to guide them back on track. One tactic is to recall the last relevant section of the interview, and once they pause for breath, ask them to return to that issue and elaborate further. Alternatively, you can thank them for what they have just told you, say you are mindful that you have much you would like to cover with them, and politely ask them to move on to your next question.

Conclusion

Interviewing is without doubt a skill that improves with experience, perhaps above all in managing the potential tension between listening closely and maintaining a sense of where you are – and where you are going – in the interview as a whole. Equally, the more you have carried out, the less likely you are to be thrown by some surprise occurrence in the course of an interview. Whatever your level of experience, though, good preparation can considerably enhance the quality of your interviews (and lack of preparation can undermine them). Thinking carefully in advance about the issues we have covered in this chapter – how you frame your questions, use probes and prompts, start and finish interviews, handle sensitive topics and status issues, as well as technical aspects of recording – should put you in a good position to gain the most from the method. Finally, it is crucial to recognise that even for the most experienced, best prepared interviewer things will sometimes not go as planned. You suddenly realise your participant has fundamentally misunderstood a whole line of questioning. You are constantly interrupted by the interviewee's colleagues, or child or dog. You hear your own voice turning your lovingly crafted question into incomprehensible gobbledegook. The trick is not to panic – take a breath, collect your thoughts and you will usually be able to find a way to deal with the situation. The key feature of the interview is that it is an extended encounter with another person (or persons). As such, it gives you the time to recover from any difficulties that arise and get back on track.

Recommended reading

Kvale, S. (1996) *Interviews: An Introduction to Qualitative Research Interviewing.* Thousand Oaks, CA: Sage.
A classic text on interviewing methodology.

McKie, L. (2002) Engagement and evaluation in qualitative enquiry, in T. May (ed.), *Qualitative Research in Action.* London: Sage.
Contains some interesting examples of issues relating to power and relationships in community-based interview research.

Rubin, H.J. and Rubin, I.S. (1995) *Qualitative Interviewing: The Art of Hearing Data.* Thousand Oaks, CA: Sage.
A good general text with useful insights into the interviewing process.

Warren, C.A.B. (2002) Qualitative interviewing, in J.F. Gubrium and J.A. Holstein (eds), *Handbook of Interview Research: Context and Method.* Thousand Oaks, CA: Sage.
A thoughtful discussion of a broad range of issues relating to carrying out qualitative interviews. One of many useful chapters in this handbook.

FIVE

Group Interviews

In the previous chapter we were concerned with the process of undertaking a face-to-face individual qualitative interview. Similarly, we will now consider process in relation to group interviews, exploring both theoretical and practical issues. There is a plethora of information to draw upon around group interviewing, and while much of the information is comprehensive and instrumental, there are certain issues to consider. In our view, it is important to fully understand why group interviews might be appropriate and what the implications might be for the research. These implications are manifest not only in terms of managing the physical encounter, but also in relation to theory. How is the subjectivity of the individual represented? Are opinions and accounts transformed when given as part of a group interview? How might opinions and accounts be transformed? In this chapter we will be paying specific attention to these issues, exploring:

- why use group interviews?
- different types of group interview
- planning a focus group
- running the focus group.

Why use group interviews?

Group interviews are not new. They were employed as early as the 1920s by Bogardus (1926) when testing his social distance scale. Consequently, with such a lengthy history, group interviews have been used in social research to explore a vast range of issues – for example, mass communication (Merton et al., 1956), health (Morgan, 1988), spirituality (Daaleman et al., 2001), education (Lewis, 1992). This list is almost endless, showing that group interviews have an enduring and broad appeal as a research technique.

Without doubt, one-to-one interviews have certain advantages, but the use of group interviews can open up an opportunity to obtain opinions or attitudes at another level. The data produced in group interviews can reveal the social and cultural context of people's understandings and beliefs. As Blumer (1969: 41) explains:

A small number of individuals, brought together as a discussion or resource group, is more valuable many times over than any representative sample. Such a group, discussing collectively their sphere of life and probing into it as they meet one another's disagreements, will do more to lift the veils covering the sphere of life than any other device that I know of.

Indeed, a situation where people are interacting as part of a group is seen to be more 'naturalistic', to be much closer to everyday life than the individual encounter with a lone interviewer. Group interviews can encourage recall and stimulate opinion elaboration. The very nature of being part of a group can engage participants in a re-evaluation of their existing position. Stated views can often be amplified, qualified, amended or contradicted when expressed as part of a group interview.

In research, getting a group of people together to discuss a topic or issue can have an explicit function. The following 'purposes', outlined by Frey and Fontana (1993: 23–4), show distinct methodological justifications for deploying group interviews in social research.

- *Exploratory*: Here group interviews are often being used in the initial stages of a research project when the researcher is unfamiliar or new to the social context.
- *Pretest*: Group interviews can be used to test questionnaire items, with respondents being asked to comment on readability, comprehension, wording, etc. These are often very structured group interviews aiming to meet very specific outcomes.
- *Triangulation*: Frequently group interviews are used to offer additional data, lending methodological rigour to, for example, one-to-one interviews or questionnaire data.
- *Phenomenological*: When applied with this purpose in mind, group interviews are *not* used either to generate provisional data or to provide additional data. Rather, the data collected may be the only source of information, potentially providing detailed insight about specific phenomena and experiences.

All the purposes presented above are appropriate, justifying the wide-ranging use of group interviews in social research. The identification of this broad spectrum of applications, as might be expected, methodologically reflects the range of theoretical and philosophical approaches taken in research. Moreover, this identification of *why* group interviews are being used should mean that the researcher is aware of the ontological and epistemological underpinnings of the research. For instance, a group interview organised in line with *positivist* thinking might be useful in identifying preliminary variables or to investigate the construct validity of an instrument (e.g. a questionnaire). Alternatively, a focus group might have a *post-positivist* grounding whereby additional data is being used to triangulate existing evidence. Yet, these applications do not preclude using group interviews to access more subjective/intersubjective understandings of human experience in line with *phenomenological* or even *postmodernist* ideologies.

Even so, it is wise to take on board comments made by Billig (1991), who suggests that data generated as part of a focus group interview are very much situated within the specific discussion that takes place, possibly being context-specific. Therefore it is unwise to extrapolate views expressed in focus group discussions as having an uncomplicated and direct relationship with an individual's subjective understanding. Morgan (1997: 29) maintains that '[f]ocus groups are useful when it comes to investigating *what* participants think, but they excel at uncovering *why* participants think as they do'. Here the benefits of group interaction and process are highlighted as a route to knowing why people express specific views. Still, a degree of caution is evident around claiming any direct access to what people think. We do not highlight this issue in order to render ineffective the use of focus groups; indeed, this wariness around laying claim to another's subjective understanding exists throughout much of social research. What we want to do is highlight the complex nature of group interviewing, bringing to the fore epistemological considerations while also providing detailed practical guidance.

Group interviews and sensitive topics

Intuitively, it might seem that group interviews are not the most appropriate research method to use if the research is to explore sensitive areas such as intimate personal relationships, sexual practices, bereavement and loss. It may seem unlikely that people would be willing to share potentially painful and/or usually private feelings and experiences as part of a group interview. However, this is a misconception. In fact, group interviews have been shown to be very useful when exploring sensitive topics (e.g. see Kissling, 1996; Frith, 2000). Having other people involved, as part of a group interview, can make it more likely that people will agree to participate in research that explores sensitive issues. Also, in a group interview participants can feel less exposed as the conversational focus is shared among the group. Even the most sensitive topics can become easier to discuss when participants are aware of others in the group with similar concerns or opinions. Claiming that group interviews are appropriate for researching sensitive topics is premised on a cautionary note. Confidentiality, and how this is negotiated and managed, is a crucial factor that will most certainly need careful consideration if group interviews are used when researching sensitive issues. This is something that we return to later in the chapter.

Different types of group interview

There are different techniques that can be adopted when undertaking group interviews – for example, brainstorming, nominal group techniques, focus groups (see Frey and Fontana, 1993) and, more recently, citizens' juries/ consultative panels (see Coote and Lenhaglan, 1997). In this chapter we will largely concentrate on focus group interviews, as this is the most widely utilised data-gathering technique that researchers adopt when deciding on qualitative group interviews. Nonetheless, we also try to give a flavour of alternative strategies when using group interviews by initially outlining some of the other techniques.

Brainstorming

Often in qualitative research we try to avoid preconceived ideas about a given topic. Therefore, brainstorming, as a research technique, can be used to facilitate the generation of initial ideas. The interviewer's role is relatively passive with no formal structure to the questioning. Ideas generated in this way can primarily be attributed to the participants. With traditional brainstorming sessions the interviewer asks group members to generate ideas, approaches or solutions to a given topic or issue, paying no regard to cost, practicality or feasibility. The interviewer asks participants not to be critical of the ideas generated by other members of the group. Rather, they are encouraged to build on ideas, suggesting modifications and improvements (Stewart et al., 2007). The emphasis is on a creative process aiming to generate a wealth of ideas, the greater the number of ideas, the higher the probability that some will be helpful with regard to the topic under investigation. Brainstorming can be a good strategy for the initial stages of a group interview, generating not only ideas but also providing an initial catalyst for group interaction.

Nominal group technique

Nominal grouping is a highly structured technique designed to keep personal interaction at a minimum during the process of new idea generation. Keeping group interaction to a minimum aims to maximise the individual contribution of each respondent. Nominal groups can be groups in name only, as the participants may not even meet, with summaries of the responses by group members provided by the researcher. Even if participants do meet, they may not interact as each member of the group is interviewed individually. If brought together, group members are asked to speak one at a time when asked a question by the interviewer. In this situation, participants hear the answers of other group members and can elaborate upon them when questioned directly as part of their turn. However, participants are not allowed to interact with other group members.

The common reason for using the nominal group technique is to avoid the influence of group opinion. In research, there may be circumstances in which interaction may inhibit the responsiveness of participants. This may happen if the group includes parents and their children, managers and their subordinates, a recognised expert in the field or even an individual with a particularly dominant personality. The nominal group technique may also be useful if the researcher believes that there is a level of conflict between group members so much so that it would interfere with discussions. Alternatively, the nominal group may be useful if it is anticipated that the majority of the group share the same opinion. With such a majority view, there is the possibility of silencing any dissenting opinions. The belief is that the nominal group technique ensures that all participants are able to give their individual responses. Sometimes this technique can be combined with the more familiar focus group discussion. If employed in this way, initially the nominal group technique is used to obtain the independent responses of individuals, providing input for the focus group discussion that follows.

Citizens' juries

Many qualitative research projects are underpinned by an ideology of social justice and inclusivity, aiming to provide avenues for exploration and consultation with participating populations. Using the imagery, and to a certain extent practices, of the trial by jury system, citizens' juries are seen as a radical participatory research method. Drawing on ideas of 'participatory democracy', citizens' juries can be situated within 'action inquiry', whereby the aim is to stimulate positive social change (Coote and Lenhaglan, 1997; Smith and Wales, 2000). The jury is made up of between 12 and 20 people who are seen to serve as a microcosm of the public. Jurors are often recruited via a random selection of people taken from the electoral roll. Over several sessions, jurors hear from a variety of specialist witnesses and are able to discuss as broad or narrow a range of issues as they see fit.

Like a trial jury, the main principle of a citizens' jury is the belief that once a small sample of a population have heard the evidence, their deliberations can fairly represent the perspectives of the wider community. Wakeford, Murtuja and Bryant's (2004) research, in Lancashire towns, used citizens' juries as a research method. The participating citizens' jury was able to analyse problems faced by people living in their neighbourhoods, proposing a range of solutions. However, making such a consultation process both accessible and attractive to people is challenging, particularly given the substantial amount of time participants need to give as part of this research method.

Focus groups

Focus groups are a familiar part of modern-day living, with retailers, employers and the government often mobilising focus-group conversations on predetermined topics. We decided to cover focus groups last as we wanted to show that this approach is distinct from the techniques already outlined. It is easy to assume that the term 'group interview' means only focus groups, and indeed the two terms are often used interchangeably. However, it is our view that the term 'group interview' represents the broad spectrum of techniques that engage groups of people in either formal or informal interviews. In this spectrum, those involved engage in different levels of interaction. Specifically with regard to focus groups, Morgan (1997: 6) says that his preference is for an 'approach that broadly defines focus groups as a research technique that collects data through group interaction on a topic determined by the researcher'.

Collecting data through group interaction clearly sets the method apart from a *nominal group technique*, which prohibits interaction. Further, the idea that the topic is determined by the researcher is distinct from *brainstorming* and the *citizens' juries*, where participants more actively create the topic under discussion. Frey and Fontana (1993), when distinguishing focus groups from other forms of group interview, suggest that focus groups are 'formal' and 'directive', having a 'moderator' who structures the discussion. However, having planned and run several focus groups, we would support Morgan (1997), who says that focus groups vary along a continuum from the more formally structured interaction to much more informal sessions. Situating the choice of approach, with regard to this formal or informal continuum, relates to the demands of the research, the aims, the setting and the participants. The second author, with a co-researcher, recently organised a focus group involving 11 young people aged 11–14 years. The focus group aimed to engage young people in a discussion that concentrated on their use of a community development project aimed at improving health. The session took place at the community project in an activity room where the young people usually met when accessing community development services. The ethos of the project was centred around community engagement, empowerment and inclusivity. The researchers were 'strangers' to the young people, who were in a familiar place, with friends. It would have been impossible to organise a 'formal' focus group with the structure comprehensively determined by the researchers. The nature of the research and the participating group determined the approach (formal/informal). In this instance, the approach taken was informal, although some activities were included. With a different set of demands the focus group approach can change, becoming far more structured.

Planning a focus group

Selecting participants

Careful consideration needs to be given to the selection of participants for focus group interviews. The aim is to facilitate interactive discussion and the sharing of understandings and views, while at the same time ensuring that the data generated are able to meet the aims of the research. Again, the aims of the research and the issues to be discussed will to a large extent determine the selection of participants. If you want to know about young people's culture, it doesn't make sense to primarily ask a group of middle-aged professionals. So, generally, focus group participants will share some similar characteristics, experiences and/or demographics that will both meet the aims of the research and facilitate conversation. The extent to which participants are similar or different will impact on the interactions that take place in the focus group interview. Homogeneous groups might be relied upon to spend more time interacting and be more compatible than heterogeneous groups. However, the homogeneity of group members will restrict the range of issues and positions discussed in the group interview (Fern, 2001). On the other hand, too much heterogeneity may have a negative impact, possibly stifling group discussion because of the incompatibility of group members.

The research aims might be met by recruiting participants who are total strangers, meeting for the first time in the interview. However, it should be acknowledged that in reality this may be difficult to achieve. Those sharing characteristics that determine their inclusion in the focus group often share wider aspects of their lives – for example, they access the same services, are of the same professional group, know the same people. An alternative sampling strategy is to actively recruit *pre-existing groups*, where clusters of people who live, work or socialise together are invited to participate in the focus group interview. Moreover, recruiting people who already have a relationship can offer a level of confidence in the group's ability to discuss and interact. Arguably, people that we already know, such as friends, family and colleagues, are precisely the people with whom we usually discuss, consider and examine ideas and issues of importance.

Group size

To be effective, it is important when recruiting participants to consider *group size*. It may be difficult to actively engage a smaller group in discussion; alternatively, larger groups may be hard to manage. Possibly the nature of the research demands a larger group. Even so, consideration should be given to how the interaction will be controlled, the time taken to include all participants and the potential for larger groups to break up into smaller discussion groups. Morgan (1997) advises that, practically, a range of 6–10 participants is advisable. Below six it may be difficult to sustain discussion and above 10 it may be difficult to control discussion. This guidance is not meant to be hard and fast; some groups will, by their very nature, be hard to engage and thus a larger number of participants might improve involvement. For highly involved participants, smaller, groups size might work effectively. For example, if the focus group is targeted at social service managers, the researcher would expect a high level of participant involvement. However, if interviewing young people who have never met before, then proceeding to ask them to discuss healthy lifestyle choices, one might anticipate a lower level of participant involvement. As always, it is the finer details of the research that will determine the practicalities of participation.

Whatever group size is selected for participation, it is important to over-recruit. In saying this we recognise that this does run the risk of a larger than expected group. However, in our experience you need to factor in the reality that there will be 'no-shows' – people who agree to participate but then for various reasons do not attend. Offering incentives to participate can reduce the possibility of no-shows (ethical issues surrounding the use of incentives are covered in Chapter 7). Yet, even then, there are no guarantees. It is better to err on the side of caution in order to avoid needing to cancel because there are too few participants to make the focus group viable.

Finding a venue

Typically, the researcher chooses the venue for the focus group interview. Finding a suitable venue is crucial as any environment creates an ambience which can affect how people behave. It is vital that the room is quiet and private, ensuring that the focus group will not be interrupted. Sometimes the research project's participating population, and the overall aims, determine where and when data collection takes place. Researching with particular communities and/or pre-existing groups might mean that the focus group takes place on the group's 'home turf'. They may have a regular meeting place that you can use that is accessible, familiar and comfortable for participants. In this situation, the researcher needs to consider if this venue is suitable for recording the interview. Regrettably, if the venue has relatively open access, or is acoustically problematic, the researcher will need to negotiate a change. We both work at universities that have fully equipped 'interview suites', where groups of participants can easily be accommodated in rooms that have inbuilt digital video-recording equipment. Importantly, the rooms have wall-mounted audio-visual recording equipment that is unobtrusive. Video-recording can be highly beneficial both in terms of capturing non-verbal communication and identifying speakers when transcribing. Even so, there are drawbacks: the cameras often have a limited coverage, with some participants inevitably having their backs to the camera. Participants may feel uneasy knowing that their conversation is being video-recorded. This may be due to feeling self-conscious or because they are concerned about confidentiality issues. However, these facilities are purpose-built, functional and very practical in terms of providing both a venue and the means to record the focus group action. Such venues can sometimes be booked. Alternatively, there are study rooms in libraries and conference venues that have meeting rooms for hire. Despite their functional appeal, we acknowledge that there may be sound reasons for not using these facilities. Such venues are likely to be unfamiliar and to a certain extent artificial – they do not therefore provide a 'naturalistic' environment where participants can feel relaxed and secure from the start. These are major considerations that can only be resolved by researchers spending time thinking through the pros and cons of different venues. Research is often about compromise; it will be hard to find the perfect venue and therefore you will need to work towards capitalising on what is available.

Setting up the room

Importantly, having secured a venue, the room must be arranged comfortably, seating participants in a way that ensures everyone has eye contact with the researcher and, ideally, all other participants. This is generally done by seating participants around a table or in easy chairs. The choice of seating style may be reliant upon availability or be dependent upon what you will be asking participants to take part in. Whatever seating arrangement is decided upon, the researcher needs to be aware of how this might 'feel' for participants. Sitting around a table will feel quite formal, with the alternative being more relaxed.

Housekeeping issues should also be considered – easy access to toilets is essential. The researcher will also need to provide participants with comprehensive directions on how to get to the venue. Checklists of essential items needed for the smooth running of the focus group are really helpful.

Wilkinson (2003) gives an example checklist of some of the supplementary materials that are needed: refreshments (water at the very least), writing materials, informed consent and expenses claim forms (if appropriate), box of tissues, name badges or cards (and marker pens to complete them), recording equipment, including spare tapes and batteries. We have covered recording equipment in a previous chapter and much of the advice is the same. However, it is crucial to thoroughly check the recording equipment. It is not necessary to have high-specification recording equipment, however, the most recent digital recorders are excellent both in terms of quality of recording and downloading. An omnidirectional, flat microphone placed among the group will give a good recording. Remember, having gone to the expense and effort of organising a focus group, it would be catastrophic to fail to record the data. If possible, have two sets of recording equipment. If this is not possible, then use new batteries and **do a test** before the participants arrive. To look unsure or have faulty equipment when doing a one-to-one interview can be somewhat endearing (although never totally forgivable as it aligns with every negative stereotype about academics and researchers), but when faced with a group of people it surely appears amateur and unprofessional.

Running the focus group

Group interaction

Focus groups are by their very nature a 'contrived' discussion where the researcher's interests and concerns are the main drivers. Yet, the essential characteristic which distinguishes focus groups is the insight and data produced by the interaction between participants. Uncertainty around how interacting in a group influences what each individual participant contributes is an enduring conundrum. A tendency to conform and develop group norms might imply that opinions expressed lack validity in a more subjective sense. Without doubt, interacting in a group will inevitably affect what some people say – some participants may initially feel more reticent as part of a group and be more vocal when in a one-to-one interview. This point probably needs to be conceded, with an acknowledgement that any method of data generation carries implications. Nevertheless, there are huge benefits to be drawn from group interaction. Box 5.1 shows the main advantages to be gained from interaction between participants (Kitzinger, 1994: 116). Encouraging participation and open conversation, the identification of group norms and the ways in which participants interact are all framed as advantageous in the generation of data. The social processes of group interaction and communication that occur in focus group interviews have the potential to develop and articulate considered understandings. Focus group interactions can provide fascinating insights into wider cultural and ideological frameworks. Our advice on running the focus group session, which comes later on in this chapter, aims to enable the researcher to capitalise on this potential.

Box 5.1   Main advantages to be gained from interaction between participants

- Highlights the *respondents'* attitudes, priorities, language and framework of understanding
- Encourages a great variety of communication from participants – tapping into a wide range and form of understanding
- Helps to identify group norms
- Provides insight into the operation of group/social processes in the articulation of knowledge (e.g. through the examination of what information is censured or muted within the group)
- Can encourage open conversation about embarrassing subjects and facilitate the expression of ideas and experiences that might be left underdeveloped in an interview

Through detailed attention to the information between different members of the group a researcher can:

- Explore difference between group participants *in situ* with them and, because participants reflect upon each other's ideas, ensure that the data is organic/interconnected
- Use the conflict between participants to clarify why people believe what they do. Examine the questions that people ask one another in order to reveal their underlying assumptions and theoretical frameworks
- Explore the arguments people use against each other, identify the factors which influence individuals to change their minds and document how facts and stories operate in practice – what ideological work they do
- Analyse how particular forms of speech facilitate or inhibit peer communication, clarify or confuse the issue (in ways directly relevant to improving communication)

Taken from Kitzinger (1994: 116, original emphasis)

Role of the researcher(s)

The role of the researcher will vary dependent upon the purpose of using focus groups as a data collection technique. We have already discussed how focus groups can be formal or informal, with the researcher taking a directive or non-directive approach. Whatever approach is taken in focus group interviews, the role of the researcher is quite distinct. The researcher facilitates participation and the sharing of understandings but is also something of a regulator presiding over proceedings. So although some of the skills involved in running a focus group are similar to those needed for one-to-one interviews (e.g. sensitivity to non-verbal cues, developing rapport, effective use of probes and prompts), the researcher using focus groups needs also to be able to 'people manage' (Wilkinson, 2004). In light of this, the term *moderator* is often preferred when referring to the researcher who coordinates a focus group. Krueger (1994: 100) explains this preference:

> ... this term [moderator] highlights a specific function of the interviewer – that of moderating or guiding the discussion. The term interviewer tends to convey a more limited impression of two-way communication between an interviewer and interviewee.

However, Hennink and Diamond (2000) refer to having a 'focus group team' consisting of a moderator, an observer and, optionally, a housekeeper. The role of the observer is to take notes during the discussion, identifying key issues, non-verbal messages and body language that can be used later in the analysis. The housekeeper, if used, welcomes participants and attends to organisational issues, for example, paying expenses and arranging refreshments. This then leaves the moderator and observer free to concentrate on the actual interview discussion. Realistically, it might be that funding demands and time constraints mean that often there will only be a moderator, and possibly an observer. The observer both takes notes and generally supports the moderator, managing the recording equipment and possibly intervening if they feel that some participants are at times finding it difficult to contribute.

Moderator characteristics and style

Most forms of qualitative interviewing are reliant upon the interpersonal skills of the interviewer. With group interviews, and particularly focus groups, the interviewer/moderator's characteristics and style are pivotal. Moderator characteristics ideally should include being a good listener, having an interest in people, having a lively personality, being warm and essentially believing in one's work. It is also important to 'blend in' with the group (Krueger, 1994) so advice on self-presentation (outlined in the previous chapter) should be carefully considered. Also, having suggested that the moderator should blend in, it is important not to be too obvious and therefore risk appearing patronising. The aim is to try to put the group at ease. If interviewing solicitors, therefore, the moderator's appearance should be smart and professional. Alternatively, for the focus group with young people, mentioned earlier, both researchers wore jeans and trainers, and while they 'blended in' they did not attempt to mimic the participants.

Moderator style is very dependent upon the purpose and aims of the research. Being welcoming when greeting participants can assist in putting people at ease. Smiling and nodding can serve as a form of positive reinforcement throughout the interview, helping to regulate the flow of conversation. Notably, listening skills are one of the most essential aspects of moderator style and, drawing on Fern (2001), we present strategies for *non-reflective* and *reflective listening*.

When using non-reflective listening, the moderator encourages respondents to participate in the discussion with minimal responses (e.g. nodding the head and 'mm-hmm'). The moderator does not participate in the discussion and remains non-judgemental, yet these minimal non-reflective responses can facilitate the participation of shy and reserved participants. Fern also suggests that this non-reflective listening can enable more dominant participants to feel that they too are being heard and thus they may be more restrained in their participation.

Reflective listening remains non-judgemental but seeks to elucidate what is being said. *Clarifying* is one strategy: the moderator asks the speaker to clarify (e.g. 'I'm not quite sure …'). The speaker is then able to explain and elaborate. *Paraphrasing* is also useful, with the moderator restating the main aspects of what the speaker has said. This enables the moderator to ensure that the meaning the speaker intended to communicate is clear. As well as sharing opinions and viewpoints participants in focus group interviews will express a range of feelings and emotions. These aspects of the interview are a vital part of the group interaction and, as such, provide important data. *Reflecting* feelings, where the moderator attempts to mirror back the feeling expressed (e.g. 'You seem to feel …'), can both reveal the feeling behind the content of what is said and acknowledge the intensity of participants' experience. In focus groups, it may be that not all speakers are able to logically communicate their views. The moderator has a crucial role in *summarising* responses, enabling the main points to be heard and understood (e.g. 'Just to sum up – I think your main points are …'). This can prompt further discussion as other participants may then understand better the points being made. These strategies of reflective listening considerably increase the researcher's confidence in having captured both the substance and breadth of participants' viewpoints and understandings.

Moderating the focus group

Ideally, there will be a moderator and an observer who assists, particularly with larger focus groups. Moderating the focus group requires consideration of process – the focus group interview can follow different formats. Focus group interviews can have short question-and-answer discussions or include activities and exercises. What we attempt to do in this section is to provide the novice focus group moderator with clear guidance on each stage of the focus group interview, while offering some variation with regard to format.

Setting ground rules

As a researcher, you want participants to enjoy taking part in the focus group interview. They should feel able to relax and talk freely. However, in order to have a relaxed and comfortable atmosphere, the moderator needs to establish some ground rules. Participants need to know what is expected, how the session will be organised and what their role will be.

- *Respect*: It is important to explain that respectful, polite and open conversation is expected and that everyone is encouraged to participate. In the focus group literature, a great deal is written about dominant participants and how they can almost 'railroad' proceedings. Truthfully, even the most experienced moderator will struggle if they are confronted with a very dominant and insistent participant who is intent on hogging the conversation. Thankfully, most people are keen to cooperate, and although at times some participants may be a little over-enthusiastic, if ground rules around respectful participation have been made clear, everyone is usually able to contribute.
- *Moderator's role*: The moderator explains that they are there to guide the conversation and that they will aim to avoid offering opinions and comments. Having a one-way conversation can be unnerving, but if participants know that this is the moderator's role they will be less concerned.
- *Format*: Always remember to explain the format of the session – will there be individual questioning (similar to the nominal group technique) where speakers are nominated by the moderator? Alternatively, is the intention to introduce a question, or raise an issue, that is then available for discussion by the whole group, with participants deciding if they want to contribute to the discussion? This kind of clarification can avoid participants feeling unsure about when, and if, their contribution is required.
- *Recording and turn-taking*: Transcribing and analysing focus group interviews is at best taxing, but if participants speak over each other it can become impossible. So referring to the recording equipment and asking participants to try their best to avoid speaking if someone else is talking is worth reiterating.
- *Mobile phones*: Mobile phones ringing can be highly distracting, so ask participants if they will please turn their phones off for the duration of the focus group interview. Occasionally participants may need to have a mobile phone turned on. If this is the case, just request that if the phone rings can they please leave the room quietly and return to the group as soon as they are able.

Welcoming, sharing information and consent

Whatever the format, all focus group interviews will require you, as moderator, to welcome participants and share information regarding the nature of the research. Getting things off to a good start by warmly welcoming participants as they arrive is fundamental and generally puts people at ease. When all participants have arrived, the moderator can make a more formal start to the session. First, the moderator will need to give their name and introduce the observer if one is present. It is then the moderator's job to explain what the focus group interview is seeking to achieve and how this relates to the research overall. This can be a brief statement carefully prepared in advance – try to avoid lengthy or technical explanations. If you have prepared a 'script' for this part of the session, try to memorise the main points so that you need only glance at the notes. Reading verbatim from a page can appear condescending to participants or reveal insecurity on the part of the moderator. Either way, the result is less than satisfactory. In Box 5.2 we offer Krueger and Casey's (2000) example of an introductory statement.

Box 5.2   Focus group introductory statement based on Krueger and Casey (2000)

Good morning and welcome. Thanks for taking the time to join our discussion about the training needs of new employees. My name is John Doe, and I will serve as the moderator for today's focus group discussion. Assisting me is Mary Doe. The purpose of today's discussion is to get information from you about the training needs of new employees during their first year on the job. You were invited because you were hired within the last year. There are no right or wrong answers to the questions I am about to ask. We expect that you will have differing points of view. Please feel free to share your point of view even if it differs from what others have said. If you want to follow upon something that someone has said, you want to agree, disagree, or give an example, feel free to do that. Don't feel like you have to respond to me all the time. Feel free to have a conversation with one another about these questions. I am here to ask questions, listen, and make sure everyone has a chance to share. We're interested in hearing from each of you. So if you're talking a lot, I may ask you to give others a chance. And if you aren't saying much, I may call on you. We just want to make sure we hear from all of you. Feel free to get up and get more refreshments if you would like. We will both be taking notes to help us remember what is said. We are also tape recording the session because we don't want to miss any of your comments. We have names here in front of us today, but no names will be included in any reports. Let's begin by having each person in the room tell us their name and the county in which they work.

It is important to confirm with participants that they understand the project and their role within the research – invite questions (Are there any questions? Please do feel able to ask for clarification.). Be prepared to answer, in a friendly and responsive manner, anything that is raised, even if the questions appear challenging or unrelated to the topic. Depending on the nature of your research, it may be necessary to request participants to sign consent forms – allow time for this. Make sure that you confirm the finish time. You will probably have booked the room for a fixed period of time and often participants will only have set aside a designated amount of time for participation. Arrangements for payment of expenses can be explained at the end of the session, if applicable.

Participant introductions

We have discussed the choice between recruiting pre-existing groups or people whom we believe to be unfamiliar with each other. Whatever sampling strategy has been used, there is a need for introductions because even if the focus group participants are familiar with each other, the researcher(s) is generally new to the group. The moderator should have already made brief introductions when welcoming participants. The next step is for the moderator to get to know the participants and, if appropriate, participants should be introduced to each other. Asking participants in turn to give their name, occupation (possibly) and one thing that they think is interesting about themselves is often used to provide an opportunity for people to become acquainted. A variation on this strategy is to ask people to chat in pairs about who they are and, for example, what kind of work they do. Participants then, in turn, introduce the person they have been chatting with. For most groups this can be fine; many people are familiar with such strategies and thus the required outcome is achieved. However, there will be instances when alternatives are needed, for example, the focus group with 11 young people referred to earlier in the chapter. Asking the young people to introduce themselves, or each other, in this way would have been hard to manage and might have appeared somewhat artificial and contrived. Having a set of badges or labels that people fill out themselves can be useful. In this instance, the young people chatted while creating a range of colourful name badges. The moderator was then able to facilitate introductions, using the information on the badges, therefore avoiding making very shy participants ill at ease and uncomfortable. If the moderator chooses not to use name badges, then there has to be another strategy for knowing individual participants' names. This can be done by drawing a brief plan of the seating arrangements beforehand and writing in people's names as they introduce themselves. Such a strategy avoids awkwardness around the moderator remembering and, more importantly, misremembering people's names.

The discussion and asking questions

If forward planning, introductions and the setting of ground rules have been effectively carried out, then the discussion will most probably be enjoyable and productive. However, it is important to carefully think through how the discussion will be focused to meet the research aims. In Chapter 3 we covered questioning and interview guides. Careful consideration of ordering, the use of open-ended questions, prompts and probes are still applicable, with most focus groups following a 'discussion guide', which is, in effect, a semi-structured interview schedule or topic guide. The guide needs to be fairly brief; avoid using too many questions but ensure that the ones you do include anticipate the discussion, having the potential to draw into the conversation as many participants as possible. Our advice is to always pilot the discussion guide if you can. This may be hard as the guide might only relate to the particular participant group you are researching. Nevertheless, it usually helps to simulate a focus group using the pilot discussion guide. Even those who do not exactly fit your sampling criteria have useful thoughts on how the discussion guide is working. Using unthreatening general questions at the start of the focus group interview is generally recommended in order to ease participants into the topic of inquiry. Experienced moderators will be able to, and most probably will, deviate from the discussion guide. This can be productive but it does require a level of adaptability, with the researcher being confident enough to 'think on their feet'.

Some focus groups will rely on 'discussion stimulus' to either break the ice or prompt conversation around a specific issue. For example, Barbour (2007) tells of using a still from a television soap, *Peak Practice*, when researching participants' experiences around primary healthcare. The still was shown, with the moderator then asking a specific question: 'This is one general practice that you're probably all familiar with. How does your own GP practice compare with this?' (Barbour, 2007: 84). Newspaper clippings, advertising campaigns and vignettes can all be used to stimulate the discussion, but such materials may not always have the desired effect. You need to be prepared to modify your discussion format if things are not working well. Focus groups are not an exact science. The researchers using this method need to be flexible and able to adjust to what will inevitably be a dynamic encounter.

Confidentiality

The issue of confidentiality when using focus groups is crucial if the researcher wants to stimulate candid and free-flowing discussions. Some participants might be reluctant to share their opinions if they are concerned about the confidentiality and anonymity of their responses in the group. Participants may fear repercussions from unfavourable opinions expressed during the session about an organisation, issue or person. For example, in a focus group with teachers, one participant might reveal their reluctance to comply with a government-led education initiative. The participating teacher would not have expected this to be reported back to the headteacher at their school. How, though, is this to be avoided if colleagues are part of the same focus group? If researching highly sensitive topics, confidentiality can become even more of an issue. Berg (2001) advocates asking participants to sign a 'statement of confidentiality' (see example in Box 5.3). All group members agree and sign the statement affirming that they will not communicate or disclose information discussed in the focus group. This kind of written statement can seem quite intimidating to participants and would need to be managed very carefully by the moderator. Realistically, such statements cannot be enforced, but they do psychologically commit participants to honour and respect confidentiality. If a consent form is used, then confidentiality should be included, with participants consenting to maintain the confidentiality of the focus group.

Box 5.3   Group agreement for maintaining confidentiality (Berg, 2001: 128)

This form is intended to further ensure confidentiality of data obtained during the course of the study entitled (place, title of the research here). All parties involved in this research, including all focus group members, will be asked to

---

read the following statement and sign their names indicating that they agree to comply.

I hereby affirm that I will not communicate or in any manner disclose publicly information discussed during the course of this focus group interview. I agree not to talk about material relating to this study or interview with anyone outside my fellow focus group members and the researcher (or moderator).

Name: _____

Signature: _____

Project Director's Signature: _____

Raising issues of confidentiality with the group, both in the participant information distributed prior to participation and when setting ground rules, does give participants the chance to reflect and consider. While there is no panacea to remove all possibility of confidentiality being breached, if confidentiality has been discussed openly participants are able to make choices. If they believe that they will be unable to keep the focus group discussion confidential, they can withdraw. Equally so, participants are alerted to their reliance upon the confidentiality of other members of the focus group. While this may mean that some information might be withheld, this is preferable to there being negative consequences arising from participation.

Debriefing

The moderator must make sure that there is time for debriefing participants at the end of the focus group interview. Participants may want to clarify some of the information you outlined at the beginning of the session. It is always useful to once again outline what the aims of the research are and how the research will progress. Asking if participants have anything that they are unsure about can often prompt discussion. The moderator should spend the necessary amount of time responding and not appear as if they are eager to depart. It is important to make sure that participants have the researcher's contact details in case they need to discuss something they are concerned about at a later date. The researcher can hand out relevant information leaflets or, if appropriate, helpline contact numbers. Barbour (2007) suggests giving participants the opportunity (directly after the session or at a later date) to request that any of their comments be erased from the transcripts. This seems ethically justified; often people will become enthusiastic when part of a group discussion, wishing later that they had been more reticent. As researchers, we do not want in any way to compromise participants' well-being, either by causing distress or coming into conflict over the inclusion of data. If you do decide to give participants the option to remove data, ensure that you set a timescale. For example, 'You will be able to request that some of your comments are erased from the data but I'm afraid no later than (insert date) as we will be in the final stages of writing up the research and after this time will not be able to remove quotes'. Offering participants this kind of option is reassuring and seldom is it the case that participants request that data be erased.

Conclusion

Focus group interviewing is one of the most popular qualitative interview methods and is used by a whole range of researchers working on different topics and with diverse affiliations. The potential benefits in having participants engage in various forms of group interviews seems obvious, enabling researchers to recognise and engage with the evolving nature of human understandings. Of course, there are epistemological implications that need to be considered, not least the way in which inter-subjectivity is theoretically managed. There are many challenges involved in planning and running focus groups, but these are compensated for by the rewards that can be achieved. It is crucial to appreciate that the skills of the researcher are paramount and that there is no substitute for hard work at the planning stage. Good preparation should never be underestimated as it has the potential to make or break the success of a group interview. This method of generating data is both exciting and demanding, but if used well and imaginatively, group interviewing can offer a wealth of opportunities for generating valuable insights.

Recommended reading

Barbour, R.S. (2007) *Doing Focus Groups*. London: Sage.
This is a comprehensive book that covers the whole process of focus group interviewing from theoretical tensions through to the challenges faced when analysing focus group data. There is a very helpful section in Chapter 6 on developing stimulus material.

Frey, J.H. and Fontana, A. (1993) The group interview in social research, in D.L. Morgan (ed.), *Successful Focus Groups*. London: Sage. pp. 20–34.
This chapter effectively discusses the breadth of group interviewing, providing a useful overview of different approaches.

Stewart, D.W., Shamdasani, P.N. and Rook, D.W. (2007) *Focus Groups: Theory and Practice*. London: Sage.
Chapter 3 gives a detailed account of the advantages and disadvantages of using focus groups.

SIX

Remote Interviewing

The conventional interview, whether individual or group, involves the researcher sitting down face-to-face with her participants, asking questions and responding to their answers. Much of the guidance we have given in earlier chapters is concerned with the ways in which you can effectively manage this interaction. However, not all qualitative interviews take place in such a setting. Telephone interviews have been used in social scientific research for many years, and more recently there has been a rapid growth in the use of online interviewing. Not surprisingly, the use of such remote interviewing techniques raises some issues that are not apparent in face-to-face interviews. Equally, different challenges arise for different forms of remote interview, associated with the time frame of data collection (synchronous or non-synchronous[1]) and the types of data collected (spoken or written word). Table 6.1 illustrates how the main forms of remote interview relate to each other on these characteristics.

Table 6.1   Main forms of remote interview

Remote interview form	Time frame	Data type
Telephone	Synchronous	Verbal
Remote video (Video-conferencing and webcams)	Synchronous	Verbal (plus visual)
E-mail	Asynchronous	Written
Instant messaging	Synchronous	Written

In this chapter we consider how the various types of remote interview should be managed and carried out, as well as any ethical issues that are different from – or additional to – those we confront in face-to-face interviews. Our suggestions and illustrative examples are organised under the following headings:

- why use remote interviews?
- doing telephone (and remote video) interviews
- ethical issues in telephone interviewing
- doing online interviews
- ethical issues in online interviewing

Why use remote interviews?

Qualitative researchers tend to use remote interviews for one (or more) of three reasons: physical distance from participants, availability of participants, and the nature of the interview topic. Perhaps the most obvious advantage of remote interviewing is that it can facilitate the inclusion of participants who are geographically distant from the interviewer, without the need for time-consuming and expensive travel or the recruitment of local interviewers. International research becomes viable for even modestly-resourced projects, especially where online methods are to be used.

In some studies, access difficulties are not due to distance so much as the ability and willingness of participants to make time to take part in a face-to-face interview. In such cases, the use of a remote technique may be an acceptable alternative for them, as it enables them to schedule a telephone interview at a time that suits them, or respond to e-mailed questions at their own convenience. In a study of health practitioners' experiences of out-of-hours palliative care, the first author and colleagues found it very difficult to persuade GPs (family doctors) to attend face-to-face interviews, due to their work pressures. However, the GPs were happy to set aside time for telephone interviews, and these proved successful in gathering the kind of data we required (King et al., 2003).

Sometimes the main reason for using remote interviewing is not the location or availability of participants but the nature of the research topic. Social scientists studying aspects of internet use have argued for the value of online interviews in preserving what Mann and Stewart (2002) call 'contextual naturalness'. In other words, where internet use is the subject of interest, online interviews will allow participants to answer the researcher's questions in the same setting as that of the activity under investigation. For instance, Kivits (2005) carried out e-mail interviews to study how people used the internet to access information about health. Remote interviews may also be preferred for some sensitive topics because the greater sense of anonymity felt by participants may help them feel more willing to disclose their personal stories than they would face to face (Joinson, 2001; Opdenakker, 2006). For some participant groups, particular remote interviewing media may be especially well suited to their needs. A good example is Egan, Chenowith and McAuliffe's (2006) use of e-mail interviews with traumatic brain injury survivors. These participants would struggle with the demands of immediate response in a face-to-face interview, due to the cognitive-linguistic impairments caused by their injury. The written and asynchronous nature of e-mail interaction enabled them to take the time they needed to reflect on questions and respond effectively.

As can be seen, both practical and methodological design issues might influence you to favour the use of remote interviewing in a qualitative study. The crucial question, then, is which form to employ. In the remainder of this chapter we will discuss the use of the main types of remote interviewing, highlighting their potential strengths and weaknesses, to help you to make an informed choice of approach.

Doing telephone (and remote video) interviews

The telephone has long been used as a means of gathering data in social sci-entific research. The literature on it, though, is surprisingly sparse, and tends to focus more on structured survey interviews in the positivistic tradition, rather than qualitative studies. Where qualitative telephone interviews are discussed, it is usually by way of a comparison with online and/or face-to-face interviews (e.g. Opdenakker, 2006; Kazmer and Xie, 2008). We suspect that this reflects the assumption that using telephone interviews is a pragmatic second choice where, for reasons of resources (time, expense), face-to-face interviews are not possible. In the *Sage Handbook of Interview Research* (Gubrium and Holstein, 2002), Shuy starts his chapter on telephone interviews with the presupposition that they are used as a method for 'reducing fieldwork time' (2002: 537). This is in stark contrast to online interviewing, about which there is a burgeoning literature that treats it as a valid method in its own right, rather than a cheap alternative to conventional interviews. We would argue that issues of research resources might influence the choice of either telephone or online interviews (indeed, the latter have the added saving of removing the need for transcription, as we discuss later). This does not obviate the need for qualitative researchers to consider seriously the nature of the communication processes in these media in order to assess how to use them effectively in a research context.

Managing a qualitative telephone interview study

In many respects the processes of designing such a study and carrying out interviews are no different from in-person interviewing, and the guidance we provided in Chapters 3 and 4 would apply here. However, there are some aspects that do require special consideration because of the nature of the telephone medium – the scheduling of interviews and the means by which they are recorded.

Scheduling telephone interviews

One of the threats to the quality of telephone interviews is the potential for participants to misunderstand the nature of the interaction. Interviewees may perceive that you want certain factual information from them, or they may see the conversation as simply an informal chat. Either way, it will be difficult for you to obtain the kind of rich account that qualitative research requires. You should, of course, seek to clarify the nature of what you are doing at the point of recruitment, through your information sheet, informal discussions with potential participants, and so on. Nevertheless, in our experience, people may still all too readily slip into their habitual mode of telephone use. The way you schedule your interviews can help to reduce this risk.

In scheduling your interviews with your participants, there are three factors you have to bear in mind. First, you must think about the likely duration of the interview, and make sure participants are clearly aware of how much time they need to keep free for it. (You may find it helpful to carry out one or two 'pilot' interviews to get a sense of what this should be.) If participants are told you require them to set aside a substantial amount of time for the interview (half an hour, an hour, or whatever), this will help reinforce the point that a detailed discussion of their views and experiences is expected. Second, you should encourage participants to arrange to take the phone call in as private a location as possible. This is both to protect their confidentiality and to reduce the danger of frequent interruptions that might harm the flow of the interview. Third, for similar reasons, you should seek to agree a time of day when the interviewee is likely to be relatively free of other demands on their time.

Recording telephone interviews

As with face-to-face interviews, telephone interviews need to be recorded in order to produce transcripts for analysis. A simple way to achieve this is to use a telephone with a monitor/speakerphone facility, but we would generally not advise this because of the poor sound quality of most such systems. Fortunately, there is a large range of devices available on the market designed to directly record from the telephone, many of which will produce extremely good quality recordings – better than in most face-to-face interviews due to the reduction in background noise. Before purchasing any such device, you must check that it is compatible with the telephone you have, and we strongly suggest that you practise using the equipment repeatedly until you are sure of your competence with it.

Style of interaction

It has long been recognised in communications research that the style of inter-action used over the telephone tends to differ markedly from face-to-face conversation. In relation to qualitative interviewing, the most important char-acteristic is the generally more task-focused nature of this form of mediated interaction in comparison with face-to-face communication. This is in part due to the lack of visual cues, which provide much of the richness and nuance that is possible in face-to-face interaction (Bruce, 1995). Qualitative researchers may therefore feel that telephone interviews will inevitably yield inferior data to face-to-face ones, and should only be used as a last resort when the latter is not a viable option. We would argue, though, that telephone interviews can provide very valuable qualitative data, if you take into account the nature of the interaction and think carefully about who you use the method with.

Getting beyond 'task-focus'

It is important to recognise that the tendency for telephone conversations to be task-focused is not an inevitable consequence of the medium itself. Task-focus (or 'instrumentality') stems at least as much from social expecta-tions regarding the use of the telephone as from its material features, such as absence of visual cues. This is demonstrated by the strong, consistent finding that women use the telephone in a less instrumental and more relationship-focused way than men (e.g. Smoreda and Liccope, 2000; Lacohée and Anderson, 2001), because of differences in gender roles and patterns of work and family life. As Ling (2000: 72) points out, there is a danger of overstressing the extent to which the medium determines the message:

> ...people are quite able to adapt communication to the medium available. A medium will develop a unique form into which we will apply meaning. The leeway for style in writing, the telephone conversation and even, among those who know it, Morse code, is broad enough to allow for the inclusion of para-language.

In practical terms, qualitative researchers using telephone interviews need to give strong cues to participants regarding the type of interaction that is anticipated. Clear briefing at the point of recruitment is especially important; if at all possible, try to discuss this directly with potential participants rather than just relying on a written information sheet. As we have seen, scheduling can play a key role in increasing your chances of obtaining good quality data, by signalling the kind of depth of discussion you expect. Also, telephone interviews may require stronger overt probing than equivalent face-to-face interviews – both to encourage participants to open up if their responses are becoming too 'factual' in tone, and to resolve ambiguities in the absence of visual information. This in turn requires very careful listening from you as interviewer.

Finally, you need to be aware that problems with the style of interaction in telephone interviews may be more likely with some demographic groups than others. As we have noted, men tend to be more instrumental in their use of the telephone than women. There may also be generational differences. The spread of mobile phones since the 1980s has encouraged the widespread use of the medium for purely social reasons, often involving the exchange of seemingly trivial information. Older people are likely to have developed their habits of telephone use at a time when the norm was not to use the medium in such a casual manner. In addition, hearing impairments become more common as people get older, which can be a serious inhibitor to effective telephone interaction (Shuy, 2002), as can mobility problems and a range of illnesses (Herzog et al., 1983; Worth and Tierney, 1993). Of course, these points about gender and age are generalisations that inevitably gloss over many exceptions. As Wilson and Roe (1998) show in relation to older people, with forethought and planning the potential pitfalls for specific groups can sometimes be avoided. Nevertheless, there may be occasions when you decide that the nature of the sample you require means that telephone interviews are not the best choice of method.

Using remote video for qualitative interviewing

There are now a number of technologies that allow synchronous video as well as audio interaction at a distance, which we refer to here as *remote video* techniques. Such media clearly have potential as a means of conducting qualitative interviews, though at present their use is in its infancy. Matthews and Cramer

(2008) piloted the use of inexpensive personal webcams in research with 'hidden' populations, and concluded that the method has much to offer, especially as both hardware and software become cheaper and more widely used. Hewson (2007), while not denying the potential of the medium for the future, argues that at present using remote video for research interviews is inadvisable, for a number of reasons. First, it inevitably restricts the sample to participants who have access to the technology – specifically a home computer, internet access and a webcam. While the majority of households in the developed world have at least the first two, there are still substantial sections of the population in most countries who do not. Matthews and Cramer (2008) argue that webcams are cheap enough for qualitative researchers to consider providing them for participants, although this brings us to a second concern of Hewson's – the reliability and quality of video-conferencing via webcam. Problems with both sound and video quality, including temporary loss of one or both, are still commonplace, especially where relatively cheap or dated equipment is used. Peaks in network traffic can cause dramatic slowdowns or breaks in transmission, even where high quality equipment and fast broadband connections are available. Some video-conferencing software will allow direct audio-recording of the interaction, but Matthews and Cramer warn that the quality of this may be poor and advise simultaneous external recording.

At present, we would tend to suggest that qualitative researchers should be cautious about the use of remote video for interviews. As Hewson suggests, it may be best if it is restricted to contexts where you can be sure that professional standard equipment and fast broadband are available, for example, where you are conducting research in organisations with sophisticated IT provision. However, this kind of technology is developing and becoming more accessible at a rapid rate. One possible approach which has the potential for widespread use is Skype, which we discuss in Box 6.1.

Box 6.1   Using Skype for remote interviews

We have recently been using Skype to have face-to-face remote conversations. Skype is a software application for an internet-based telephone system and is available to download free at www.skype.com. Many people are complementing their mobile and landline telephones with Skype, thus using their computers to make worldwide calls *for free*. Once downloaded, by both the researcher and participant, Skype will enable you to speak face to face using PC to PC audio/video technology. There is no expense beyond your internet connection fees, the cost of an efficient personal computer with speakers and microphone (with essential system requirements – see below) and a webcam. As we have already acknowledged, the need for specific equipment does have implications and we would not want to underestimate the potential impact this might have with regard to specific populations. However, Skype is very easy to use, enabling you to hold an intimate conversation with someone on the other side of the world. It is necessary to accommodate a slight time delay when interviewing and indeed this can be a little hard to get used to. Yet, with audio only conversations there are no visual cues and when there are periods of silence it is hard to discern why this is occurring. This is not the case when using Skype audio/video technology – by selecting 'video full screen' you can almost experience the person being in the room with you. We should say that we have not yet used this technology in our actual research but Pretto and Pocknee (2008) are encouraging, suggesting that Skype was the most reliable and preferred method of communication for their research project. They say that video connections worked well except for peak periods during the day; this is our experience too so you will need to bear this in mind. Also, there does not appear to be any facility to record audio/video sessions and the technology does seem less successful with multiple callers. Nonetheless, the possibilities of this free technology for qualitative remote interviewing are exciting, indicating that some of the potential problems with telephone interviewing and video-conferencing can be overcome.

System requirements

- PC running Windows 2000, XP or Vista. (Windows 2000 users require DirectX 9.0 for video calls.)
- Internet connection – broadband is best (GPRS is not supported for voice calls).
- Speakers and microphone – built-in or separate.
- For voice and video calls we recommend a computer with at least a 1GHz processor, 256 MB RAM and of course a webcam.
- For high-quality video calls you will need a high-quality video webcam and software, a dual-core processor computer and a fast broadband connection (384 kbps).

Ethical issues in telephone interviewing

Telephone interviews do not raise any significant ethical issues above and beyond those we cover in detail in the next chapter, but there are a few points where particular care is needed. First, it is essential that even where written consent to record has been granted in advance (which we would expect to be the norm), you ask again at the start of the telephone call. Second, to protect confidentiality and anonymity you should not only encourage the participant to take the call in as private a setting as possible, but also ensure that you cannot be overheard at your end of the conversation. You must treat the participants' phone numbers as confidential and ensure that no one outside the research team can have access to them. Third, we would advise that where possible you use a telephone at your university (or other workplace) to ensure that your home number does not get into the hands of anyone who might misuse it. Alternatively, you may be able to use a service that prevents anyone you call from home from tracing your number. A final point concerns the establishing of participant identity in telephone interviews. It is inevitably harder to be sure that the person you are interviewing is who they say they are when you can only hear their voice than it is if you can see them as well. In most studies there is little reason to suspect that people might be motivated to engage in impersonation, but where a topic is particularly sensitive and may require very strict protection of confidentiality, you might be advised to take some additional precautions to make such an eventuality even less likely. In such circumstances, it may be advisable to communicate with the participant by a medium other than telephone initially, perhaps by e-mail or letter. You can then arrange the interview call at a convenient time, making it less likely that someone might opportunistically pick up the telephone and attempt to pass themself off as your participant. The best protection is to meet the participant first, though this will often be impractical. Where positive identification is an especially important issue, video-conferencing may be a better choice of method than telephone interviewing. We would stress, though, that in the great majority of studies, impersonation is not a significant concern, and making sure your contact details come from a trustworthy source should be sufficient. (Impersonation is a much bigger issue for online interviewing, as we will see later in this chapter.)

Remote video interviews raise an additional issue in cases where the participant is video- as well as audio-recorded, in terms of threat to anonymity. You will need to be especially vigilant about who has access to the recordings (e.g. for transcription purposes). Should you anticipate that you may want to use extracts from the recording in public – for instance, in a conference presentation or in teaching – you must make this clear to the participants in advance and gain their explicit consent for it.

Doing online interviews

Online qualitative interviewing has generated a substantial and rapidly increasing methodological literature in recent years. The internet can be used in a variety of ways to collect data from people, but the main distinction drawn is between asynchronous and synchronous methods. The e-mail interview is the most commonly used technique and exemplifies the asynchronous approach, where participants are able to answer questions sent by researchers in their own time. This can be contrasted with the use of technologies that enable synchronous communication, such as chat rooms and Instant Messaging (IM) services, where a real-time exchange between researcher and participant(s) takes place. Both types of internet-based method allow the researcher to carry out either individual or group interviews. We will consider the main issues for asynchronous and synchronous approaches in turn. We will then conclude with a discussion of the ethics of online interviewing.

Asynchronous online interviews

Although there are other possible ways of conducting asynchronous online interviews, the e-mail interview is by far the most commonly used and we will concentrate on it here. The growing popularity of e-mail as a medium for qualitative research is easy to understand: it is widely available and highly familiar to very many people, is simple to use and of course enables researchers to reach potential participants worldwide. At the same time, its asynchronous, text-based nature means that it differs in important ways from face-to-face and telephone interviewing.

Scheduling e-mail interviews

In most cases, an e-mail interview does not consist of a single set of questions from the researcher and a single set of answers from the respondent. Rather, there is usually a series of exchanges between the two, varying in number from just two or three to many dozens, and in time period of a few days to a year or more. The potential to deepen the relationship by repeated contacts over a substantial time span is seen by some writers as one of the most valuable aspects of this method (e.g. Illingworth, 2001; Hewson, 2007). It is, though, a feature that creates challenges for you as a researcher in terms of scheduling. Do you tell participants in advance how long the research will continue for, or how many exchanges between you there are expected to be? Do you set any time limit for responses to your questions?

Most writers agree that it is best to set in advance the duration of the data collection period as a whole, both to ensure the participant knows what they are committing to and to facilitate management of the project. Just how long that period should be will depend on the nature of your study and its practical constraints. On the former, the more your research requires you to gather very rich data from each participant, the longer the contact you are likely to need with the participant. Kivits' (2005) study showed the benefits of extended relationships (here up to a year in length) in terms of participants' increasing willingness to open up to the researcher as the online relationship developed.

There is more variation in practice regarding whether researchers decide in advance the number of e-mail exchanges that will occur in the course of a study. In some cases participants are told from the outset that there will be a certain number of exchanges, perhaps even with an indication of the types of question to be asked at each step (e.g. Hunt and McHale, 2005). In others, including Kivits' (2005) study of health information-seeking mentioned above, a much more flexible approach is taken, responding to the developing interaction and relationship between the researcher and each individual participant. There are strengths and weaknesses to either approach, which you would need to consider when planning an e-mail interview study. Setting the number of exchanges in advance helps you to manage the project efficiently, and may reduce the difficulties that can arise in closing the online relationship with participants (see below). At the same time, this may restrict the building of rapport because as the researcher, you are controlling the pace at which relationships develop. The opposite approach is much more like 'ordinary' e-mail interaction and is more likely to lead to a genuine sense of relationship with interviewees, but raises the attendant danger that the direction of the interaction may become hard for you to control.

Whether or not you set the number of exchanges in advance, it is a good idea to give participants some guidance as to how soon you expect them to reply to your messages. While you can suggest a response time when you recruit participants to your study, as Hunt and McHale (2007) point out, you may need to negotiate variations on this in the light of individual interviewees' patterns of internet usage. If you do not agree response times, it can be very awkward knowing when it is appropriate to send a reminder e-mail to an interviewee who has not replied to you. As we discuss later, one of the main threats to e-mail interview studies is that of participants drifting out of the research without ever formally withdrawing.

Recording and managing the data

Undoubtedly, one of the attractive features of e-mail as a medium for qualitative interviewing is the fact that it removes the need for transcription. This represents a major saving in time and cost for projects. It is important, though, to recognise that e-mail interview data will require a fair amount of work to organise into a form that facilitates analysis – a series of saved e-mails is considerably messier than a nicely typed and formatted transcript. You need to allow time for the task of organising the data, which is likely to involve cutting and pasting material into a word-processing programme, standardising information about dates of messages, and so on. As Kazmer and Xie (2008: 273) point out, the time saved 'over having to do transcriptions from audio recordings is large but not as huge as we are tempted to think'. We would also concur with Illingworth (2001) that convenience alone should not be the basis for your choice of interview method – you need to bear in mind all the characteristics of different interview forms and media to select the one most appropriate for your study.

Building and maintaining relationships online

As we have highlighted in previous chapters, the quality of the researcher–participant relationship plays a key role in qualitative interviews. This naturally creates a challenge for e-mail interviews where the interaction is purely by text. There has been a considerable volume of research examining the nature of social relationships conducted via the internet. As Joinson (2005) points out, early research into the internet as a site for social relationships and interaction tended to emphasise what was lost in comparison to face-to-face relationships (e.g. Rice and Love, 1987). More recent research argues that it is entirely possible for 'genuine' relationships to be established and maintained on the internet (e.g. Markham, 2004; Derks et al., 2008), although these may take longer to attain a deep and nuanced character than in face-to-face circumstances (Ling, 2000). This shift in the way online relationships are viewed reflects changes both in technology and in people's familiarity with the internet as a medium for social interaction. For qualitative researchers, it means that we can reasonably expect that rapport *can* be built with online participants (Kazmer and Xie, 2008), allowing interviews of real depth to be carried out.

When we consider the e-mail interview as a particular form of online research, it is important to think carefully about the impact of its asynchronous nature on the interviewer–interviewee relationship. The fact that an e-mail interview can continue over weeks or months may be an advantage in terms of building rapport (note Ling's (2000) point above). Unlike a face-to-face or synchronous online interview, as a researcher you have time to reflect on how to respond to the interviewee in a way that will help develop the relationship as well as elicit useful data. Kivits (2005) argues that mutual self-disclosure is essential if a relationship of any depth is to be built with participants. She began her interviews by telling participants about herself – for example, about her interests and family as well as about what she hoped to achieve with the research, and invited them to share something about themselves. Her goal was to encourage an open and informal tone that would 'create a comfortable and friendly context for interviewing' (Kivits, 2005: 40). The amount of personal disclosure that is appropriate will vary according to your topic and who your participants are. Of course, you need to be careful about protecting your own security in the information you give out about yourself, but again, one of the strengths of the e-mail form is that you have time to think carefully about what you communicate to your participants about yourself.

Although we would agree with Kivits about the value of setting a tone in e-mail exchanges that encourages openness from participants, you need to be careful that you remain focused on your research topic. You may find it necessary to send some messages that are purely concerned with maintaining the relationship – for instance, enquiring sympathetically about the interviewee's health if they have apologised about a slow response due to illness. However, if you find yourself over several exchanges being drawn into details of the participant's private life, with little or no focus on the research topic, you need to gently steer them back towards it. Failure to do so may not only be detrimental to the quality of your data, it may also place you in an ethically difficult situation (as we discuss further below).

Closure and non-response

The e-mail interview method raises a further challenge in terms of how your relationship with your interviewees is brought to an end. In face-to-face and synchronous remote interviews, this is generally quite clear – you get to the end of the interview, thank your participant(s) and leave (or log off). You might get in touch with them once more for dissemination of findings, but in the great majority of cases there will be absolutely no doubt that the research relationship has come to an end. Things are very different in an e-mail interview, especially one in which interchanges continue for weeks or months, rather than just days. The relationship-building described above can make it very hard to simply 'sign off'. In her study with social work practitioners, looking at the ethical dilemmas they faced in their work, McAuliffe (2003) noted how both she and her participants were reluctant to bring the contact to a close. Kivits (2005) too found closure difficult, after building relationships over many months. In contrast, Hunt and McHale (2007: 1419) present the closure point as rather straightforward:

> The interviewer will know when the interview is completed. There are no more questions to ask that are likely to lead to further useful information. ... At this point the interviewer should inform the participant that the interview is over, thank him or her for participating, and ask if there are any questions or comments the participant would like to make.

This difference in view may well be due to the fact that Hunt and McHale place much less emphasis than the previous two authors on relationship-building as part of the interview process. It also reflects their more structured approach to the method: elsewhere they insist that interviewees 'should always be told about the number of questions they will be asked, including the likelihood of subsidiary questions' (2007: 1418). This may be possible in studies that have quite a tight focus and a detailed set of questions prepared in advance – as could be the case in some evaluation studies – but would be very difficult to achieve in more exploratory and open-ended studies such as McAuliffe's or Kivits' work. In the latter type of project, clearly setting the overall duration of data collection should help you as a researcher to negotiate closure without it becoming too drawn out. Attending to our earlier warning about not letting purely personal exchanges dominate the interview is also important. Finally, we would always recommend that if you are uncomfortable with any aspect of the way an e-mail interview is progressing, discuss it with a supervisor or experienced colleague (maintaining appropriate confidentiality, of course).

Another challenge distinctive to e-mail interviews is how to react if a participant fails to respond to a message from you within the agreed or expected timescale. How long do you wait before sending a reminder? How many reminders do you send? If you do not hear from the participant again, should you use the data they have already provided? As a rule, we would suggest that you send an initial reminder quite soon after you begin to have concerns about whether the participant has stopped responding. (How soon this is will naturally depend upon the response times expected in a particular study.) This message must include a request to reply within a set time period. Should there still be no response, we would suggest a further reminder, this time with an explicit question as to whether they wish to cease involvement in the study and, if so, whether they wish to withdraw the data already provided. You may repeat this second reminder, although you need to think carefully about whether you feel that it would be appropriate in the context of your study. Box 6.2 provides examples of the use of reminders in two quite different e-mail interview studies.

Box 6.2   Using reminders in e-mail interview studies

We present here a comparison of the reminder process in two e-mail interview studies. These are hypothetical but based on real-world examples. Note the change in both scheduling of reminders and the tone of the messages in relation to the nature of the two projects and their participants.

Study 1: Interprofessional relationships in architecture	Study 2: The lifeworld of online role-playing game players
This study sought to examine how architects manage relationships with clients, colleagues and members of other professions over the course of a project. Ten architects and 20 others took part in e-mail interviews, based on quite a detailed interview guide that covered a number of key practical and theoretical concerns.	This study sought to explore the personal meanings associated with playing online multi-player role-playing games. It focused on young adults (aged 18–25), and recruited a sample of ten (six men and four women) involved in a wide cross-section of games.
At the start of the study, participants were told that the data collection period would last one calendar month, and that there would be four main groups of questions sent – though follow-up e-mails to clarify responses might be used. They agreed to respond within two working days of receiving a message from the researcher.	The study was very open-ended in character, being located within a phenomenological perspective (see Chapter 10 for more on phenomenology). Data collection continued over a year. There was not a fixed schedule of questions, but participants agreed that they would try to respond to the researcher's messages within a week of receiving them.
Reminder 1: sent when no response to researcher's message after four working days (i.e. two days beyond agreed deadline) Re: research project Dear Stella I hope this finds you well. I am sending this because I am a little concerned not to have received your response to the questions I sent on Thursday of last week. As you have	*Reminder 1: sent when no response to researcher's message after two weeks (i.e. one week beyond agreed deadline)* Re: research project Dear Lee Hope all's well with you. Wanted to check you got my last lot of ques-tions. If so, it would be really help-ful if you could reply in the next few days – but if you need a bit longer,

(Continued)

(Continued)

Study 1: Interprofessional relationships in architecture	Study 2: The lifeworld of online role-playing game players
previously always responded very promptly, I wanted to make sure you had received my questions, and if so to check there were no other reasons for the delay. I would be very grateful if you could confirm that this has reached you, and forward your response to my questions as soon as is convenient for you. With best wishes Gerry	that's no problem, just let me know. If they never got to you, please tell me – I'll send them again. Cheers Nicola
Reminder 2: sent one week after reminder 1 if no response Re: research project Dear Stella I contacted you last week, to ask about the delay in responding to my last set of questions in our ongoing e-mail interview. If you have not received these messages, or have mislaid them, could you let me know so that I can forward the questions to you. If, however, you have decided not to continue your involvement in this study, that is fine – I would just be grateful if you could reply to confirm this. Also, could you let me know whether you would be happy for me to use the information you have already supplied or whether you would like me to withdraw all your data from the study? With thanks for your help so far, Gerry	*Reminder 2: sent two weeks after reminder 1 if no response* Re: research project Dear Lee I sent you a message a couple of weeks ago because I'd not heard from you since I e-mailed the last bunch of questions for my research project to you. As I've still not heard from you I thought I'd better check what's happening – did you get my message? Let me know if you didn't and I can send the questions again. I hope you still want to help me with this project, but if you've decided you've had enough of it that's absolutely fine – could you just drop me a message to confirm this? And if that's the case, are you happy for me to use your earlier answers, or do you want me to pull all your data from the study? All the best Nicola
Reminder 3: sent one week after reminder 2 if no response Re: Research project	*Reminder 3: sent two weeks after reminder 2 if no response* Re: Research project

Study 1: Interprofessional relationships in architecture	Study 2: the lifeworld of online role-playing game players
[forward text of previous reminder, and preface with the following message] Dear Stella I sent the message below to you a week ago, about my research project on interprofessional relationships in architecture. As I have not heard from you I wanted to check one more time that you had received this and previous messages. I realise that you may simply not wish to respond any further, so I will not contact you again for this study, unless you confirm your continued wish to be involved. Many thanks for your contribution to my research Gerry	[forward text of previous reminder, and preface with the following message] Dear Lee I sent the message below to you a week ago, about my research project on online RPGs. Don't want to hassle – but as I've not heard from you I wanted to check one more time that you had received this and previous messages. I realise that you may simply not wish to respond any further, so I will not contact you again for this study unless you let me know you still want to be involved. Many thanks for taking part in my research Nicola

Should your respondent fail to answer all your reminders, you will be left with the question of what you should do with data already received from him or her. We will return to the ethics of this below, but in purely practical terms you need to consider whether there are aspects of your planned interview that are crucial to meeting your research aims that you have not covered. For example, imagine that in your study you were interested in users' views of specific aspects of a website providing advice on housing issues. You planned to start your interview by eliciting some biographical information, followed by details of why the interviewee had consulted the site. You would then move on to specific questions about four key features of the website in question. If your participant 'vanished' before getting on to any of the questions about the site itself, you might well conclude that there would be no point incorporating their answers to the early part of the interview in your analysis. In contrast, if they covered the questions on two of the four features of interest before responses stopped, you would probably be well advised to include that data.

Asynchronous group interviews

The opportunity offered by online research to access geographically remote participants is especially valuable when it comes to group interviews. It enables you, as a researcher, to bring together not only people who live at a great distance from each other, but also to sample from very small populations. Thus, for example, it might be possible to convene a focus group of people suffering from an extremely rare genetic condition, or of experts in a highly specialised field, whom you could never otherwise gather in one place. As with individual online interviews, you must bear in mind that your potential samples will be restricted by access to and willingness to use the technology involved. The lower uptake of the internet among older people compared to the rest of the population is an issue that is commonly raised (e.g. Hunt and McHale, 2007).

In terms of asynchronous methods, there is a range of options available for conducting online group interviews. You could use ordinary e-mail and simply address messages to a group of people. This can, however, be quite cumbersome to manage. For instance, if someone replied just to you rather than to the whole group, you would need to check whether she had intentionally sent you a personal message or had simply clicked on 'Reply' instead of 'Reply to all' inadvertently. A more efficient alternative is to set up an e-mail distribution list for the research project, to which you subscribe all the group participants. Such lists are very easy for participants to use as they just involve sending and receiving e-mails. They are also straightforward to set up and enable you to take on a 'moderator' role – allowing you to anonymise sender information, organise different discussion 'threads', insert prompts, and so on (Stewart and Williams, 2005).

An alternative to e-mail discussion lists is to use a web-based discussion board or forum. These can be made much more visually appealing than an e-mail-based system, and enable links to other material that is relevant to your study to be made available for participants. For example, the front page of your project discussion board could include links to detailed participant information pages, to other sites of relevance to your topic, or could even incorporate a parallel online survey as part of a mixed methods design. On the downside, participants may be less familiar with this technology than e-mails, and web-boards require much more technical expertise to set up and manage than a discussion list (Stewart and Williams, 2005).

Synchronous online interviews

A number of technologies have developed on the internet to allow the exchange of messages instantaneously (or nearly so) online, offering the qualitative researcher the chance to carry out synchronous interviews. While sharing some features in common, this form also differs in significant ways from the asynchronous e-mail interview, and it is these differences that we will concentrate on in this section. These relate particularly to issues concerning recruitment, the impact of the medium on interaction style, and the management of the interview process and its resulting data.

The most commonly discussed medium for synchronous online interviews in the literature is Instant Messaging (IM). IM is a facility that enables two or more people to engage in text-based, real-time 'chat' and, depending on the specific service used, also exchange such things as pictures, music files and video clips. There are numerous services available, although the best-known are probably Windows (MSN) Messenger and Yahoo! Messenger. IM can be used for both individual and group interviews. Another option for the latter is the use of internet chat rooms that enable real-time discussion relating to a specified topic of mutual interest. We will say more about chat rooms later, when we discuss synchronous group interviews, but in the main our focus will be on the use of IM as a research medium.

Recruitment on IM services

A study by Stieger and Göritz (2006) examined the recruitment of participants for IM-based research. As part of a world-wide web-based survey, they asked participants to provide their IM names if they were willing to take part in a subsequent IM interview. A full year later, they used buddy/friend lists on the relevant IM services to search for the potential participants and, if successful, send them a request to be interviewed via IM. Of those found to have valid user names, 33% went online within the 15-day field research period and received an invitation to be interviewed, and 45% of these agreed and were interviewed. This is a higher response rate than the average of just under 40% calculated for 68 studies where participants were invited by e-mail (Cook et al., 2000), and is all the more encouraging for the long gap between the initial request via the WWW survey and the IM contact. Stieger and Göritz's study suggests that using IM itself in the process of recruiting participants for an IM interview study can be a viable option. It would be possible to use information elicited in the initial web survey to sample IM contactees purposively, in the manner commonly used in qualitative studies, and there may be additional advantages where the researchers introduce themselves via the same medium in which they will be carrying out data collection.

Interaction style

There is general agreement among researchers that the use of IM rather than e-mail encourages a more spontaneous and lively style of interaction than e-mail. Stewart and Williams (2005: 405) argue that 'while asynchronous communications are literate, synchronous communications are more oral'. This reflects not only their real-time nature but also the conventions of IM usage, which include a more chatty style and greater use of emotion indicators such as emoticons and forms such as 'LOL' (for 'laughs out loud'). This difference in style will almost certainly be reflected in the kind of interview data generated, and should be borne in mind when you chose the online method to use in a piece of research. If your approach and/or topic are best served by eliciting thoughtful reflections, then e-mail is likely to be best suited, but if you require immediacy and spontaneity, IM would be a good choice.

There is evidence to suggest that people may be more willing to disclose personal information online than they would be face to face (Joinson, 2005), probably due to the sense of anonymity they feel through communicating only by text. This tendency is likely to be present in any online interview technique, but the chatty, spontaneous style of IM may be especially likely to facilitate openness from participants. The likelihood that participants will talk openly via IM may therefore be an important factor in your choice of method, especially if your research is on a topic that people may be reticent about face to face. At the same time, the potentially unguarded nature of comments via IM raises ethical issues for you as a researcher. Voida, Mynatt, Erickson and Kellog (2004) report a case where a participant herself reflected at the end of an IM interview on how she had been so immersed in the conversation that it came as a 'shock' to be reminded that the research project's findings would be made public. We will return to this subject in the concluding section of this chapter.

Voida et al. (2004) also highlight another feature of everyday IM interaction style that you may need to address if using the medium for qualitative interviews – the tendency for users to multi-task when engaged in IM conversations. Users will very frequently maintain several IM conversations at once, clicking between them as new contributions arrive. They may also be simultaneously logged on to other services, such as social networking sites. In qualitative research, we normally seek to encourage our participants to be strongly engaged in the interview, so the divided attention that is a commonplace of IM use may be problematic. Worse still, as the interviewer, you cannot be sure whether your interviewee is fully engaged with your interaction or is dipping in and out of it alongside various other online activities. One way to address this issue is to ask participants at the start of the interview not to multi-task. This may produce more focused interviews, but it may also inhibit the spontaneity that we have emphasised as a key characteristic of IM. There is an argument that if you want carefully considered, focused responses you would be better off using e-mail interviews in the first place.

Managing the IM interview process and its resulting data

Technical characteristics of IM services provide some helpful features as well as challenges for qualitative interviews. One of these is what Voida et al. (2004) refer to as 'persistence': the fact that a record of the ongoing conversation is kept, enabling both interviewer and interviewees to 'scrollback' and check on what they said earlier in the interaction. As a researcher, you can very quickly and easily go back to earlier parts of the interview to check for seeming contradictions that might need to be explored further, or to ensure you have not omitted any important topic areas from your interview guide. You can also invite your participant to do the same – perhaps in a final question where you ask them whether there is anything else they want to cover.

Some IM services (including Windows Messenger) incorporate a 'typing indicator', which shows you when someone is engaged in composing a response to your posting. In an interview, you can tell from this how long a participant has taken to compose a response to one of your questions. For instance, Voida et al. (2004) described how a typing indicator showed that their respondent had taken five minutes to compose a message, but what they actually posted was a bland, three-word comment. This might be a sign of self-censorship, which could be worth carefully probing further, and should certainly be borne in mind when interpreting the data.

It is important to note that although in most cases IM services keep a persistent record of active conversations, these will be lost when the conversation window is closed. Naturally, this makes it crucial that you save your IM interviews carefully. Some programs will give you an option to download and save conversations in a word-processing or rich text file (rtf) format. Alternatively, you may have to manually highlight and save the information yourself. In case of a technical problem occurring which disrupts the connection and possibly loses the ongoing record of interaction, you may be advised to save periodically during the interview, rather than waiting until the end of the session to do so.

Synchronous group interviews

The IM medium can work very well for group interviews, in part because in everyday use multi-party conversations are commonplace. Given that in group interviews we are generally interested in the dynamics between members as well as the content of what they say (see Chapter 5), the synchronous form may be preferable to the asynchronous one. Stewart and Williams (2005) argue that the immediacy of IM encourages more expression of emotion and more heated exchanges between participants than normally occurs in asynchronous group methods. The impact of status differences between members is likely to be reduced in online compared to face-to-face groups (Kiesler and Sproull, 1992) and Stewart and Williams argue that this difference will probably be more evident in synchronous than asynchronous interviews. However, they also warn that participants may tend to exaggerate their views and accounts in IM groups, and adopt more extreme positions than they would in other settings, so researchers need to bear this in mind when analysing and interpreting their data.

Ethical issues in online interviewing

There is considerable debate about the extent to which the development of online research methods raises entirely new ethical issues for qualitative researchers (e.g. Holge-Hazelton, 2002; James and Busher, 2007). We would argue that although the ethical principles we work to do not change in the online environment, the nature of that environment sets up some distinctive challenges for decision-making in research ethics. These relate to: the lack of visual or aural contact with participants in internet-based research (we except here online video-conferencing which we covered alongside telephone interviewing earlier); the cross-national and cross-cultural nature of the internet; and the blurring of the division between public and private space in online environments. Below we will consider how these and other characteristics of online research impact on ethical considerations. First, though, we will look more closely at the public/private divide in the online world.

Public and private spaces on the internet

Ethical guidelines commonly make a distinction between public and private spaces in terms of whether permission is required from those using such spaces to have their activities observed and studied by researchers. Thus the British Psychological Society's (BPS) code states that where people are in a public space in which they might reasonably expect to be observed, their consent is not required (BPS, 2006). So, a psychologist might observe queuing behaviour at a bus stop without asking permission, but would certainly need consent to observe family interactions in the home environment. Inevitably, there are grey areas regarding what counts as 'private' – for instance, would consent be needed to record a personal conversation in the same bus queue? – but conceptually, the distinction is relatively straightforward. Furthermore, for qualitative researchers using interviews, the decision is unambiguous: a face-to-face interview is unquestionably a private conversation and, as such, would always require consent.

Things become much less clear when we look at definitions of public and private online. Many writers have pointed out that there is a blurring of these categories when we look at interaction on the internet (e.g. Waskul and Douglass, 1996; Bowker and Tuffin, 2004). For example, a chat room or discussion list may be open to anyone to join, but interactions in them may, in effect, be private conversations. Your university e-mail account, which you may use to conduct internet-based interviews, will be accessible to system administrators. Equally, internet users may not be aware of the limitations to their privacy when they communicate through particular services (Ess, 2002). Qualitative researchers using online methods therefore need to be very sensitive to the ambiguous nature of the public/private divide on the internet when addressing such key ethical issues as gaining informed consent and protecting participants from harm.

Establishing authentic identities

Just as establishing the authentic identity of your participants is harder in telephone interviews than when face to face, so for online interviews it is harder still. This is not only because participants are even more physically remote from researchers than they are over the telephone – you cannot see them *or* hear them – but also because assuming alternative or fictitious identities is a common aspect of online interaction. Misidentification, whether through a genuine misunderstanding or through impersonation, is of real concern where a study requires that specific groups should be included or excluded. For example, an online focus group study of women's experiences of harassment at work could be compromised if men took part pretending to be women. Equally, there would be serious ethical problems if children could easily impersonate adults to take part in e-mail interviews which involved explicit discussion of sexual behaviour. As with telephone interviews, seeking confirmation of identity through media other than the online one can reduce the risk of misidentification. James and Busher (2007) acknowledge that it was an advantage in their use of e-mail interviews in educational settings that they had had prior face-to-face contact with their participants in a professional capacity. In many online interview studies, this would not be possible. In fact, the impossibility of face-to-face contact might well be one of the main reasons for using the internet in the first place! Video-conferencing (or Skype) may be an option in some cases, and telephone contact in many more. Potential participants may also be able to send documentation to support identification by post or fax.

The lengths to which you should go to reassure yourself of your participants' identities depends on the risks you perceive from misidentification. Where the risks seem very high, you may feel that online methods are not appropriate if you cannot operate an extremely robust identification procedure (BPS, 2008). Conversely, where risks are low, and where a few cases of misidentification would not be fatal to your design, fairly simple procedures can be used. As with most ethical decisions, it is a matter of weighing up risks and benefits in your specific study context, rather than applying absolute rules.

Informed consent

The issue of accurate identification of participants has implications for the process of obtaining informed consent; you need to be as sure as possible that the person giving consent is actually the person you will be interviewing. It can be a good idea to request that a signed consent form is sent or faxed to you, rather than just relying on e-mail or another online medium (Meho, 2006). In qualitative research in general, it is common not simply to obtain written consent at one point at the start of the study, but also to check during data collection and afterwards that the participant still understands what is happening in the research and is happy to continue taking part in it. This notion of so-called 'process consent' is discussed further in Chapter 7.

The 'informed' part of informed consent creates a challenge for online research. Simply sending an information sheet by e-mail, or directing potential participants to a project website, may not be enough to ensure the information is actually read and understood prior to interview. Of course, this can also be true in a face-to-face interview, but in that context it is easier to check levels of understanding before commencing. In addition, as the BPS guidelines point out (BPS, 2008), it is commonplace in internet use to be presented with terms and conditions that a user has to agree to before signing up to a service. Many people get into the habit of ticking the agreement box without reading the 'fine print' of the terms and conditions, and there is a danger that the same will happen with research project information sheets. To reduce this risk, it is important not to make information sheets/pages too long-winded and complicated. Where a project website is used, providing links to more detailed information for those interested can be helpful. Also, contact e-mail and/or telephone numbers for queries should normally be provided.

Early in this chapter, we flagged up another issue for online interviews that has ethical implications: what to do when people cease responding without letting the researcher know that they have decided to quit the study. In such circumstances, you are left with the question of whether this should be counted as a withdrawal, and if so, whether that means that data up to the point where non-response was identified should also be withdrawn. Researchers take different positions on this. For example, Hunt and McHale (2007) suggest that non-response should normally be viewed as a full withdrawal from a study, while Kivits (2005) was comfortable including data from participants who had ceased replying to her e-mails. An ethical case can be made for either of these positions. We suggest that the crucial thing is to think about *your* position from the start of the study and inform participants what you intend to do with partial data from those who cease responding. This can then be considered part of the conditions of the study to which participants are giving consent.

Confidentiality and anonymity

The nature of the internet means that you can never promise absolute confidentiality and anonymity to participants. At the very least, online interactions are potentially accessible to service providers, who can be forced to provide records to law enforcement agencies in certain circumstances (with different regulations operating in different countries). If you are carrying out e-mail interviews from a university account, system administrators may also be able to access your exchanges with participants. Furthermore, as James and Busher (2007) point out, it is very easy to inadvertently pass on e-mails to people not involved in a study – one mistaken click of the mouse is all it takes!

Where you are using media such as IM, it may be possible for people outside a study to locate identifiable contributions by search engine. Also, when you are researching a well-defined online community, identity may be revealed through characteristics of writing style that are familiar to community members. Stewart and Williams (2005) describe a case where a participant points out that her messages have stylistic features (e.g. habitual use of certain emoticons and persistent mis-spelling of 'remember') which are likely to make her identifiable to other members of her online community, however carefully the researchers anonymise her.

While complete anonymity and confidentiality cannot be assured, there are many things that can be done to minimise the risks of inadvertent disclosure. You must take great care in removing potentially identifying headers, tags and so on from messages – for example, senders' e-mail addresses, user IDs, etc. We would recommend that even where a participant uses a pseudonym in their communications – as many IM users commonly do – you should consider replacing it with a project pseudonym in reporting findings. Great care must be taken in storing any non-anonymised 'raw' data securely, and separately from anonymised material.

Protection from harm

Many decisions about ethical practice in online interviewing need to be guided by considerations of the potential harm to participants should things go wrong. The greater the potential harm, the more careful you would need to be about confidentiality and anonymity, the more rigorous in your procedures for ensuring informed consent, and so on. For example, in a study about viewers' responses to reality television, there are not likely to be particularly negative consequences should a participant's identity be inadvertently revealed. However, if the project was examining young people's personal involvement in bullying or anti-social behaviour, identification could be seriously damaging to the participant involved.

In studies where you have many exchanges with participants over a long period of time, perhaps on sensitive issues, you need to be careful not to drift into a personal relationship that goes far beyond that between researcher and participant. The appropriate boundary can be difficult to judge, given that you quite legitimately do want to develop some degree of personal rapport in such situations, to help the participant feel comfortable in discussing their experiences and views with you. It is helpful to set limits to the duration of the study from the start (whether in terms of time or number of message exchanges expected), and send a message that clearly indicates the end of the interview at the appropriate point. In the course of the interview, if you feel that interactions are becoming uncomfortably personal in areas that seem unrelated to the study topic, try at first to guide the participant back to more pertinent issues. Should this not have the desired effect, you may need to state directly to the participant why you feel uncomfortable with some aspects of the interaction.

Although the risks to your own safety as a researcher are generally lower in online research than in face-to-face interviews, you must still bear them in mind in your research design. You should consider setting up a separate e-mail or IM user account to carry out interviews, rather than use your normal personal or university one. This may help both you and your participants to be clear about the boundary between research and personal interaction, and may offer some protection in the unlikely event that an interviewee interacts with you inappropriately. We would also caution you to think very carefully about agreeing to meet with online participants offline. If you are sure that such a request is legitimate, and relates to the research topic, you must follow the advice regarding safety in face-to-face interviews that we provide in the next chapter. We suggest, though, that you discuss any such request with a more experienced colleague or supervisor first.

Conclusion

Remote interviewing techniques have a great deal to offer the qualitative researcher, as we hope this chapter has illustrated. They can enable you to include participants whom you would not otherwise be able to reach. They offer the opportunity to use different modes of interaction to suit the needs of different studies – from the spontaneity of IM group interviews to the more considered and reflective e-mail interview. In online settings, they also remove the need for the lengthy process of transcribing interviews – though the work involved in properly managing and preparing records of online interactions should not be underestimated. But remote techniques also present a series of methodological and ethical challenges that we have described in some detail above. We would argue that the key to the successful use of remote interviews is to think carefully about the nature of the media you might use, and how they are suited to the requirements of your particular study – its topic, characteristics of the sample you are interested in, its philosophical assumptions, and so on. To choose telephone or online interviews purely for convenience can undermine the quality of your project. Finally, it is important to bear in mind the rapidly changing nature of information technology and the impact of this on social scientific research. One thing we can confidently predict is that the future will bring us yet more ways to technologically mediate interviews.

Recommended reading

Hunt, N. and McHale, S. (2007) A practical guide to the e-mail interview. *Qualitative Health Research*, 17 (10): 1415–21.
A useful, concise introduction.

James, N. and Busher, H. (2007) Ethical issues in online educational research: protecting privacy, establishing authenticity in email interviewing. *International Journal of Research and Method in Education*, 30 (1): 101–13.
Thoughtful consideration of some of the main ethical challenges in online interviews. Relevant beyond the specific context of educational research.

Kazmer, M.M. and Xie, B. (2008) Qualitative interviewing in internet studies: playing with the media, playing with the method. *Information, Communication and Society*, 11 (2): 257–78.
Compares face-to-face, telephone, e-mail and IM interviewing.

Kivits, J. (2005) Online interviewing and the research relationship, in C. Hine (ed.), *Virtual Methods: Issues in Social Research on the Internet*. Oxford: Berg.
A rich account of relationship issues in e-mail interviewing.

Voida, A., Mynatt, E.D., Erickson, T. and Kellogg, W.A. (2004) *Interviewing over instant messaging. Extended Abstacts of CHI 2004 Conference on Human Factors in Computing Systems, Vienna, Austria*, 1344–7, New York: ACM.
Provides some very pertinent insights into the nature of IM as a medium for conducting research interviews.

Note

1 'Synchronous' refers to media in which the exchange between interviewer and interviewee happens in real time. 'Non-synchronous' (or 'asynchronous') refers to those where there is not an immediate real-time exchange between the parties. As we will see later, Instant Messaging is an example of synchronous communication and e-mail of non-synchronous communication.

SEVEN

Ethics in Qualitative Interviewing

The ethical practice of social research with human participants is a complex and demanding responsibility. Throughout the social research process, from initiation to completion, ethical issues will exist and emerge – often raising moral dilemmas that are not easily resolved. Nevertheless, whatever the design, context or structure of the research we must always be mindful of the ethical implications for all those involved in the process. In light of this imperative, most qualitative and quantitative research texts include sections or chapters that outline the main issues that researchers need to consider. This book is no different in this regard, but it is prudent to be alerted to the extensive literature that already exists on this subject, spanning disciplines and ideologies. It would be impossible with such limited space to offer an all-embracing account that accommodates the breadth of historical, philosophical and political thinking underpinning ethics in social research. For this reason, what we offer in this chapter is insight into the main debates, but also practical guidance and advice that is directly targeted at ethical issues in relation to qualitative interviewing. Being aware of the need to be comprehensive yet targeted and succinct, we will cover the following main areas:

- morality, epistemology and ethics
- research governance and ethical principles
- professional codes of ethics and ethical review committees
- qualitative interviewing and informed consent
- confidentiality and anonymity
- physical safety and welfare of the researcher

Morality, epistemology and ethics

We begin by outlining some of the contemporary thinking and debates that surround social research ethics and qualitative research more specifically. Our justification for initially offering a more conceptual view is that it is important to have a sound appreciation of why you are taking a particular course of action. We have made this point in earlier chapters in relation to specific theoretical orientations in qualitative research. Similarly, an undertaking to be conversant with the moral reasoning, surrounding a certain course of action, should prevail when thinking through the ethics of qualitative interviewing.

As researchers we all bring to the research process our own individual morality, which is an accumulation of understandings, feelings, positions and principles around particular issues. Our moral outlook has been shaped by the different experiences, events, and social and cultural locations that constitute our lives. Morality is therefore not merely a matter of simple universal dichotomies such as good and bad or right and wrong. Rather, we each have our own individual moral viewpoints which, although not necessarily consistent and coherent, we nonetheless feel strongly about. This moral compass is there in research and while there is the possibility of embracing certain general ethical principles, the way in which these are taken up and acted upon is very much reliant upon notions of individual morality. The following quote by Edwards and Mauthner (2002: 16) captures how ethics and morality are intertwined:

> Ethics concern the morality of human conduct. In relation to social research, it refers to the moral deliberation, choice and accountability on the part of researchers throughout the research process.

It is important to note not only the prevalence of morality, choice and account-ability here, but also the idea of the whole research process. As qualitative researchers we need to ethically consider, for example, the framing of our research question, how this is impacted upon by interested parties and what might be the implications and applications of research framed in this way. Yet interestingly, ethical concerns are often only directed at research practice (methods, consent, confidentiality) with knowledge construction seen as an epistemological issue that is not situated within the ethical domain (Doucet and Mauthner, 2002). This is an unsustainable position, not least because different approaches in qualitative interviewing are founded upon complex, competing and often political understandings of human experience. Thus there is an obligation to consider the morality of not only research practice, but also the various practical, epistemological and ontological assumptions that surround and define the research.

In previous chapters we have questioned notions of objectivity and the epistemological integrity of searching for one universal truth, suggesting that with qualitative interviewing there is the potential for multiple realities. Taking these ideas on board necessitates the researcher having to reflect on how the production of knowledge has the power to shape and determine particular and often powerful versions of social reality. Early feminist researchers (Oakley, 1981; Gilligan, 1982) have shown how an epistemology founded upon men's experience, as an all-encompassing norm, introduced a powerful bias that discriminated against women. There are regrettably many instances of knowledge construction where underlying epistemologies have mobilised detrimental cultural, social and gendered beliefs that have until recently remained unchallenged. Embracing qualitative methods, with their more contextually located and constructionist roots, prompts careful deliberation around knowledge production that is inclusive of inherently complex ethical relationships and responsibilities. We have ethical responsibilities not only to those who participate, but also to those for whom the knowledge is produced. As qualitative researchers engaged in producing knowledge, we are required to act responsibly, being aware of how the research we produce will be read, re-interpreted and used. Being attentive and transparent regarding the personal, theoretical and epistemological assumptions that underpin, and generally inform, the research therefore has an ethical as well as reflexive dimension (we cover *reflexivity* more comprehensively in the next chapter).

Research governance and ethical principles

The governance of research has become a primary issue for those involved in undertaking, funding and supporting research. While research governance is often seen to be prevalent in the domain of health and healthcare research, it is fair to say that its impact is becoming far more widespread. In the UK, the Economic and Social Research Council's *Research Ethics Framework* (REF) (2008) gives full and accessible information around the relationship between ethics and research governance. While ethical principles concern the rights, dignity and safety of research participants, research governance focuses on the development of joint standards and processes that permit the proper management and monitoring of research and, if necessary, allows sanctions to be brought in cases of research misconduct. Managing, monitoring and ensuring the ethical undertaking of research is therefore becoming more of a transparent and accountable process. Consequently, it is highly likely that as researchers you will need to go through a process of ethically justifying your research. Within this process your topic of inquiry and research methods will be thoroughly reviewed and evaluated against certain ethical principles.

Utilitarian ethics

In the previous section we stressed the importance of moral and epistemological issues with regard to ethics. While there is a wealth of debate regarding the theoretical origins and application of ethics in qualitative research (e.g. Christians, 2003), here in this chapter we have taken a pragmatic approach. With the growing prevalence of governance, it is probable that the principles used to assess the ethical credentials of research will be broadly drawn from what are referred to as *utilitarian ethics*.

According to utilitarianism, actions are judged right or wrong in proportion to their propensity to produce the most happiness or pleasure, for the greatest number. This model of ethics is founded upon the ability to predict the consequences of an action with rightness or wrongness being dependent on the consequences of an act. Utilitarian ethics have generally been deployed because of compatibility with scientific ways of thinking, drawing on rational thought and the assumption of a single and consistent view of moral action. This is often the kind of rationality we use in this chapter. For example, when recruiting participants we consider whether it is appropriate to include those who might be identified as 'vulnerable'. This consideration is generally framed in terms of predicting the possible consequences that participation might hold for the participant. Utilitarian ethics emphasise the role of human happiness as a consequence of our actions, but this does then translate into a concern with achieving the maximum good. Theoretically, the infringement of an individual's rights may be acceptable in order to maximise the happiness of the majority. In research terms this might translate into including the vulnerable participant because, although as a consequence their well-being may be compromised, the well-being of the majority might be served by their inclusion.

There are serious difficulties with the use of utilitarian ethics in qualitative interviewing, not least the inherent problems associated with predicting the future consequences of actions. Qualitative interviewing seeks to be fluid and flexible, thus having to accurately predict consequences is generally not desirable or realisable. Also, if we return to questions of morality, how might different people, agencies and institutions view the consequences of certain actions? In actual fact, our individual morality may make it impossible to align ourselves with an ideology that justifies a potentially detrimental act based on maximising benefits for the majority. Indeed, the assumption that one moral code might encompass the complexity of qualitative social research seems hard to sustain both morally and methodologically. In spite of this difficulty, generally speaking there are certain moral principles, drawn from utilitarianism, that are often used when formally evaluating both qualitative and quantitative social research: *respect for persons*, *beneficence* and *justice*.

- *Respect for persons* demands that individuals participate voluntarily, having had adequate information about what involvement in the research will entail, including possible consequences. This means dealing with people as free to choose, but also acknowledging more vulnerable people's rights to be protected. There are thus two aspects to respect for persons: autonomy and protection. Being free to choose with regard to participation is generally related to information-sharing. The participant should be given comprehensive information such that they are able to give their informed consent. There are particular target groups (e.g. children, older people, those with literacy deficits or mental health disabilities) where the individual's ability to understand and fully appreciate the process and consequences of participation is hard to determine. Indeed, there will be persons whose vulnerabilities require that they are protected against involvement in research. Respect for persons is a wide-ranging principle that for social researchers goes well beyond simplistic notions of respecting people's freedoms.
- *Beneficence* relates to the researcher's responsibility to secure the well-being of participants. The principle is to avoid harm, although whether this means to avoid harm altogether or minimise it is much debated. As already stated, underlying this debate is the ideology of maximising benefits or securing the 'greater good', whereby it is understood that to achieve substantial benefits there may be certain risks. Some might think that this utilitarian argument is a slippery slope, with researchers being able to justify unethical research by pointing towards gains in knowledge. While we can historically point towards the catastrophic misuse of this principle (e.g. the 'medical' research undertaken by the Nazi regime) most researchers have the well-being of all participants foremost in their minds.

- *Justice* is a principle that is often less talked about when looking at generic guidance on the ethical practice of research. Implicit in the term justice is the notion of 'fairness' and in research terms this translates into the fair distribution of both the benefits and burdens of research (for a review, see Porter, 1999). Take, for example, how the benefits of research have not been equally distributed, with men's and women's priorities failing to receive the same attention. Such injustice in research also works in the other direction, when some groups are overburdened in terms of involvement (e.g. the institutionalised, certain ethnic groups, particular service users). While there are no easy solutions to such matters, having the principle of justice present does offer the likelihood of discussion and, possibly, accountability.

Social and communitarian ethics

Principles founded upon utilitarianism do, without doubt, extol notions of individual autonomy, rather than a more relational view. The scientific furtherance of knowledge – as the overall aim – is also evident. Indeed, the existence of explicit principles does point towards a consensus worldview of what constitutes good ethical practice in social research. However, this consensus is seldom evident in qualitative research practice. As we said previously, different approaches to research mobilise their unique understandings of ethical practice, which are underpinned by certain theoretical, cultural and moral ideologies. Hence, many researchers have been engaged in working towards a more *social ethics* (see Code, 1991; Taylor, 1991) where a complex and situated view of moral judgements is adopted. Within this broad approach, conventions of distance and impartiality in research are replaced with notions of *caring*, interdependency and collaboration. For example, Carol Gilligan (1982) characterises the female moral voice as an 'ethics of care'. Here, merely avoiding harm is seen as inferior to embracing an ideology of participation founded upon compassion and nurturance.

There are obviously inbuilt tensions in arguing simplistically to typify women as caring/relational and men as being engaged in a more rational approach within social research. Even so, the overall challenge to individualistic utilitarianism is evident, with Denzin (1997, 2002) referring to 'feminist communitarianism' as an alternative ethical theory that can take qualitative research forward. He argues that we are now in a period were there is an abiding concern with moral discourse that is inclusive of politics, gender, freedom, nation and community. The idea that we can appeal to an objective, morally neutral viewpoint (e.g. university review boards) is rejected, and is replaced with a more localised morality, an ethics of care and 'shared governance'. Research becomes ethically situated in a mutually cooperative domain where the community is served, rather than the producers of knowledge and the policy-makers. Within such a model, participants have a say in how the research is conducted and may have a part to play in its actual undertaking. Research then becomes far more about social action with the researcher and researched participating together, acting in the best moral interests of both the individual and the community (see, for example, Shaw, 1999, on 'participatory inquiry'). Of course such approaches have their own challenges, not least how to achieve the participatory ideal when confronted with differences around methodological know-how (Heron, 1996). Those facilitating the research may find it hard to engender full participation when knowledge and power are so unequally dispersed.

Professional codes of ethics and ethical review committees

Returning to the idea of research governance, there are a number of professional codes of practice that now specifically outline ethics in relation to social research (e.g. British Sociological Association, 2002, updated 2004; British Educational Research Association, 2004; British Psychological Society, 2006). It is fair to say that professional codes of practice have been viewed with caution by some (see Homan, 1991), arguably because they may have been produced to establish a minimum standard of ethical practice. Our view is that while such documents are a useful starting point, it is the practical operationalisation of these codes of practice that presents challenges in social research, and qualitative interviewing in particular.

Most professional codes of ethical practice outline a set of *basic ethical considerations* such as the ones outlined by Willig (2001: 18):

1   *Informed consent*: The researcher should ensure that participants are fully informed about the research procedure and give their consent to participate in the research *before* data collection takes place.
2   *No deception*: Deception of participants should be avoided altogether. The *only* justification for deception is when there is no other way to answer the research question *and* the potential benefit of the research far exceeds any risk to participants.
3   *Right to withdraw*: The researcher should ensure that participants feel free to withdraw from participation in the study without fear of being penalised.
4   *Debriefing*: The researcher should ensure that, after data collection, participants are informed about the full aims of the research. Ideally, they should also have access to any publications arising from the study they took part in.
5   *Confidentiality*: The researcher should maintain complete confidentiality regarding any information about participants acquired during the research process.

These basic considerations, some of which we cover later in greater depth, offer sound initial guidance for enabling researchers to protect participants from harm, aiming to preserve their well-being and dignity. The important thing to bear in mind is that these are *basic* ethical considerations that will normally be developed and expanded upon in the process of undertaking qualitative interview research. Indeed, we later elaborate, extend and, in places, take exception to each one of these considerations, showing the ways in which ethics in qualitative interviewing are both individually, epistemologically and ideologically located.

Alongside the development of professional codes of ethics a number of government agencies now have stringent ethical processes that must be adhered to before any research can commence. For example, the National Health Service (NHS) requirement is that any research involving patients or staff must go through the National Research Ethics Service (NRES) process. This involves completing and submitting for approval a lengthy document where the researcher is required to give explicit details about the aims, methods and outcomes of the proposed research. The researcher is required to identify and comprehensively respond to a range of ethical issues, and is asked to explain in detail how these will be addressed. In order to accommodate the inductive fluidity of qualitative research it is possible to gain phased ethical approval. Although this is time-consuming, it does mean that researchers can return at a later date with, for example, a more fully developed interview schedule or, indeed, a change of focus. Whatever the strategy, failure to comply with the strict guidance provided will almost certainly result in the proposed research being denied approval. Universities also have ethical review boards and although, in relation to the NRES process, they may require the information in a less prescribed format, they will nevertheless call for similar information and detail. Such processes are not there to hinder research but should be viewed as providing an opportunity to thoroughly engage with the ethical implications that research with 'human subjects' presents. The question often asked by researchers is 'how is approval secured?' There is no secret formula; all ethical review boards have guidance that is readily available. This guidance needs to be meticulously read through with a view to identifying the information required and the level of detail needed. If possible, speak to other researchers who have been through the process and ask if they might be willing to share their 'approved' documentation (providing this, of itself, does not have ethical implications).

Researchers do sometimes tell stories of difficult encounters with ethics committees. While we do not deny that this may occasionally happen, our experience (having submitted proposals to a range of ethical boards, and having been members of ethics committees), is that the process is demanding but usually fair. Indeed, often the process and advice given can enhance methodological rigour and pre-empt potential problems. This said, it may be the case that some ethical review boards are limited in their understanding of qualitative research. This can prove to be testing and it is therefore important that the documentation submitted is written in a style that is accessible and clear. In earlier chapters we have stressed the importance of philosophical theory, and while some of this information might be relevant, in terms of orientation or analysis, for example, such detail should aim to inform not alienate any committee.

Finally, when thinking about these processes it is useful to remember that such committees have a demanding remit, often aiming to be supportive of research while still being accountable for its ethical undertaking. It is in everyone's interests to engage in ethical research practice and therefore governance processes that regulate may be time-consuming and demanding, but they are also necessary.

Qualitative interviewing and informed consent

Ethical codes of practice emphasise the importance of gaining the informed consent of participants prior to taking part in the research. Participants should be giving their 'knowing consent' (Berg, 2001), making choices free from duress or inducement. The key word here is 'knowing' – are participants fully aware of what they are consenting to when they agree to participate in a qualitative interview? Do participants know if they are consenting to answer any and all questions that are asked in the qualitative interview? Are participants knowingly giving you the right to use the data no matter what is said? Do participants share the researcher's perspective regarding what counts as data? For example, did the interviewee agree to have their body language, personal appearance, home situation described in detail? We are not suggesting that these aspects of a person's life are not relevant details in qualitative interviewing, but rather we are asking whether consent was given for the use of these data.

In this section we aim to raise central issues, making it plain that working through the specifics of informed consent is a crucial aspect of ethical research practice. It is fair to say that while it is important to obtain informed consent, participants will only be in possession of fuller knowledge of what participation entails when they have experienced the interview. While accepting this conundrum, there is a great deal that can be done to ensure that the qualitative interview is a productive and/or enjoyable experience that holds no unwelcome surprises.

Process of negotiation

In order to get to the point of being able to conduct a qualitative interview the researcher is, in our view, required to enter into what is, in effect, a *process of negotiation*. The researcher should provide as much information as possible so that the participant is able to consider, and potentially negotiate, the terms of their involvement. In social research there are of course tensions, as offering explicit and detailed information may have implications for data production. If you state, for example, that you are interested in the power dynamics between managers and workers, you may inhibit what certain participants will discuss. Participants may perceive certain consequences if they reveal too much about the relationship. There is no hard-and-fast rubric here. Rather, the researcher needs to be conscientious in their efforts to share relevant, understandable and honest information. Of course, in this information-giving process your concern will be to protect the open-endedness and fluidity of the qualitative interview. Even so, participation in social research should not have unforeseen negative consequences and nor should information-giving be partial in a way that hides any potentially detrimental effects in order that the researcher is able to secure data.

When using qualitative interviews researchers are better positioned than those carrying out other kinds of research to recognise ethical issues, to obtain information that could help in making ethical decisions and to engage in a genuine process of negotiation around ethical concerns (see Rosenblatt, 2000). While such flexibility means that prospective participants can be engaged with and informed in a variety of ways, there are specific issues that need to be covered. In Box 7.1 we suggest a framework for producing a participant information sheet that explains the purpose of the research, the nature of participation and what will happen to the data that is generated. Of course, this will not be the same for different approaches to qualitative interviewing and we are not suggesting the standardisation of such processes. Rather, the framework aims to highlight key information that researchers should consider providing.

Box 7.1   Information for interview participants

What is the purpose of the research?

- You can give the aims of the research here but ensure that these are presented in a format that participants can appreciate and understand.
- If appropriate, describe the potential benefits that the research might have for informing service delivery, enhancing knowledge and so on. Be cautious though – don't overstate the potential of the research.

Why have I been chosen?

- The research needs to have relevance with regard to the proposed participant's involvement so be specific.

Do I have to take part?

- Participation is voluntary and this always needs to be stated.
- If appropriate, make it clear that choosing not to participate will not have any negative consequences.
- Make participants aware that they have the right to terminate their involvement in the research whenever they please.
- Participants also need to know that they can decline to respond to questions or prompts at any point in the interview.

What do I have to do?

- Explain exactly what the participant needs to do if they are willing to become involved in the research. This is dependent upon the nature of the research but generally participants will need the contact details of the researcher in order to initiate their participation.
- Provide some general information about the interview. It is good practice to make participants aware of the kinds of questions that will be asked before they consent to participate. This outline need only be general but it should both alert and prepare the participant for their involvement in the research.
- Give details of the expected duration of the interview and an indication of where and when this might take place.
- People don't like surprises when they are consenting to something that is unfamiliar so mention that, with their permission, you will need to record the interview.

(Continued)

(Continued)

What happens to the information I give at the interview?

- Explain concisely how confidentiality of the data and anonymity will be handled.
- For some research you may need to explain the limits of these arrangements.

What will happen to the results of the study?

- Give details of dissemination and this should include feedback to participants.

Who is organising the funding of the study?

- If appropriate, provide this information.

Who has approved the study?

- Giving this information can allay people's concerns so, if appropriate, provide this information.

Contact for further information

- This information may have already been given. However, presenting contact details again in a way that encourages the seeking of further information can enable participants to seek clarification and therefore increase participation rates.

Thank you for reading this information sheet and considering taking part.

This information can be presented in a range of formats. Possibly, the required format is a letter with the information sheet enclosed. Alternatively, this information can be verbally explained to participants as part of an initial individual or group discussion with the researcher. The information might be presented as text-based but with a more engaging graphic format. The way this information is presented will very much depend upon the researcher adapting and responding to the needs of the participant group. It would be foolish to use the information sheet in Box 7.1 in its current guise with young schoolchildren. Something more aesthetically appealing and interactive would be needed. However, providing information with this general information structure enables the researcher to outline the specific nature of the research. Participants are given information detailing what involvement will entail and the potential benefits and consequences of participation. With such information, the participant is able to make an informed choice and will know what to expect if they consent to participate in the research.

The giving of consent can often be a verbal agreement between the researcher and researched and we are not suggesting that these kind of verbal agreements are to be avoided. However, often ethics committees and review boards will require the active giving of consent by way of a consent form. Box 7.2 gives two examples of consent forms, one that can be informally completed before the interview commences but after information has been shared (Form A), the other (Form B) with a more personal tone and including of specific information that can be sent to participants in advance. The important thing to keep to the fore is that informed consent is about being open, truthful and respectful of people's right to choose. While informed consent in social research is not generally a legalistic process (although there may occasionally be a time when such documentation has a more bureaucratic purpose), the consent form endorses the process, making it visible, memorable and, most importantly, something that can be returned to if necessary.

Box 7.2   Consent forms – two different options

Form A

Title of Project:

Name of Researchers:

Please initial box

1. I confirm that I have read and understood the information sheet dated (insert date) for the above study. I have had the opportunity to consider the information, ask questions and have had these answered satisfactorily. ☐

2. I understand that my participation is voluntary and that I am free to withdraw at any time without giving any reason and without any consequences for me. ☐

3. I have been informed that the interview will be tape recorded and I give my consent for this recording to be made. ☐

4. I understand that all information I provide will be treated as confidential and will be anonymised. ☐

5. I agree to the use of anonymised direct quotes from my interview in publications and presentations arising from this study. ☐

6. I agree to take part in the above study. ☐

Name of Participant	Signature	Date

Researcher	Signature	Date

(Continued)

(Continued)

Form B

Informed consent for Masters project

Title: Women's experiences of reproductive choice

Dear (name of participant)

I am a Masters student in the School of Social and International Studies at the University of Bradford. I would like to invite you to participate in research I am undertaking as part of my studies. The research has been approved by the University's Departmental Ethics Panel. My research project explores the experiences of women as they consider reproductive choices and the prospect of becoming a parent for the first time.

If you agree to participate, this will involve being interviewed once and it is expected that the interviews will last no longer than one hour. I can undertake the interview at a time and place that is convenient for you and I would want to record and transcribe the interview. All interview data will be treated with the utmost respect and will be stored securely. However, information about the project, including interview data, will be shared with my dissertation supervisor and other appropriate staff at the University.

You may be concerned that other people will be able to know what you've said in the interview. I will do my very best to protect you from this by removing identifying information, for example, changing your name and your exact age. You will be able to withdraw from the project at any time until 1 May 2009. After this time I will be at the point of writing up my research and therefore will not be able to remove quotations from the final dissertation. The final dissertation resulting from this project will be publicly available through the University Library.

I appreciate your giving time to this study and if you have any questions please do call me at _____ . You can also contact my dissertation supervisor, Dr _____ at _____.

Thank you

(Name of researcher and signature)

If you are willing to participate in the Masters project outlined above please sign below.

Signature _____

Print name _____

Date _____

The right to withdraw and managing emotions

Participation in social research is voluntary and, as such, participants have the right to withdraw at any point in the process. The important factor to remember is that informed consent is a *process*. This recognition of process is not helped by the term 'informed consent', where past tense is inferred. Past tense suggests that when consent is given it is completed – over and done with. This one-off approach to informed consent is generally not acceptable in qualitative interviewing. Think about how frequently qualitative interview research stretches over a period of time and therefore people may have forgotten and thus need to be reminded of their right to withdraw. Equally, some qualitative interview research might require a change of direction that necessitates returning to the process of informed consent. If we consider research that relies on grounded theory, perhaps the topics we originally gained consent to focus on in the interview have changed. This kind of 'process consent' (Ramos, 1989) can also take place within the interview situation. When interviewing parents who had experienced the death of a child, Rosenblatt (2000: 204) gives the following example of how he sensitively used process consent within the actual qualitative interview, giving participants the implicit right to withdraw from aspects, and even all, of the interview:

> I don't know if that's an appropriate question to ask or not...
> I feel like maybe all these questions are too personal. You can tell me to shut up anytime you want...
> Can I ask you...?

Therefore consent to participate in qualitative interviewing is not a one-off conversation but is ongoing, requiring renegotiation and enabling participants to be aware of their right to withdraw throughout the process. In reality, participants rarely withdraw once they have consented to participate. However, if participants do exercise their right to withdraw, data and other material related to that person's participation must be destroyed immediately.

The right to withdraw can be deployed mistakenly when participants become emotional and distressed during an interview. This is often the reaction of a novice researcher who assumes that someone's distress necessitates the termination of the interview, perhaps in relation to the ethical principle of beneficence and the undertaking to do no harm. Understandably, interviewers can often fear the emotional reactions of participants, but automatically invoking a distressed participant's right to withdraw from the process is often not the outcome that the participant wants or needs. Of course the aim of the interview is to gather information and not to elicit a participant's extreme emotional response. On the other hand, interviews aim to provide rich, detailed and in-depth information and it is hard to imagine how this might be achieved without layers of emotional input. Although dependent on the type of interview, in general, as an interviewer you should acknowledge, and if necessary try to verbalise, the emotions you observe (e.g. 'does this make you sad?'). You should not ignore such emotions. Sometimes it is useful to suggest a short break (make a coffee, etc.), after which the participant can be asked if they want to continue. Having been involved in research that, by its very nature, gives rise to emotions (e.g. drug misuse, intimate partner relationships, care of the dying), we can say with confidence that it is often more useful for participants to finish the interview. Emotional life is an essential part of our experience and therefore will be an integral part of the interview process.

'Off the record'

In our experience of using qualitative interviews in various research projects, there is one thing that seldom varies. Almost always, participants breathe a sigh of relief when the recording equipment is switched off but then continue to talk. Often this part of the qualitative interview encounter is crucial, with participants sharing sometimes highly sensitive information that has direct relevance to the research. This appears to occur regardless of the tenor of the interview. We have known many different researcher responses to this kind of 'off the record' extended conversation – a conversation that at times is about personal disclosure. In our view, there is only one ethical response that takes on board the ethical principle of *respect for persons*, and that is to renegotiate with the participant. As the researcher, you can sensitively ask if it might be acceptable to turn the tape recorder back on or if you might be able to write down what is being said. Whatever course of action is taken in terms of recording data, the choice regarding the inclusion of 'off the record' data should always remain with the participant. If the participant refuses permission, then any data that has been recorded should be destroyed.

Payment for participation

Paying participants to take part in research is controversial and may be seen as an inducement that changes the fundamental nature of the process. With payment, instead of participation being voluntary, the research relationship is seen to be founded upon tangible rewards that may impact not only on consent but also any data generated. Drawing on an uncomplicated account of power relations, participants who have received payment may feel obliged to respond in a particular fashion, having thus relinquished their free choice regarding participation. An alternative view is one put forward by Hollway and Jefferson (2000: 84–5) that takes a far more relational view of power. Payment for participation may have the effect of 'equalising the relationship (our money for their time) … a mark of respect for their participation'. However, the authors avoid oversimplifying the case, recognising that 'equalising' is set within a structural understanding of power. This understanding suggests that power is unevenly distributed between the researcher and the researched. Such power differentials are often multifaceted, reflecting involved and contextually located fields of inquiry. While conceding that, in some ways, payment may induce participation, this does not negate the relational nature of the research process. Each party in the research process has inputs and investments that facilitate and mediate involvement. Of course, there will be any number of factors to consider when making choices regarding payment for participation: when, how much, to whom is payment made? However, situating payment for participation within a relational dynamic, rather than framing it as inducement, does provide a convincing ethical argument.

Confidentiality and anonymity

Confidentiality and anonymity are often taken to mean the same thing in research. This is a mistake. While the concepts are related, they have quite distinct meanings that are critical in relation to qualitative interviewing. In the ethics literature, confidentiality is commonly viewed as equivalent to the principle of privacy. Therefore, to assure someone confidentiality appears to suggest that what is said in the qualitative interview will remain private and not be repeated. Obviously this can't be what we want to imply in social research, and more specifically qualitative interviewing, since as researchers we undertake to report the findings/outcomes of research. It is hard to imagine how this might be done, when using qualitative interviewing, if what is said is not to be repeated. Rather than assuring confidentiality, as researchers we can seek to offer *anonymity* when using the data generated in qualitative interviews. Anonymity refers to concealing the identity of the participants in all documents resulting from the research, therefore actively protecting the identity of research participants.

The British Sociological Association's, *Statement of Ethical Practice* (2002: 5, updated 2004) provides the following guidance which is fairly representative of professional bodies' views on this issue:

Anonymity, privacy and confidentiality

(34) The anonymity and privacy of those who participate in the research process should be respected. Personal information concerning research participants should be kept confidential. In some cases it may be necessary to decide whether it is proper or appropriate even to record certain kinds of sensitive information.

(35) Where possible, threats to the confidentiality and anonymity of research data should be anticipated by researchers. The identities and research records of those participating in research should be kept confidential whether or not an explicit pledge of confidentiality has been given.

This guidance links privacy, confidentiality and anonymity to the underlying principle of respect. What we try to do overleaf is to offer specific guidance on how these discrete aspects can be addressed in relation to qualitative interviewing.

Confidentiality of the data

When participants agree to be interviewed they have the right to expect that the data as a whole will be handled with due respect and discretion. Participants do not expect their interview data to be available for general consumption. The data was generated for a specific purpose, and no other use should be made of the data unless this is renegotiated with participants. With the introduction of the Data Protection Act 1998, which came into effect on 1 March 2000, the consideration of anonymity and confidentiality goes beyond the moral and ethical domain. There can be legal implications, with the fundamental principle of the Act being the protection of the rights of individuals in respect of personal data held about them and this includes research data. Concerns relating to the misuse of personal data have surfaced because of the vast amount of data that new technologies now enable to be stored on individuals and their lives. While electronic storage is a concern, it should be noted that the Act applies to both electronic data and manual data (paper, card indices, files, and so on).

A straightforward reading, with regard to confidentiality of the data, means that participants should be able to rely on their data being kept secure, with identifying information removed and known only to the researcher, or research team if appropriate. A process for managing the separation of personal information from the data needs to be put in place before the collection of data. For example, numbering interviews (Participant 1) and keeping a record of actual names in a secure and separate location that can only be accessed by the researcher (lockable filing cabinet or password-protected computer). Indeed, you should consider if you need to actually maintain a record of participants' actual names – what purpose is this serving? You may need to keep a record if you have agreed to enable participants to look through the transcript (a practice we will return to later), or you may be doing follow-up interviews. Whatever your decision, such information should be well organised and kept secure. You can also assign pseudonyms at this point – this helps with anonymity. Also, assigning pseudonyms at this point avoids becoming familiar with the data using one name, and then switching to a pseudonym at a later date, which can be perplexing.

One of the principles of the Data Protection Act 1998 is that personal data shall not be kept for longer than is necessary. Ethics committees now often ask how long the data will be stored and the expectation is that unless agreed otherwise the data will be destroyed once the stated period has expired. We can hear qualitative researchers protesting at the loss of data that can be reworked and reanalysed. Such measures do not preclude the archiving of qualitative data that can be made available for further or secondary analysis (see ESRC Qualitative Data Archival Resource Centre: http://ideas.repec.org/a/sro/srosro/1996_73_/.html). Actually, it can be argued that the principle relating to the length of time personal data is kept does not relate to data that has been anonymised because the data is no longer 'personal'. This is a view that many researchers take and, indeed, is one that makes logical sense. However, serious consideration needs to be given to those data that are not so easily anonymised. Equally, we need to think about notions of good practice in scholarly research. If the data are destroyed too early, how might findings be validated if challenged? As you can see, it is hard to give categorical advice on this issue, particularly when thinking about work such as Catherine Reissman's 'A Thrice-Told Tale' (2004b). In this work Reissman returns many years later to previously used data, reanalysing it, for a third time and offering new insights into the experiences of someone living with multiple sclerosis. To suggest that such data should have been destroyed seems almost barbaric. What we are saying is that it is the researcher's duty to be aware of the responsibilities surrounding the storage of interview data and that these should be at the forefront of any decisions that are made with regard to confidentiality of the data.

Transcription

Transcription is always a time-consuming and demanding task and often this is contracted out to people with the essential skills. Of course there is the consequential impact that you do not develop the same level of familiarity with the data if someone else does the transcribing. Nevertheless, realistically, time constraints may mean you need to employ others to do this task. This is not necessarily a problem, and can greatly reduce the demands placed on qualitative researchers. Often those who take on this work have experience working with confidential data. Even so, the researcher must ensure that the transcriber is aware of confidentiality issues and agrees to respect the confidentiality of the data. In a similar vein, researchers are very enthusiastic about their work and novice researchers can become eager to share their fieldwork experiences. Discussing the data professionally (with co-researchers, colleagues) is fine, but relating this in a way that identifies individual participants is not, and researchers need to quickly develop the ability to use, at all times, the assigned pseudonyms.

Anonymising the data

Generally, as already mentioned, the advice given in textbooks is to use pseudonyms, replacing the participant's name with an alternative one. This is, of course, sound advice and does go part way to making sure that participants are not identifiable. There are, however, many instances in qualitative interviewing when this simply will not suffice. For example, in a narrative interview a participant will describe in great detail their personal experiences, relationships and life events. The *story* that is told, its structure and fabric, remains transparent – knowable to others. The name of the participant is therefore not the only way in which the participant can be identified. In a semi-structured interview with a 'key informant' (someone who has specific information relating to the research, e.g. a headteacher, a public health manager), the position that the person occupies and/or other attributes and characteristics will be both relevant to the interview and identifiable to others. Take the example of interviewing a group of young mothers where one of the participants has three children while all the other participants have one or two children. The mother with three children is distinct in relation to the other young mothers participating in the research. If this specific information is included, the young women participating in the research, and others reading the subsequent research report, may be able to directly link quotes to the mother with three children. Evidently, the use of a pseudonym would not suffice to protect anonymity in this instance. A decision needs to be made about the use of such identifying information. Its removal may in many instances have profound relevance in terms of research aims. The young mother already referred to has her experiences and understandings rooted in the fact that she has three children and therefore omitting this information from your analysis may have an impact in terms of contextually locating the data.

There are no simple solutions to such dilemmas and it is the responsibility of the researcher to comprehensively think through the impact that participation might have for people taking part. It might be argued that the nature of qualitative interviewing makes anonymity a highly challenging concept. Participants are invited to share their personal thoughts and opinions, and these are always set within their own lives, which have distinctive features. Therefore the researcher needs to have considered in more detail how to anonymise, and perhaps even explore with participants if anonymisation is possible and/or desirable. You could also enter into a process of negotiation with participants with regard to the use of specific quotes. Participants will have insight into what might be fine to use and which quotes may hold potential dangers with regard to the disclosure of identity.

Regrettably, all too often issues around anonymity are left until the later stages of the research when the costs to both the participants and the research have escalated. Removal or omission of data can profoundly affect the overall outcome of research, yet inclusion without anonymity may have reverberating consequences. Our advice is always to be upfront and clear when discussing the potential benefits and effects of participation when seeking 'informed consent'; this should most certainly relate to anonymity if this is a concern. Also it is important to consider that there exists a growing awareness of how some research participants, particularly children and young people, may want to be identified and not anonymised in research outputs (see Grinyer, 2002). Even if this is the case, it is still the researcher's responsibility to decide if such a strategy is ethically sound. In these circumstances, researchers are advised to obtain written consent that an individual wishes to waive their right to anonymity.

Ownership of the data

Participants, commissioners and other interested parties all want to be represented in a positive light and at times this may bring about serious clashes and disagreements around who actually owns the data. Even when consent has been undertaken as a process of negotiation, there may still be points of conflict around ownership of the data. Based on the 'democratic principle' (Simons, 1984), data is the property of the interviewee and they have the right to negotiate what information is made public. This principle most probably guides the practice of sending interviewees transcripts, and sometimes analysis, to read through and validate. When set within the complex theoretical field of qualitative research we are often left questioning such practices. When sent a transcript, it is perhaps fair to say that participants can edit aspects that with hindsight they may not have wanted to reveal; ethically and morally this does have merit. Often though, participants will edit with a view to removing colloquialisms and poor grammar, which usually the researcher is keen to maintain as they speak to the contextual and cultural grounding of the research. However, it is hard to comprehend how participants might actively determine the validity of research findings as these have often been set within reified, expert understandings which the participant is unlikely to fully appreciate. This is not suggesting that participants should not have access to the findings of research. Rather that the theoretical location and process of analysis are generally reliant upon specific expertise which makes participant validation tricky.

Ownership of the data may also be claimed by the funders of research and there are certainly instances when findings have not been disseminated because the commissioners have withheld permission. It is therefore important to consider the contractual claims that might be placed upon actual raw data and research insights when embarking on funded research projects. Leaving aside the contractual aspects, there may be other challenging moral issues. What if handing over data has implications for interviewees? While for some researchers there may be codes of conduct that bind people not to release information without the permission of interviewees (client), this may be neither robust nor generally applicable. The advice is to be circumspect when first embarking on research, try to think through and negotiate how data will not only be stored and anonymised, but also the potential for coming into conflict over ownership. This way you can take action to secure the appropriate use of interview data.

Physical safety and welfare of the researcher

Having covered moral, epistemological and ethical research practice, the physical safety and welfare of the researcher can easily be overlooked, becoming a seemingly minor issue when planning a research study. This is a potentially dangerous error that should always be addressed. Thankfully, with the introduction of more rigorous ethical processes, such concerns have become more formalised. If we first critically consider the physical safety of the researcher; in our personal lives we are cautious about entrusting our safety to others. For example, we check out the background of those who care for our children, and if someone uses a dating agency, they are advised to ensure that any first meeting is in a public place. Similar levels of care need to be taken when undertaking research. The researcher should first and foremost be encouraged to consider the potential dangers when meeting participants who are often also 'strangers'. Of course, we would not want to overstate the point; qualitative interviewing is primarily a fulfilling and enjoyable method of collecting data. Even so, being safety-conscious from the start can ensure that problems do not arise.

It is the naturalistic nature of qualitative interviewing that presents the most intense concerns around researcher safety. Qualitative interviews can be undertaken in numerous places, with the researcher often able to negotiate the location. If this is possible, then the interviewer can ensure that they control the environment – they can access a telephone, notify another person that they are interviewing and make that person aware of where they are and when they will be finished. On the other hand, sometimes the interviewee may be unable to travel, or it may just be convenient that the interview will take place in people's homes or another place that provides easy access for the interviewee. When making these arrangements the researcher needs to consider if there are safety issues. Merely to arrange an interview without any strategies in place to ensure researcher safety is irresponsible in the extreme. It is essential to have a *safety protocol* (a set of practices) as an effective way of dealing with such issues. Here we offer what we believe to be a useful, but far from exhaustive, safety protocol.

- Always carry a mobile phone. Make sure it is charged and has credit, do not be careless and think it will be OK this time if the battery is running low.
- Always inform someone of the time and place of the interview and let them know that you will call once the interview is complete. The person you inform and call can be your PhD supervisor, the research principal investigator/co-investigator or a friend. The most important point is that they know when to expect your call and are alerted to the need to act should you not call.
- If you inform your contact by e-mail, check that your message has been received and can be acted upon if necessary. Often the person you designate as your contact will be a busy person; if they don't read your message, your safety may be compromised.
- Throughout the interview be aware of safety issues and reflect on whether you feel safe enough to continue. If you feel unsafe, politely suggest rearranging the interview. Once you have terminated the interview, you can consider the next course of action – possibly using a different interviewee or deciding that this interview needs to be abandoned.
- Always call your contact once the interview has been completed. Ingham, Vanwesenbeeck and Kirkland (2000) suggest making a phone call to your contact in the presence of the participant so that they are aware of the precautions being taken. This may indeed be good advice if you have specific reasons to be concerned, for example if interviewing particular target groups with a history of challenging or confrontational behaviour. Whatever the timing of the call, forgetting to ring will, and should, have consequences. Primarily your contact will take action and will be very angry to find that you merely forgot to get

in touch after the interview. A further consequence if again you fail to ring, is that they will be unsure whether this is just another instance of forgetfulness or a potentially dangerous situation. They may delay taking action, thus further compromising safety.

Finally, issues of researcher safety also relate to the potential personal impact of qualitative interviewing on the interviewer. Earlier we referred to debriefing in relation to participants; it can often be the case that researchers themselves need to debrief. By its very nature, qualitative interviewing can place researchers in situations where they hear and learn about experiences and events that are not easily put aside when the day's work has ended. It is important that the researchers themselves are able to discuss and talk through what may have happened in the course of an interview. This should be done in a way that takes on board all we have been discussing in relation to confidentiality and anonymity. Therefore the researcher/interviewer debrief should most probably be an arrangement with co-investigators or research supervisors. While it would be naïve to suggest that the safety of all those involved in qualitative interviewing can be completely and easily assured, the strategies we have suggested can uphold your confidence in having undertaken qualitative interview research that is ethically considered and responsible.

Conclusion

The ethical practice of qualitative interviewing is a wide-ranging and often demanding enterprise. Throughout this chapter it has been our intention to be inclusive, aiming to offer theoretical and conceptual ethical understandings, alongside meeting the more functional demands when undertaking qualitative interviews. Our account, situating ethics in qualitative interviewing within a moral and epistemological frame of reference, does place a great deal of responsibility on the researcher. Still, it is important to recognise that often an all-encompassing solution to some of the ethical dilemmas you will come up against will not be feasible. Ethical codes of practice can be of help, as can the guidance and support of other experienced researchers and wider research governance systems. Be that as it may, it is essential to constantly have a critical stance towards the whole research process, knowing that ultimately it is the researcher who is accountable. When we say this, it is not to instil a level of trepidation, but rather to encourage the thoughtful ethical practice of qualitative interviewing where care and respect are intertwined.

Recommended reading

Economic Social Research Council (2008) *Research Ethics Framework (REF)*. Swindon: ESRC (pdf available at: www.esrc.ac.uk).

The REF provides a comprehensive account of issues that resonate in numerous professional codes of ethics relating to research.

Hollway, W. and Jefferson, T. (2000) *Doing Qualitative Research Differently*. London: Sage.
This book gives a very honest and thought-provoking account of how ethics are conceptualised, developed and applied when engaged in qualitative interviewing. Using very detailed examples, the authors enable readers to access the moral and theoretical reasoning surrounding certain ethical decisions.

Mauthner, M., Birch, M., Jessop, J. and Miller, T. (eds) (2002) *Ethics in Qualitative Research*. London: Sage.
This is an edited collection covering complex epistemological and political issues relating to ethics and research practice.

EIGHT

Reflexivity and Qualitative Interviewing

The emergence of qualitative research in the social sciences has brought about a more questioning approach, not only around topics of investigation, but also around social inquiry more generally. In qualitative research, much of this deliberation is exemplified in what is now referred to as *reflexivity*. The word itself implies reflection and thoughtfulness but this intuitive reading belies the extensive complexity and impact of reflexivity in terms of theoretical understandings and the practicalities of 'doing' qualitative research. Reflexivity in qualitative research specifically invites us to look 'inwards' *and* 'outwards', exploring the intersecting relationships between existing knowledge, our experience, research roles and the world around us. This exploration can be both illuminating and confusing, possibly threatening our certainties around research process and evidence. This 'uncertainty' is, in our view, a good thing, opening up possibilities around additional, and often radically different, ways of seeing and comprehending people's lives and experiences. We concentrate here on how reflexivity formulates, enhances and indeed exemplifies the qualitative interview. However, as with previous chapters, this often necessitates engaging with more generalised debates within qualitative research, and therefore we will take you through:

- discovering reflexivity
- reflexivity and accountability
- reflexivity and co-construction

Discovering reflexivity

We were recently at a well-attended workshop on reflexivity. The number of people there surely echoed the growing interest in qualitative research and more specifically reflexivity, with seasoned researchers and those who were less experienced all seemingly eager to learn more. Interestingly, while we did experience great enthusiasm in the room, there was also considerable variation evident, both in terms of understanding and engagement. Some of those attending were new to the area of qualitative research and were experiencing difficulty with regard not only to the concept, but also to the underlying relevance and justifications for reflexivity in research. This apparent unease perhaps stemmed from the breadth of philosophical grounding among those taking part in the session. Some attendees appeared to hold firm to the scientific model of research, including an ideology of objectivity and researcher detachment, while others suggested variations around critical realism and relativism. This experience prompts us to begin this chapter by exploring the wide-ranging conceptualisations of reflexivity. Rather than aiming to give a categorical definition, we want to enable you to discover the variations and differing manifestations and applications of this somewhat elusive concept.

Reflexivity: a critical approach

There are numerous uses of the term 'reflexivity' in qualitative research. In its broadest sense, reflexivity responds to the realisation that researchers and the methods they use are entangled in the politics and practices of the social world. This realisation brings about the unavoidable acceptance that doing social research is an active and interactive process engaged in by individual subjects, with emotions and theoretical and political commitments. Yet, in the scientific account, the role the researcher plays in shaping the outcomes of research is most often ignored. Gergen and Gergen (1991) explain how in the social sciences, as in the natural sciences, researchers have attempted to safeguard against what is viewed as researcher bias by, for example, deploying field experiments or unobtrusive measures (e.g. observation). The assumption is that with due caution 'scientists can safely avoid disfiguring the picture of nature with their own fingerprints' (Gergen and Gergen, 1991: 76).

As committed qualitative researchers, we have in preceding chapters encouraged a critical stance towards research that takes a detached and overwhelmingly authoritative view based upon 'objectivity'. Qualitative research in general does not claim to be objective; all research is carried out from a particular 'standpoint' (Banister et al., 1994) by researchers who bring their subjective values and meanings to their endeavours. This subjectivity is not treated as a problem to be avoided, but as a resource that can be developed in ways that augment and intensify social research. For most qualitative researchers, reflexivity enables a critical stance to be taken towards the impact of both the researcher and the context in which the research takes place. This can include a wider political context and more subjective, personal perspectives. For example, we both have experience working in partnership with local healthcare providers where, at a political level, there is extensive government policy around inclusivity and community engagement. Perhaps when discussing research with a potential funder, we might become aware that there is an expectation that focus groups will be employed as they appear to be in line with the commissioner's notion of community engagement. On a more subjective level, our thoughts and anxieties around the efficacy of focus groups as an effective model of community engagement may have brought about a certain level of resistance that could have been evident when we were running the focus groups. Both levels of critical reflection have a place in informing and revealing the processes of knowledge production. But this example also aims to demonstrate the way in which complex relationships and power dynamics play a part in how research gets done. The detached, depersonalised and 'uncontaminated' account of research that is often presented is arguably a very powerful and well-rehearsed 'illusion' (Mair, 1989). All research is funded and/or undertaken by (and with) people with motivations, agendas and needs. Leaving these unexamined presents an incomplete picture which arguably misrepresents research and the research process. Different dimensions of reflexivity enable us to engage with these highly influential aspects of research. Using reflexivity, we are able to critically assess and acknowledge the manner in which the research may have been transformed.

Reflexivity and theory

Unsurprisingly, Gough (2003: 25) says that, as a general rule, reflexivity focuses on revealing 'hidden agendas' as these will have a direct impact not only on how the research is undertaken but also on the whole research process from start to finish. He goes on to discuss 'practising reflexivity', explaining how, when doing so, it is useful to articulate a theoretical position. We would take this further, arguing that if we are to understand better why researchers offer particular interpretations of events and people's lives, then there is a necessity to critically appreciate the theoretical lens through which they are being viewed. Payne (2007), when writing about taking a grounded theory approach, argues that reflexivity allows the researcher to acknowledge their role in the creation of the analytical account. She maintains that one's theoretical and disciplinary background should be recognised before undertaking data collection to ensure that the research remains open to new ideas. Indeed, in Chapter 2 we explained how Willig's (2001) *epistemological reflexivity* encourages us to reflect upon assumptions about the world that have been made in the course of the research. So it follows that having a critical appreciation of what drives the research stretches beyond challenging value-free objectivity.

When discussing different theoretical orientations in research, Alvesson and Sköldberg (2000) explain that, given the task of investigating the same non-trivial research question, ten different researchers would come up with ten different results. Taking the time to examine why this might be the case will reveal a variety of ideas about how social reality is constructed and represented. Without doubt, each researcher is interpreting, and investigating, the research question by weaving together quite particular social, political and theoretical ideas. The qualitative interviewer who relies on social constructionism will concentrate on language and discursive practices. Another researcher may be fruitfully mobilising psychoanalytic concepts to shed light on the same topic of investigation. Take, for example, Hollway and Jefferson's (2000: 76) research. They take time to explain how their research is rooted in psychoanalysis, enabling the reader to fully appreciate how the interview techniques used reflect the theoretical foundations of the research:

...both theoretically and methodologically: our subject is one that is not only positioned within the surrounding social discourses, but motivated by unconscious investments and defences against anxiety; our data production is based on the principle of free association; and our data analysis depends on interpretation.

So in this guise reflexivity is a critical approach that both reveals and opens up for scrutiny the underlying beliefs and ideologies that formulate and drive the research. We are required to take account of not only social and political power relations, but also the theoretical orientations that inform our research questions, the methodological approach, the choice of interview technique and the analysis. For these reasons, reflexivity, and the critical approach it engenders, has become a central facet of qualitative interviewing.

Bringing the 'personal' into our research

We have already referred to one of Willig's (2001) two kinds of reflexivity in the previous section – *epistemological reflexivity*. We discussed how theoretical assumptions about the world can impact on the research and how epistemological reflexivity involves revealing and considering the impact of such assumptions. *Personal reflexivity* is Willig's second kind of reflexivity and has possibly become the most familiar manifestation of reflexive practice in social research. As we explained in Chapter 2, personal reflexivity involves giving consideration to the ways in which our beliefs, interests and experiences might have impacted upon the research. In qualitative research there are many instances where the personal has been made explicit, impacting on research questions, data collection, analysis and write-up. Take, for instance, Arthur Frank's (1997) research around the experience of illness. His work is known to be inextricably linked to his own personal experience of serious ill health and his subsequent 'survivorship'. In much of his writing, he makes visible the ways in which his ongoing personal experiences permeate the research:

> My current research on long-term survivorship after illness crystallized after a large public lecture I gave several years ago to a cancer support organisation in Montreal. The first question came from a woman sitting far in the back of steeply banked medical lecture theatre. ... 'Why isn't it enough,' she asked, 'to have cancer and go through treatment. Why do we then have to do more?' In the context of the talk I had just given, 'more' meant finding some meaning in illness and then finding ways for that meaning to change one's life. (Frank, 2003: 217)

Conceivably, many of us have stories of how personal experiences have set in motion our own particular research journeys. These accounts are often revealing and highly informative, providing useful insights into the grounding, direction and motivations pervading the research. The researcher using this form of reflexivity should, however, take care not to allow this to develop into a rather embarrassingly subjective form of self-indulgence, where the researcher takes centre stage. Rather than providing critical and usable information, such forms of reflexivity can at times be used to pre-empt criticism, or serve to reinforce the authority of the researcher. For example, we have read research were the author provides a highly detailed account of their life, laying claim to sharing similar experiences to those of their participants. The author then almost appears to adopt a position of 'knowing' what participants are feeling and experiencing rather than recognising that they can only ever interpret the data from their own very particular perspective. We offer these observations as a gentle note of caution rather than any kind of disapproval. The sharing of personal thoughts and information can be extremely brave, and necessary, adding much to the research and possibly requiring that we transgress our more formalised understandings of research process. Yet if such forms of reflexivity are to be successful, there is a need to resist the worst excesses of personal exposé. The second author once overheard an immensely useful piece of advice regarding speaking out in discussion groups: 'Only contribute if you think what you have to say will *add* to the discussion. If what you have to say is only about your need to hear your voice, then say nothing.' Rather stark but always valuable advice. The message remains the same regarding reflexivity and the sharing of personal information. Consider if such personal revelations add to the process of knowledge production. If they do not, then ask yourself why are they being shared?

Having identified how research more generally is a personal enterprise, we also want to take up the point that qualitative interviewing is itself a highly personal activity that necessitates *critical self-reflection*. When we make the decision to use qualitative interviewing as a method of data collection, we are stepping forward to embrace our personal (often face-to-face) involvement in the activity of research. A crucial aspect of qualitative interviewing is to have the sensitivity and understanding to engage in self-reflection: How might my presence and reactions have influenced the participants? Did I say too much and therefore the responses given were somehow swayed by my involvement? Or perhaps did I say too little, and fail to establish rapport with the interviewee? This level of self-reflection is one of the necessary skills of the qualitative interviewer. Hence, Wilkinson (1988: 493) says that at its simplest reflexivity can be considered to be 'disciplined self-reflection'. Yet, the following quote, reflecting the interviewer's thoughts before an interview, conveys the depth of personal investment and risk that can be required when qualitative interviewing. To fully appreciate the quote, it is important to know that the interviewer and interviewee are women who both experience bulimia and the research is about life and history as a bulimic woman.

> ...although Lisa was a peer and a colleague, we didn't know each other that well. I began thinking about how much of myself I would reveal to her and what parts of my story I would conceal. ... I knew that by revealing I would facilitate a connection between us. I also knew that by concealing certain aspects of my story I could protect myself. (Ellis et al., 1997: 127)

Often in qualitative interviewing we focus on the interviewee, spending considerable time thinking about the potential impact participation in a qualitative interview may have on their life. We rightly agonise over how participation may provoke a level of self-reflection that could be detrimental for interviewees, trying to balance participation with the need to avoid causing harm. The focus on participants can often mean that we overlook how interviews are opportunities for participants *and* researchers to engage in self-reflection. In positivist research, the interests, values and indeed passions of the researcher are apparently laid aside, with research being an essentially procedural and technical activity. In contrast, qualitative research, and more particularly qualitative interviewing, involves entering meaningful relationships with people ('participants', 'respondents'). With this kind of personal activity the researcher is ever present and therefore they will, without doubt, influence how the research develops. In Box 8.1 we present an excerpt from Miller (1998: 62) where she gives a reflexive account of her experiences when engaged in longitudinal research on childbirth. She writes about the interview situation and her relationships with participants, critically reflecting on how her silence around her own birthing experience may have reinforced the 'publicly held silence around pain in childbirth'.

Box 8.1   Entering into relationships with participants

In the excerpt below Tina Miller writes about the interview situation and her relationships with participants, critically reflecting on how her silence around her own birthing experience may have reinforced the publicly held silence around pain in childbirth.

> The relationship between the researcher and participant is also brought into focus in longitudinal research which follows women through a period of transition *already* experienced by the researcher. Whilst I have sought to establish an interview situation in which women can place me, and feel able to voice their experiences without fear of 'judgment' from me, I am also aware that I am already a mother and that what I choose to reveal during the interviews about my own experiences actually reinforces much of the silence which exists around childbearing. So, whilst endorsing notions of reciprocity and equality within interviews, I find that in reality these aims are only sometimes achieved. (Miller, 1998: 71)

So when trying to understand and interpret the experiences of others, the interviewer's self-reflections on how they feel during the interview and how they use their feelings and experiences, can provide insights that add to and enrich the research.

Keeping a research diary

Many qualitative researchers keep a research journal or diary where they record their thoughts and personal experiences. You can record dates and times of meetings, including what was discussed and decided upon. At a later date you may want, or even need, to justify why certain courses of action were taken, a point we take up later in relation to accountability. You can also keep a record of detailed thoughts about process – how the research is unfolding, what is occurring as it happens and, most importantly, why certain courses of action were taken. At a later date such information could prove to be invaluable, providing access to what you thought and felt at the time. All too often time passes and we retrospectively create a shorter, more sanitised version of events, possibly leaving out crucial information that could be pivotal in furthering our appreciation of the topic under investigation. These are not field notes in the strictest sense, whereby you record and reflect on unfolding interactions, thus forming the basis of your research data. Rather, the research diary contains the uninhibited, candid and personal thoughts of researchers as they work on a specific project. Nevertheless, for those of us using qualitative interviewing, some of the thoughts and reflections recorded in our research diary may indeed, at a later date, be used as data that can be analysed in its own right, offer elaborations that enhance our analysis and/or provide methodological insight.

In Box 8.2 some excerpts from the research diary of one of our PhD students are shared to show how such personal reflections develop and progress the research. Kim was then at the beginning of the second year of her three-year PhD research focusing on a new criminal justice intervention targeted at persistent but low-level offenders. She had completed phase one, which involved quantitative data collection. The second phase involved interviews with 'clients'. The interviews aimed to enable an appreciation of participants as situated people, with friends and family, and leading complex and comprehensive lives. Rather than focusing on the offending, participants were invited to set the parameters for the interview. The method of interviewing was reliant upon participants engaging in a specific exercise. Kim had enthusiastically piloted the technique and on previous occasions, as one part of the interview, she had successfully invited interviewees to construct a time line (thus the Blue Peter exercise and the request to write down age 25, referred to in Box 8.2). Using the time line, participants could reflect on aspects of their offending behaviour at certain times of their lives but they could choose where to start – wherever they thought appropriate. The account in her research diary tells of a very difficult and tense interview, in which Kim felt disappointed and frustrated. The participant clearly felt uncomfortable and compromised by Kim's chosen interview method. Although Kim did provide a participant information sheet prior to the interview, she obviously had not been explicit enough regarding the exercise. If she had been more explicit, perhaps the participant would have made the decision not to take part in the interview. This perhaps prompts questions for Kim around sampling. Of greater interest to us when reading the excerpts was Kim's revelation that she believed that she had been disrespectful, in that she had tried to 'push' creativity on to other people. Of course the discomfort of the interviewee is paramount, but Kim's recognition in her research diary that not all people will respond to such a task in the way she might is a valuable piece of critical self-reflection that can be taken forward. Here, personal reflexivity is being used to reflect on the research process, but also evident is a revision of the underlying expectations we might have with regard to how other people experience, understand and operate in the world.

Box 8.2   Excerpts from Kim's research diary

I've found this interview very difficult today. She was very reserved in her responses and didn't want to do the 'Blue Peter' (my name for the activity incorporated into the interview) exercise AT ALL. She didn't protest verbally, she was quite the opposite and just kind of froze when I began to lay all the stuff out on the table. I think I made her quite nervous and uncomfortable at first, but as soon as I disregarded the exercise she seemed to be more at ease. I'm feeling very disappointed with myself. But I need to move on. I think my initial thoughts about interviewing women have been thwarted as, clearly, not all woman want to talk about themselves all the time!

Later reflection (same day)

Today was a difficult day for me. I have plenty of experience around interviewing (mainly women). This shouldn't have been a problem for me and my thoughts before the interview were that I would be in my 'comfort zone' interviewing women who, in my mind, (up until this interview) were much easier to interview (compared to men).

I still remember the sheer panic on her face when I emptied my bag of felt tip pens and rolls of paper onto the desk – happily setting my stuff out! She looked terrified. I continued, immediately noting her reaction and I began to compute this in my mind realising that this was probably a huge mistake. I began my preamble about the interview, and still received no positive reaction. I asked her to think of an age at where she would like to begin her interview, to which she replied, 'I don't want to talk about early stuff, I had a happy childhood'. 'OK' I said. At this point I was trying to reassure her that we could talk about whatever she felt comfortable with. We agreed that she would begin at age 25 where, for her, she felt things began to go wrong in her life. I then asked her to write down '25' so we could develop a time line. The scared look came back. She was really not comfortable with this. She held the pen in a child-like way and shakily wrote the number 2 then the number 5 while I looked on in horror of what I had asked her to do (the assessment showed that she was literate?). I immediately moved the attention away from the pen and paper and began to ask her about the treatment programme. The interview immediately became a little more relaxed and we never referred to the paper again.

Today I learned a huge lesson. I am glad that instinctively I could see that the client was uncomfortable and had the flexibility to be able to respond to that. I now accept that trying to 'push' creativity onto other people cannot work. Participants are people and not children, they will have a pre-conceived idea of what an interview will be like and therefore may not always respond well to different techniques, especially as I am a stranger to them.

Reflexivity and accountability

In previous chapters we have discussed how different stages of the research process are reliant upon the decisions we make. As researchers, we are therefore accountable for the work that we do. Reflexivity can be used in ways that formalise this accountability. Finlay (2002: 210) uses the following comments from Coffey and Atkinson (1996: 191) to show how reflexivity can be used to monitor and audit the research process:

> Transactions and ideas that emerge from [the research process] ... should be documented. The construction of analytic or methodological memoranda and working papers, and the consequent explication of working hypotheses, are of vital importance. It is important that the processes of exploration ... be documented and retrievable.

In using this example, Finlay is alerting us to the ways in which forms of reflexivity (keeping a research diary, documenting process) can be used to support validity claims. Validity is generally understood to be a positivist criterion, used for assessing the extent to which our research describes and measures what it claims. Such categorical and precise claims pose a challenge for qualitative researchers who often operate with data and theory that are more fluid and shifting. As such, validity is a highly debated topic for qualitative researchers. In Chapter 9 we will explore three broad positions with regard to quality criteria, ranging from using the same criteria as quantitative research (e.g. validity and reliability), the development of separate criteria for qualitative research (e.g. credibility, transferability, trackable variance and confirmabilty) and a final position that resists any suggestion that such criteria are applicable for qualitative research. These three positions are founded upon differing philosophical and methodological positions. We accept Seale's (1999) point that we should resist research being overburdened with fulfilling philosophical and methodological prespecified rules. Nevertheless it is useful to consider these rules if we are using reflexivity as some form of quality technique that conforms, or indeed is in conflict with, our particular research approach (e.g. realism). If we subscribe to a realist position, possibly we can adopt a form of reflexivity that seeks to document and audit with a view to promoting reliability and validity. We say this somewhat unenthusiastically as we firmly believe that the researcher's subjectivity will always shape and transform the research process. Seeking to replicate even with detailed, meticulous information would seem to us to be destined to fail. Indeed, unlike those working within the positivist domain of science, many qualitative researchers assume multiple, contextually located, socially constructed realities and therefore using reflexivity to make positivistic validity claims would be incongruent. Having an eye to such tensions will help you to maintain the overall integrity of your research.

Steier (1991) maintains that reflexivity is about *you* taking *responsibility*. We take this to infer that the researcher makes visible their part in the production of knowledge – thus, as a researcher, you are accountable. There appears to be a distinction between making validity claims and showing the quality and worth of the research. While more traditional approaches to research foster a somewhat abstract, formalised and value-free objectivity, within the qualitative paradigm it is good research practice to consider and describe the differing facets of researcher involvement and influence, using these to inform and enhance understandings. Indeed, rather than resisting notions of accountability, Gill (1995) uses the term 'accountable reflexivity' whereby, having accepted that research cannot be value-free, we should actually be explicit about particular agendas. Here Gill is referring in particular to the political agenda(s) of feminist research where there is a concern with gendered inequality, power, resistance and emancipation.

By engaging in the reflexive practice of research, the author (researcher) and the reader become more closely connected to the research and its undertaking. Reflexivity in its differing forms can be presented as a process of validity checking or as an alternative to the more problematised positivist criteria. Without doubt, taking the time to reflect upon, record, review and incorporate information relating to the role of the researcher are practices that are seen to be enriching in qualitative interviewing. Reflexivity invites people in, opening up the research process for examination and enabling others to scrutinise and judge the quality of the work.

Reflexivity and co-construction

Earlier we discussed the 'personal', taking what might be called an 'inward' approach to reflexivity. Social constructionists, and other researchers with a theoretical grounding in interaction and relational dynamics (e.g. those using narrative interviewing, Interpretative Phenomenological Analysis (IPA) etc.), would argue against only taking an inward approach. Instead, they invite us also to look 'outwards' at interaction, discourse and shared meanings. Hence, the interview is a site where people socially interact. Using language, they have the chance to author their experiences into particular versions of events. Yet these versions of events do not pre-exist the interview. Rather, through shared meanings they are co-constructed within the interview situation. For these reasons it is necessary to explore the researcher–researched relationship, examining the intertwined and shaping features of qualitative interview encounters.

Multiple 'selves'

From the moment of conceiving the research through to completing the interviews, analysis and write up, interviewing is an 'interactional project' (Gubruim and Holstein, 2003a). As qualitative interviewers, we are actively shaping and managing how the interaction will unfold. Therefore, we unavoidably co-create or *co-construct* the events that take place. Finlay and Gough (2003: ix) explain the co-constructed nature of research by showing how reflexivity locates researchers as involved and implicated in the entire process of knowledge production:

> Reflexivity requires critical self-reflection of the ways in which researchers' social background, assumptions, positioning and behaviour impact on the research process. It demands acknowledgement of how researchers (co-)construct their research findings. Reflexivity both challenges treasured research traditions and is challenging to apply in practice.

This quote moves us beyond a reporting of personal thoughts and experiences in a way that has been conceptualised as 'confessional'. The inference Finlay and Gough make is that we are all 'situated actors' and as such we bring to each interview our own histories, political affiliations and a myriad of other aspects that constitute who we are. As Guba and Lincoln (2005: 210) say, 'reflexivity is the process of reflecting critically on the self as researcher'. Here they refer to the *multiple selves* we bring to our research. Each of these selves has the potential to be present in the research, having a part to play in the production of knowledge. Therefore, a central facet of reflexivity is to consider how we might account for these different selves and the part they play in co-constructing the qualitative interview and our research more generally.

One of the ways in which we can begin to unravel what we bring to the process of knowledge production is to follow the lead of Shulamit Reinharz (1997), who provides a framework for exploring the different 'selves' we bring to the field of research. When Reinharz analysed the field notes from her study of an Israeli kibbutz, she identified approximately 20 different selves that she categorised into three major groups: *researcher-based selves*, *brought selves* (the selves that socially, historically and personally create our standpoint), and *situationally-created selves*. Thus Reinharz argues that being a researcher is only one aspect of the researcher's self in the field, and although one may consider being a researcher one's most salient self, there are other selves to take into account. For example, when we interview we bring our understandings of how people exist in the world (social constructionist, critical realist selves), we bring our political agendas (feminist, ecologist, socialist selves), our caring roles (father, daughter selves), our professional selves (nurse, academic, social worker, teacher selves). We also situationally *create* different selves in the field – being a member of a group, being a friend, being sympathetic.

Often there is a sense of unease around created selves; producing such selves can challenge and test our existing standpoints or *brought selves*. The second author, when involved in research with former mining communities, needed to negotiate and challenge aspects of her brought selves. In this particular research there was a call for both appreciating and understanding how the loss of the mining industry had in many ways taken away historically entrenched gender roles. Many of these gendered practices were viewed by the second author as oppressive of women, both at a structural and more relational level. Yet, the self created in the field at this time acknowledged a very specific set of cultural practices and social norms: man as breadwinner, protector and brave – many of these men had spent their whole lives underground working for their families. This growing understanding of specific social norms brought about a thoughtful respect and at times 'silencing' with regard to voicing aspects of the brought self (feminist ideals). Reflecting on how her brought self interacted with sexist jokes and overtly oppressive gendered assumptions, the second author felt a sense of disquiet and personal unease, resulting in a questioning of what this clash of ideologies might mean for the actual research. What would feminist ideals have brought to the field research if made explicit? How might this aspect of the brought self influence the analysis? Was the behaviour exhibited by the researcher in the field disingenuous or even hypocritical? Possibly, at a political level, the behaviour was both of these things. But in terms of ethical research that involves respect for persons, we would argue that selves created in the field are necessarily mutable, often inconsistent and relative to the circumstances. Taking time to reflect on the co-construction and interaction of these different selves can be illuminating, enabling us to see not only who we are but also who we *become*. Research as a process of discovery has many facets and the different selves we co-construct will each have something to add if we actually take the time to critically self-reflect.

Participatory and democratic collaboration

There is a range of methodologies that embrace research as a co-construction, for example, cooperative inquiry research (Heron and Reason, 2001; Reason, 2003), feminist approaches (Ramazanoğlu and Holland, 2002) and narrative inquiry (Mishler, 1986). These methodologies share a broadly 'participatory' approach whereby the tradition of separating the researcher from the researched is replaced with an emphasis on *collaboration*. We might argue that qualitative research in general breaks down the distinction between the researcher, who does the thinking, and the researched, regarded as the 'object' of study. However, for many qualitative researchers there is still a distinct differentiation whereby the parameters of the study, the how of data collection, analysis and dissemination, remain under the absolute control of the researcher. Questions around the nature of power – who has power and who does not – are critical, and have political and ethical implications for the way knowledge is produced. Participative forms of inquiry aim to confront the ways in which power is distributed not only in research but also in society more generally. Research participants are not 'subjected to' the decisions made by the researcher, but rather participate in and contribute to the process as 'co-researcher'. Hence all co-researchers (including the more traditional roles of researcher and researched) are acknowledged as knowing subjects who bring with them their motivations and intentions and their ability to both reflect on experience and collude, rationalise and even self-deceive (Reason, 2003). In qualitative interviewing such participative collaboration changes the power relationship between interviewer and interviewee to one that is far more relational, breaking down familiar power differentials.

Further, the participatory perspective asks us to 'see inquiry as a process of coming to know, serving the democratic practical ethos of action research' (Reason and Bradbury, 2001: 7). Here the political dimension of participation is highlighted, aiming to educate and develop people's capacity for reflection and taking action in their lives. Reason and Bradbury explain that participation affirms people's right and ability to have their voices heard in relation to decisions that impact upon them. The concept of *voice* can be used to introduce an awareness of how influence is exerted, not only with regard to research practice but in society more generally. For us here, it is important to recognise that some people, and groups, have their voices heard while others do not. It is therefore important to acknowledge both the potentially oppressive and emancipatory aspects of research. This relates not only to the actual impact of any subsequent knowledge produced, but also to the act of participation. Research undertaken in collaboration with others requires a more equal relationship. Indeed, a primary aim for participatory research is to empower people, and while this is a multifaceted ideal, the sentiment has philosophical and practical significance.

In a very tangible way, the research will produce knowledge that relates to participants/co-researchers, so they should have an authoritative part to play in how the research is conceived and undertaken. In qualitative interviewing this will mean a collaborative approach to sampling – negotiating who will be interviewed rather than the more traditional process of the researcher purposively identifying who will be interviewed. You will need to develop together the form of interview encounter that takes place, if indeed interviews are agreed upon as a method of data collection. Within the interview there is active avoidance of 'interviewer dominance', striving to actively empower those who take part (Mishler, 1986). With regard to reflexivity, this requires careful, collaborative reflection aiming to recognise thoroughly the creative co-constructed nature of the research. Still, Birch and Miller (2002: 92), when reflecting on participation, talk of wanting to have 'honest and reciprocal relationships', going on to describe how this ideal was difficult to achieve:

> We found that the research ideals of participation that we embraced at the outset eventually came into conflict with our personal goals of completing our projects and fitting into the requirements of the academic world. This conflict led us to desert the 'moral high ground' and re-interpret our earlier understandings of what participation should involve.

In this reflexive account we are able to see how critical self-reflection involves exploring the competing demands of ideology and our ever-present, more material concerns. We make no judgement on the decision Birch and Miller refer to, whereby they changed the formulation of participation in their research. Rather, we want to highlight the challenges that participatory approaches present and the importance of reflecting on the nature of participation. We are thus able to see the ways in which collaboration in its many forms brings about differing ways in which the co-construction of knowledge can operate and be incorporated into research process.

Writing and representation

Although our focus is qualitative interviewing, we felt that having outlined and explained reflexivity we should include a final section that briefly discusses reflexivity in relation to writing about your research. For the qualitative researcher, writing about research involves far more than simply outlining methods and reporting findings. At the more reflective level there is the constructing influence of language, and indeed the limitations of language, to consider, alongside interpretation and representation. When we write about our research we are inevitably offering an interpretation and therefore our style of writing and how we describe and depict people, events, literature and theory all impact on what we produce.

Writing up and presenting our work can be daunting for several reasons. Josselson (1996: 70) shares reflections that suggest ethical conflict when writing about people who have taken part in qualitative interviews:

> My guilt, I think, comes from my knowing that I have taken myself out of relationship with my participants (with whom, during the interview, I was in intimate relationship) to be in a relationship with my readers. I have, in a sense, been talking about them behind their backs and doing so publicly. Where in the interview I had been responsive to them, now I am using their lives in service of something else, for my own purposes, to show something to others.

Certainly, when writing up the analysis of qualitative interview research the act of *representing* people is a very personal and moral activity. Josselson's critical self-reflection regarding the guilt that he experienced when writing about other people's lives is a form of personal reflexivity that shares the moral dilemmas of the research with those reading, utilising and evaluating the work. Using different forms of reflexivity, we can take this personal reflection further, again encompassing a concern with 'voice' focusing on the process of representation and writing. The voice of the participant is almost always filtered through the account of the researcher who authors the write-up. As you sift and organise material, working from literature search, through data collection and analysis, you will inevitably create a 'representation' that is directed at a particular audience. As part of our reflexive practice we should consider what impact this audience has on the representations we intentionally produce. Have we emphasised certain areas at the expense of others? If so, was there a rationale for this and how might other relevant findings be included? Also, how do those who receive our findings (organisations, supervisors, participants and other stakeholders) make sense of what we give them? What perspectives do they bring when reading the research write-up and how might this affect what we have reported? Of course, as a researcher it would be impossible to have perfect knowledge of all these positions, but being self-aware and conscious of what messages are represented in our work is broadly achievable. While some researchers resist such expectations, we would argue that researchers have a wider social responsibility, particularly in relation to applied research and evaluation, to present their work in ways that are understandable, useful and accountable. Practising reflexivity can be a means of achieving these ethical objectives.

Continuing with notions of responsibility, the turn to language and the embracing of multiple realities bring about a concern that research can often provide a 'totalising' description of a certain reality. By this we mean that when writing, the researcher speaks with such authority that they appear to be claiming to speak for the 'Other' – to be speaking on behalf of those who participated in the research (we mentioned this briefly earlier in relation to personal reflexivity). This is a perilous way to proceed, having the potential not only to misrepresent but also block alternative voices, with the subjectivity of the researcher taking the prominent position in the research. We have to take authorship very seriously, questioning the way we present our work and the representations of other people's lives that we ultimately convey. It is so disappointing to read qualitative research where there are only glimpses of the participants' voices. Of course there will be quotes, but the rhetoric, focus and perspective of the writing are predominantly overlaid with the authoritative voice of the researcher. While this is in many ways inescapable, having an eye to what is selected or not selected for analysis, the values and interests that are expressed, keeps us focused on the co-constructed nature of knowledge.

Providing 'pen portraits', which give biographical information about participants, can make them more alive and present in your write-up. In Box 8.3 we offer two different approaches to introducing participants – one is the more familiar pen portrait of Rucksana, a woman who took part in a project examining Asian women's access to primary healthcare. The second portrait is a reflexive account of the first encounter with Beth, a young woman who had recently left local authority care who participated in a longitudinal research project for young people. The research involved taking part in a 'leaving care' interview (exit interview) and life story interviewing. Both 'portraits' effectively bring the participants into the research, aiming to both inform and personalise the write-up.

However, such strategies should always be mindful of the potential conflicts, discussed earlier in Chapter 7, with regard to maintaining the anonymity of the participant. Indeed, it is worthwhile taking time to appreciate that for those of us who resist the objective, scientific paradigm, research constructs rather than depicts what we are researching. Therefore the ways in which we 're-present' versions of reality (people's lives) are crucially important and we should think carefully and creatively about how, and in what way, our research brings people's lives to a wider audience.

Box 8.3   Bringing participants into the research

Rucksana

Rucksana is a 23-year-old British-born Pakistani woman. She has three very young children who are all below school age. Rucksana is a full-time mother and her husband works full-time in clothing manufacturing. Her husband also attends college on an evening so Rucksana is at home with the children on her own most of the time.

Beth

When I first met Beth she was 17 years old and unemployed, having recently moved back into her family home. The social worker, with my assistance, explained the *exit interview* initiative. Beth's reaction unnerved me at the time:

> 'What a waste of time. They don't want to know what kids in care think. They all say they're listenin but are they fuck – they just do what they like. Social Services don't care what kids in care think.' (taken from field notes)

The worker who was 'on duty' asked Beth to *'watch her language'*. Beth then flounced out of the Scheme followed by her friend. Neither the worker nor Hannah (Beth's friend) seemed surprised or bothered by this outburst. I for my part felt exceedingly guilty and somewhat embarrassed; guilty that I had invaded Beth's space with the end result being her leaving, and embarrassed at the vilification the *exit interview* initiative had received.

Nevertheless, Beth did rather surprisingly give an *exit interview*. The following 'care' history information was, as with other young people, primarily taken from information given at that time. Beth's first local authority placement was: with foster parents when she was 13. During the one-year period that followed Beth moved three times; two were foster placements, the other a period at the Assessment Centre. Her response when asked why she moved was: *'I haven' got a clue.'* Beth had two more placements. One at a local authority residential unit with education where she stayed for six months. Her final move was on the same site as the Assessment Centre but in a residential unit where many of the young people placed there were among those who were difficult to place. Beth remained there for almost three years leaving because, in Beth's words, she, *'got kicked out'*.

Conclusion

Reflexivity is an ever-evolving concept in qualitative research and we have, in many respects, been selective in this chapter, aiming to provide a sound, but by no means comprehensive, review. The most enduring feature is surely the critical stance taken in relation to knowledge production. The distant and objective researcher is replaced with a more thoughtful and ever-present subject who throughout has an impact on the what, why and how of the research. What are we interested in researching? Why are we doing the research this way? How will we proceed? Critical self-reflection in the form of *personal reflexivity* is evident but so too is *epistemological reflexivity*, whereby we begin to engage with the complex process of co-construction. Reflexivity is one of the most challenging facets of qualitative research and qualitative interviewing; it is also a far-reaching means of extending our understanding and insight.

Recommended reading

Gough, B. (2003) Deconstructing reflexivity, in L. Finlay and B. Gough (eds), *Reflexivity: A Practical Guide for Researchers in Health and Social Sciences.* Oxford: Blackwell Publishing.

Gough provides an accessible account of different forms of reflexivity, making explicit the links between 'reflexivities' and different philosophical positions.

Lyons, E. and Coyle, A. (2007) Appendix 2: Reporting qualitative research, in E. Lyons and A. Coyle, *Analysing Qualitative Data in Psychology.* London: Sage.

This appendix consists of four different research reports where there are good examples of 'practising reflexivity'. Researchers provide personal, theoretical and practical insights into the process of knowledge production.

Nicolson, P. (2003) Reflexivity, 'bias' and the in-depth interview: developing shared meanings, in L. Finlay and B. Gough (eds), *Reflexivity: A Practical Guide for Researchers in Health and Social Sciences.* Oxford: Blackwell Publishing.

In this chapter Nicolson sensitively considers the dynamic nature of the qualitative in-depth interview and the relationship between interviewer and participant. The subjective emotionality of interview encounters is explored, coming to the fore as a central facet of the research process, but also as promoting personal change for researchers and participants.

NINE

An Introduction to Interview Data Analysis

In this chapter we will introduce you to some of the basic principles of the analysis of qualitative interview data, and provide you with practical guidance on their use. As we noted in Chapter 2, interviews are used within a wide range of methodological traditions in qualitative research. Naturally, this leads to some very different approaches to the analysis of interview data. Since this is not a specialist text on data analysis, we have had to be selective in what we have chosen to cover here. We have been guided by the techniques you are most likely to come across in research literature based on qualitative interviewing, and that you are likely to find helpful for your own research.

When considering the many different forms of analysis available, one distinction that is often made is between approaches that are strongly focused on language and those that are more concerned with the content of what participants have to say. The former are generally located within the social constructionist tradition (Burr, 2003) and include varieties of discourse and narrative analysis. They seek to examine how language is used to achieve certain ends in social interaction, or to create a story that makes sense of aspects of the teller's life for a particular audience. The latter usually come from either contextualist or realist philosophical positions, and include phenomenological approaches (Langdridge, 2007), grounded theory and most qualitative or mixed-method case studies (Hartley, 2004). They are principally concerned with understanding their participants' lived experience from their own position – to step inside their shoes, as it were. In this chapter we will focus on thematic approaches to analysis, which are normally associated with experience-focused methodologies. In doing so, we will cover the following topics:

- transcription
- principles of thematic analysis
- thematic analysis: a basic system
- assessing the quality of qualitative analysis
- writing up a thematic analysis
- alternative styles of thematic analysis

Transcription

Transcription is the process of converting recorded material into text and, as such, is usually a necessary precursor to commencing the analysis of your interview data. Indeed, if you are doing your own transcribing, it can be seen as the first step in the analysis itself, as it inevitably helps you to become closely familiar with your data (Langdridge, 2004). Before you begin transcribing there are key decisions you have to make that will have a major impact on what you produce from your analysis. Will you transcribe all your tapes in full? What system of transcription will you use? If you employ someone else to carry out transcription, what guidance or training do they need? In answering these questions you need to bear in mind the methodological position of your study, the resources you have available for the task, and the main potential threats to the quality of transcripts that you need to guard against.

Full or partial transcription?

There are really two issues at stake here: whether you transcribe every second of every interview word for word (verbatim), and to what level of detail you need to transcribe. While it might seem self-evident that verbatim transcripts are the preferred option, you must consider how very time-consuming transcription is. Even at the simplest level – where only the actual words spoken are recorded – you can expect the transcription of an hour's interview to take between four and eight hours, depending on the quality of the recording and your typing skills. For studies involving a relatively large number of interviews – say, 20 or more – full verbatim transcription is thus a huge investment of time and effort (and if you are paying someone else to do it, money). Those methodologies that are focused strongly on how language is used generally require a much more detailed level of transcription than the basic kind, with notation used to indicate length of pauses, overlapping speakers, voice intonation, and so on. In approaches such as discourse analysis and conversation analysis, transcribing one minute of interaction can take many hours. While these approaches generally prefer to work with natural conversation rather than interview data (see Chapter 11), narrative techniques – which commonly *do* use interviews – may well need to include at least some of the more detailed information that helps to convey meaning in the spoken word.

The golden rule to avoid becoming swamped by the transcription process is to think carefully about what needs to be transcribed, and at what level of detail, from the very start of planning your research project. For some methodologies, you may be concerned to identify broad patterns of common themes across quite a large number of participants – for example, in an organisational case study or in an evaluation study. In these kinds of instances, recording everything verbatim may not be necessary. You might decide to listen through the tapes to identify main areas of interest and then only transcribe those sections in full, summarising the rest. Alternatively, you may, on some meaningful grounds, identify certain respondents as key informants for your study and just transcribe their interviews in full, summarising the rest. In contrast, approaches that seek to examine personal experience in depth (e.g. narrative and phenomenological approaches) will require full verbatim transcription, probably involving a level of detail beyond the basic. Economising on resources by summarising or transcribing more superficially is not a sensible option here. Instead, you need to factor in a substantial amount of time for transcription when deciding how many interviews to carry out.

Systems of transcription

It is crucial that you adopt a consistent style for your transcription, so that it is clear to you and to anyone else reading your material what features of speech your notations indicate. Numerous authors have offered transcription systems, especially for discourse analysis and conversation analysis. The best known of these is Jefferson's (1984) highly complex system, although Silverman's (1993) more concise version of it is also widely cited. Such systems seek to capture every aspect of speech that might indicate something about the way verbal interaction operates and what it achieves. Pauses are timed to the tenth of a second, changing intonations within individual words are recorded, and so on. There is less standardisation among the simpler forms of transcription, although certain conventions are commonly seen, such as the use of capitals to indicate emphasis. Poland (2002) provides some useful suggestions for transcription notation, and we present a relatively simple system based on this and other sources in Table 9.1.

Threats to the quality of transcription

Over the last five to ten years, the discussion of quality issues in qualitative research has become prominent in the literature (e.g. Seale, 1999; Golafshani, 2003; Lincoln, 2004; Johnson et al., 2006). However, relatively little attention has been paid to transcription quality, despite the fact that inaccurate transcripts will inevitably have a deleterious impact on the process of data analysis. Poland's (2002) careful consideration of this topic remains a notable exception to the rule. Although not an exhaustive list, we would suggest three main threats to the quality of transcription that you need to take steps to minimise: recording quality, missing context, and 'tidying up' transcribed talk.

Recording quality

Good transcripts depend on good quality recording equipment and its effective use, issues we have already discussed in some detail in Chapter 4. In addition to these points, there are things you can do during the interview and afterwards to aid transcription. Ask your questions in a clear voice and at a measured pace – it is very easy to find yourself talking too fast if you are feeling at all nervous. While we would caution against drawing too much attention to the recording device, if your participant is particularly unclear and/or rushed, it would be advisable to ask them to speak a little slower and more clearly. Similarly, if they say something that strikes you as particularly important but in a way that is garbled or confused, you can ask them to repeat themselves just to make sure you have understood their point. It is a good idea to record an identifying statement at the start of the tape – giving the date and time of the interview, who the participant is and (if more than one is involved

Table 9.1   A basic transcription system

Interview feature	Representation	Notes
Emphasis	Capital letters	
	Ptp: I NEVER thought that!	
Pauses	Very short pauses, use: (p) Longer pauses,use: (pause)	We would suggest under half a second is a 'very short' pause. You might want to note particularly long pauses – perhaps those over two seconds – either wth the notation:
	Ptp: I (p) I had been there a few times, but (pause) had never had that (p) kind of problem before.	
		(long pause)
		or by actually timing the pause:
		(three sec pause)
Interruptions	Place a hyphen at the point of interruption.	
	Ptp: She said she'd meet me – Int: Sorry, who said that?	
Overlapping speech	Use a hyphen as for interruption, but precede the overlapping comment(s) with: (overlap). Where the overlapping section ends, note with: (end overlap).	You may sometimes be unsure whether to count an exchange as an interruption or an overlap. We would suggest you only use the latter where there are more than a few syllables of simultaneous speech by both parties.
	Ptp: The dog wouldn't stop bark – Int: (overlap) Was the dog in the room with you then? Ptp: (overlap) –ing, yes, she was. Yes. (end of overlap) I did feel safer with her there, even though she wouldn't hurt a fly.	
Audibility problems	If a word or phrase is completely inaudible, use square brackets to indicate this:	
	Ptp: I examined his [inaudible] but it seemed quite normal	
	If the word or phrase is unclear but you have some idea what may have been said, put the speculative transcription in square brackets, followed by a question mark.	
	Ptp: I examined his [ankle movement?] but it seemed quite normal	
Laughing, coughing and similar features	Note the feature in round brackets. If both parties are (for instance) laughing at the same time, make this clear.	
	Ptp: I couldn't believe what I was seeing! (both laugh)	

(Continued)

Table 9.1   (Continued)

Interview feature	Representation	Notes
Tone of voice	Where the participant's (or indeed interviewer's) tone of voice clearly indicates how a section of speech is intended to be understood, mark this in brackets Ptp: I mean (ironic tone) we REALLY need bright sparks like that in this company! Ptp: After that (frustrated/angry tone) I was a bit narked with her, I have to say.	It is particularly important to note tone of voice where without doing so the meaning would be very likely to be misinterpreted. Thus in the examples to the left, you could get away without noting the tone in the second case, as the feeling of frustration is evident in the words spoken. However, in the first case, without the annotation there is a danger that the comment could be read as praise rather than the opposite.
Direct speech	If the participant is directly quoting another person or themselves, put this section in speech marks. Note in brackets if this is accompanied by a clear mimicking of another's voice, or a distinctive change in tone to their own voice. Ptp: I said (angry tone) 'where are you going with that?', and he just sort of stammered and said (mimics) 'er, I just needed to, er, check it out'.	
Non-verbal communication	Where you have recorded distinctive NVC that strongly reinforces meaning, this can be noted in brackets. Ptp: It was a HUGE cock-up, just huge (stretches arms wide to indicate size)	

Based in part on Poland (2002)

in the study) who the interviewer is. Make sure you label tapes or name mp3 files straight after the interview in a way that makes them easily identifiable. (See Patton, 1990, for more discussion of these issues.)

Missing context

It is often essential to be aware of contextual features beyond the immediate words spoken to accurately prepare a transcript for analysis. This includes both the immediate context of what is being said – non-verbal communication and paralinguistic aspects (voice intonation, volume, pitch and the use non-linguistic utterances such as laughter, sighs and pauses) – and the wider context of the interview itself. For example, consider the following exchange:

Interviewer: So how did you like the new job?
Participant: Oh it was great, just great.
Interviewer: Did anything in particular make you feel like that?
Participant: Everything!

Read as a simple verbatim transcript, this would reasonably be seen as indicating her very positive feelings about 'the new job'. However, if you knew that the participant's first comment was made with a falling intonation and emphasis on the two 'greats', accompanied by a facial grimace, while her second utterance was preceded by a bitter-sounding laugh, you would almost certainly come to the exact opposite conclusion regarding her feelings. This shows that even where basic verbatim transcription may seem sufficient in the light of a study's aims and methodology, there are always likely to be occasions where a failure to record immediate contextual factors will seriously undermine transcript quality. The extract above, with some fairly simple additional notation, would be much more helpful to the analyst:

Interviewer: So how did you like the new job?
Participant: Oh it was GREAT, just GREAT (ironic tone on 'great', facial grimace).
Interviewer: Did anything in particular make you feel like that?
Participant: (bitter laugh) Everything!

Paralinguistic features will naturally be present on the recording and incorporating them is just a matter of being clear about when and how they should be included in the transcript. For many studies, it will be sufficient only to note them when they clearly impact on the meaning of what has been said. In contrast, non-verbal communication will not be recorded (except in the rare event of the use of video). The only way to enable them to be incorporated is to take handwritten notes of any particularly expressive examples. This is one reason for trying to get transcripts prepared as soon as possible after the interview, as it makes it easier to match any such observations to the correct point in the interaction.

The wider context of the interview includes such things as the level of formality, the setting, and the social dynamics of the participants' lives, where these relate to the topic of the interview. For example, if you were interviewing adolescents about their sexuality, knowing that a parent was present might be pertinent to the sense you make of what they say. Similarly, your knowledge of aspects of an organisation's history might alert you to meanings in the talk that would not be apparent to a researcher unfamiliar with the background. The first author and colleagues (King, Melvin and Ashby, 2008) came across a good example of this in a recent project looking at community nursing roles in palliative care (the care of terminally ill people). One group of nurses we interviewed were members of district nursing teams. We found that when we asked them about the role of a new kind of nurse – the community matron – many of them briefly laughed before speaking. To someone unfamiliar with the setting this might have just been overlooked. Because we had a good knowledge of the history and politics behind these professional roles and relationships (both locally and nationally) we felt confident that this repeated reaction was indicative of some degree of difficulty in relationships between the two groups of nurses. We therefore made sure these laughs were noted in transcripts.

This example illustrates the challenges posed by the wider context of interviews. There is undoubtedly a danger that the kind of prior knowledge we had as researchers could blinker our interpretation – we might make too much of contextual features noted in the transcript because of our expectations. However, if we ignored this knowledge, we might at best produce a shallower understanding than we could have, and at worst have missed important aspects of participants' experiences. There is no simple and universal solution to this dilemma. However, it can be useful to include comments on contextual features in a speculative manner, as shown below:

> *Interviewer:*   So what role have the community matrons been playing with these patients?
>
> *District nurse:*   Hmm, well (laughs lightly) I'm not sure if I'm in the best position to comment on that. (n.b. tone perhaps defensive?).

This should alert you in your analysis to be cautious about your interpretation, and to seek other evidence to strengthen or reject it elsewhere in the transcript.

'Tidying up' transcribed talk

Language in spoken form is almost always messier than it is in writing. It can be tempting when transcribing to 'tidy up' mispronunciations, mangled grammar, and so on, especially if the transcriber is used to working in a secretarial role where it might be expected that they should correct 'errors' of this kind. Researchers themselves may be tempted to do the same because they are concerned not to make the participant (or themselves!) appear inarticulate (Poland, 2002). However, it is not the purpose of transcription to produce a corrected version of what people have said, but rather an accurate one. Employed transcribers should be given clear instructions to record what they hear and not to change even obvious 'errors' in talk. In particular, where they cannot work out what has been said, it is important that they do not simply insert a best guess. Rather, they should mark the word or phrase as *inaudible* or *unclear*, in the latter cases perhaps including some comment in parentheses, as in the example below.

> *Interviewer:*   What are your relations like with the doctors in that practice?
>
> *Nurse participant:* Well, it depends err depends on who you mean and err (laughs) you'd have to say (unclear – perhaps 'time of day?'). Doctor (name inaudible) is a real sweetie though!

Technical terms and jargon can create a particular problem for transcribers. In an interview with a family doctor carried out by the first author, the participant said of a patient that 'her ESR was within normal limits'. The ESR (Erythrocyte sedimentation rate) is a test used to help diagnose certain inflammatory diseases. The transcriber, evidently unfamiliar with this terminology, recorded the doctor as saying 'her ears were within normal limits'. In this instance, the unlikeliness of the transcribed phrase alerted the research team to the need to return to the tape themselves, but sometimes mishearings may be less obvious. Where possible, you should provide transcribers with a glossary of technical/jargon terms that they might come across in the course of an interview.

When it comes to presenting quotes to support your analysis, in a paper, dissertation or report, we would accept that it is sometimes appropriate to carry out minor tidying up in order to aid comprehension. This should be done with great care, to minimise any distortion of meaning, and we would normally argue against making any changes to dialect – where this could be obscure to readers it is better to include an explanatory comment in brackets or as a footnote.

Principles of thematic analysis

There are many different styles of thematic analysis, each with their own distinctive procedures. Before we look at examples of these, we will focus on some basic principles that apply to thematic approaches in general. First, though, we need to consider what is meant by the term 'theme' itself. There is surprisingly little discussion in the methodological literature of what is meant by the concept. It is often used in a common-sense way to refer to patterns in the data that reveal something of interest regarding the research topic at hand. An exception is Braun and Clarke's (2006) paper on the use of thematic analysis in psychology, which includes a useful discussion of what counts as a theme. We would agree with them that while it is impossible to set hard-and-fast rules as to what should be identified as a 'theme', there are some guidelines that can be offered. First, identifying themes is never simply a matter of finding something lying within the data like a fossil in a rock. It always involves the researcher in making choices about what to include, what to discard and how to interpret participants' words. Second, the term 'theme' implies some degree of repetition – an issue raised just once (however powerfully) should not be called a theme, although it may still play a part in the analysis. Usually repetition means across two or more cases (interviews), but we would argue that it can sometimes be useful to identify themes unique to an individual case. Third, themes must be distinct from each other. Although some degree of overlap is unavoidable, if there is widespread blurring of boundaries between the themes you identify, they will be of little use in clarifying the interpretations you have made to those reading your work. With these points in mind, we suggest the following definition of a 'theme' in thematic analysis:

Themes are recurrent and distinctive features of participants' accounts, characterising particular perceptions and/or experiences, which the researcher sees as relevant to the research question.

Balancing within-case and cross-case analysis

Since qualitative research emphasises the importance of context, analysis must make sense of particular experiences against the backdrop of the particular participant's full account (as presented in the interview transcript). Equally, in any study, thematic analysis is concerned with saying something about the group of participants as a whole. This means looking at patterns of themes across the full data set, highlighting what interviewees have in common as well as how they differ. All techniques of thematic analysis therefore face the challenge of striking the right balance between within-case and cross-case analysis. If the within-case aspect is neglected, your themes are, in effect, treated as variables in the positivist tradition – abstract notions detached from the particularities of personal experience. If cross-case analysis is not properly developed, you are likely to produce a disjointed collection of case studies that do not allow you to effectively address your research question. Naturally, studies will differ in whether their emphasis is towards the within-case or cross-case end of the spectrum. For example, a project looking in depth at five participants' experiences of moving home would want to devote a considerable amount of attention to individual cases. In contrast, a study in an organisation examining how a new IT system impacts on perceived job roles, involving 40 interviews, would strongly emphasise cross-case analysis.

Organising themes

In all versions of thematic analysis, the researcher is required not only to produce a list of themes but also to organise those themes in a way that reflects how they are conceptualised to relate to each other. This is almost certain to include some degree of hierarchical relationship, in which main themes encompass sub-themes. Thus, in the hypothetical example above of a study into the experience of moving house, a main theme of anxiety might incorporate sub-themes such as *anxiety about the cost of moving, anxiety about new neighbours* and *anxiety about children's responses to moving*. The number of levels of hierarchy used varies between approaches. The guidelines presented by Braun and Clarke (2006) suggest two levels, while it is common to have some aspects of the data coded to four or five levels in template analysis (King, 1998, 2004b).

The organisation of themes can also include links between hierarchical groups or clusters. This method is often used where the researcher aims to develop a conceptual model of the phenomenon under investigation, as is the case in grounded theory (Corbin and Strauss, 2008). Sometimes, within a mainly hierarchical thematic structure, the researcher may want to indicate that certain themes permeate so much of the data that they cannot be restricted to any one hierarchical grouping. In a study of patients' adaptation to diabetic renal (kidney) disease, the first author and his colleagues found that issues relating to *stoicism* (as a coping strategy) and *uncertainty* thread through many aspects of almost all the participants' accounts. We therefore defined these as 'integrative themes', cutting across the otherwise hierarchical thematic structure (King et al., 2002).

Balancing clarity and inclusivity

Qualitative research is interested in providing analyses that are rich and deep. This argues for including as much of the relevant data in your themes as possible. At the same time, a major purpose of developing a thematic structure for your analysis is to help you explain your thinking about the data to other people. Themes therefore have to be well defined and distinct (as noted above) and the thematic structure clear and comprehensible. To some extent, these two goals can be conflicting. If you have a very large number of themes and a poorly organised or over-complex thematic structure, it will be hard for a reader to get an overview of your analysis and to understand how different aspects relate to each other. If you minimise the number of themes you include and oversimplify the structure in the name of clarity, you may fail to explore and interpret your data in sufficient depth to justify a qualitative approach. Again, just how you respond to this challenge will depend on the nature of your study and the kind of output you are producing. In a postgraduate thesis you may err on the side of inclusivity, as you will want to demonstrate the depth of your analysis, and you have the space to explain quite a complex thematic structure – although even here you should seek to present it as clearly as possible. In a 4,000-word journal article, perhaps addressed to a readership that is not necessarily expert in qualitative research, you may be advised to sacrifice some inclusivity to ensure clarity.

There are several ways in which you can present your thematic structure to your readers. The simplest is a list, with a numbering system (and successively wider indentation) to indicate levels of themes. This can also be shown in table form, with columns representing levels. Another style that is quite popular is a 'tree' diagram, with sub-themes branching off each main theme (e.g. Langdridge, 2004; Braun and Clarke, 2006). This is visually effective, though hard to use well if you have a large number of themes (and levels). In this case the list/table form probably works best.

Where you are organising your themes to present a conceptual model with lateral as well as hierarchical relationships, a diagram similar to a 'mind-map' can be a very useful form of presentation. You may include explanatory comments on the lines or arrows, linking themes to help explain your thinking. Note that you need to be particularly careful with this kind of diagram not to make it over-complicated. Bear in mind that you do not always have to present your entire thematic structure when you a reporting your findings. In postgraduate theses, where the writer has a large and/or complex thematic structure to present, it is quite common to use an abbreviated version in the main text and place the full one in an appendix. Similarly, in other publications you can present a short form, so long as you explain what you are doing.

Auditability

Part of the process of carrying out a thematic analysis is being able to demonstrate how you developed your themes and arrived at your final thematic structure. Such 'auditability' of analysis is proposed as an important quality criterion by several writers (see the discussion of quality issues, below). It means that you must keep a record of all the major stages of developing and organising your themes. For example, you should store successive versions of your thematic structure in numbered and dated files to enable you to remember the process. In a thesis or dissertation, you would normally include some discussion of how you developed your themes and their structure, usually within your 'Methods' section, and place key documents illustrating the process (your 'audit trail') in appendices. In other publications, such as journal articles, you are unlikely to have the space to include much of this sort of material, but you should at least give a brief account of the main steps in the process.

Thematic analysis: a basic system

In this section we will present an example of a basic system of thematic analysis, incorporating the principles noted above. We draw particularly upon the guidelines offered by Langdridge (2004), but also on other sources, including Braun and Clarke (2006). As is pretty much universal, we break the process down into a series of stages (and steps within these), but would note that in reality carrying out an analysis does not progress in a purely sequential manner. There is often the need to cycle back and forth between stages – for instance, recognising the need to go back and rethink aspects of interpretative coding (level 2) while being engaged in defining overarching themes (level 3). Figure 9.1 illustrates the steps we suggest in this kind of analysis.

Stage one: descriptive coding

At this stage your goal is to identify those parts of your transcript data that are likely to be helpful in addressing your research question. The emphasis is on trying to describe what is of interest in your participants' accounts, rather than seeking to interpret its meaning. The first step is to read through the transcript you wish to analyse at least once without making any attempt to code it, to familiarise yourself with it as a whole. This is important because when you are analysing any particular section of the transcript you need to do so in the context of the interview as a whole. To make sense of what your participant says at one point will often require you to refer back to something they said earlier or forward to something they said later (or both).

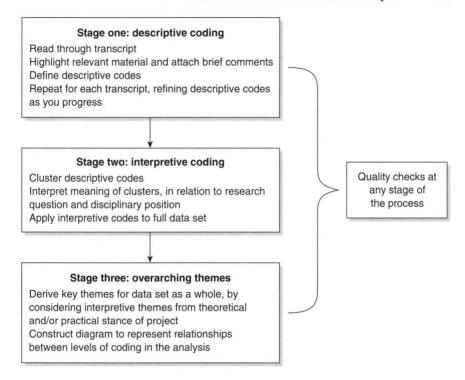

Figure 9.1   Stages in the process of thematic analysis

The next step is to highlight anything in the transcript that might help you to understand the participant's views, experiences and perceptions as they relate to the topic under investigation, and to write a brief comment indicating what is of interest in the highlighted text. The mechanics of this are up to you. You might want to use coloured highlighter pens, or simply underline by pencil. You might write comments in the margins next to highlighted sections, or use some kind of numbering system and compile your comments on a separate sheet. If you are using a computer software package to help your analysis, such as NVivo or Atlas TI, it will have its own system for carrying out these tasks. We suggest you experiment to find out which way of handling the data works best for you, though if carrying it out by hand we would always advise that you lay out your transcripts with wide margins on both sides (4–5 centimetres should do) and double spacing, and with line numbering inserted.

The final step of this first stage is to use your preliminary comments to define descriptive codes. These should stay relatively close to the data, avoiding the temptation to speculate on what might lie behind what the participant has said or to interpret it in the light of psychological theory. There is no need to incorporate every bit of text you initially highlighted within a descriptive code: you may decide when you read through your initial comments that some are not actually relevant to your analysis (although we would urge you to err on the side of caution if in doubt about this). Label your descriptive codes with single words or short phrases (which can include abbreviations), ensuring that these are as self-explanatory as possible. You want to be able to see at a glance where each of your descriptive codes occurs on each page of transcript. In Figure 9.2 we show an example of a section of interview transcript with highlighting, initial comments and descriptive codes attached. This is from a study on the experience of mistrust. In the interview the participant (Lorna) describes an episode in which her would-be business partner (Helena) betrays her trust.

Note that one segment of text may have more than one descriptive code attached. For example, in Figure 9.2 you can see that the descriptive codes *attempt to discuss* and *failure to discuss* relate to the same section of text (lines 5–7). Some overlap between codes is inevitable, because as researchers we are imposing distinctions on free-flowing accounts of complex experiences. If you find, however, that certain codes are coinciding almost every time they occur, it would suggest that it is not really useful to maintain them as separate codes and that they should be merged.

Once you have identified descriptive codes in a whole transcript, you should read through again and see if you can merge some together, where there is a high degree of overlap between them. Then moving on to the next transcript, you read through, highlight and add comments as before. Where these comments can be encompassed by a descriptive code you have already defined in your first transcript, you can use that code – otherwise, define a new one. Again, at the end look through for overlapping codes and merge or redefine where necessary, and then repeat the whole process with the rest of your data set. As your thinking about your coding develops in the analysis of successive transcripts, you may well need to go back and modify some of the coding on earlier ones. This process of defining, applying and redefining codes could, in principle, carry on *ad infinitum*, so at some point you need to make a pragmatic decision to move on to the next stage. You can usually recognise the law of diminishing returns taking effect: if you are taking hours to make minor changes to coding, you have probably reached a stage where the descriptive codes are 'good enough'.

Stage two: interpretative coding

At this stage, you try to define codes that go beyond describing relevant features of participants' accounts and focus more on your interpretation of their meaning. In the main you do this by grouping together descriptive codes that seem to share some common meaning, and creating an interpretative code that captures it. However, in the process of looking at your descriptive codes, and referring back to the transcripts to help keep them in context, you may see where you could usefully define an interpretative code that is not directly related to particular descriptive codes. Note that it is important to go back to the data to clarify your thinking about coding at all stages of the analysis.

Like Langdridge (2007), we would recommend that you do not try to apply specific theoretical concepts in your coding at this stage; this can lead to your analysis becoming rather blinkered, picking up only on those aspects of the data that fit neatly with your theoretical framework. However, we would

Interview extract (with highlighting)	Comments	Descriptive codes
1 So I was kind of developing this relationship along the	Might be running a business together	*Future busn. plans*
2 lines of, that we would possibly be running a business		
3 together, but as the weeks and months went by, um, the	Time went by without communication re business	*Failure to discuss (H)*
4 business was actually changing hands but my		
5 involvement was never really discussed, in spite of me	– in spite of Lorna's attempts to raise it – dismissed by Helena	*Attempt to discuss(L)* *Failure to discuss(H)*
6 sort of approaching Helena and saying 'how's it getting		
7 on? Where do you see me fitting in to this?' etc etc and,	Lorna sees self as not mistrustfull	
8 um, I guess not being a mistrustful kind of person I just	Husband raised questions re what Helena was doing	*L's self-percept: trusting*
9 sort of accepted any, um, excuses or explanations that		
10 she gave me, and it was only when my husband sort of	Only then did Lorna even begin to have suspicions	*Doubts about H (L's husband)*
11 said to me 'hold on a minute, what's going on here?' that		
12 I started POSSIBLY to think about it. So that was the		*L's reluctance to doubt H*
13 example that I was going to give you.		

Figure 9.2   Example of descriptive coding stage

expect your broad disciplinary approach to guide you as well as your research question. If you are a clinical psychologist, for example, you might reasonably pay particularly close attention to sections of the interviews that relate to psychological dysfunction, but you should not use specific concepts from psychodynamic theory, cognitive-behavioural theory (or whatever) to frame your interpretative codes. The same principle applies if your project is one driven more by practice or policy issues, rather than academic theory.

Figure 9.3 shows how we might move from the descriptive to the interpretative codes in the interview extract on the experience of mistrust. As you can see, the two descriptive codes *failure to discuss* and *attempt to discuss* both feed in to an interpretative code of *communication issues*. Similarly, the descriptive theme *future business plans* feeds into *expectation of common goal*. This is because we interpret the former as suggesting that Lorna assumed she and Helena were working together towards the target of creating a joint business venture. In contrast, the interpretative theme *Lorna's naïvety* does not stem from particular descriptive themes we had identified. Rather, it is a result of our realisation when looking again at the data that as well as describing herself as not mistrustful by nature, she also suggests that she should have recognised grounds for being suspicious in the 'excuses' Helena gave her. We felt that although related, the self-perceptions of *trustfulness* and *naïvety* are sufficiently distinct to warrant two separate interpretative codes. In this case, we could now go back and add a descriptive code *accepting explanations/excuses*, but it is not essential that you do this.

It is possible for the same descriptive theme to feed into more than one interpretative theme. We see here that *future business plan* relates to *Lorna's trusting nature* as well as *expectation of common goal*. This is because we felt that her comments implied that she accepted Helena unquestioningly, which seemed to us another example of the way Lorna presents herself as 'trusting'. However, if you find that almost all of your descriptive codes feed into several interpretative codes, that would suggest that you have not defined them clearly and distinctly enough, and some revision would be advisable.

As before, you will need to add to, redefine and reapply your interpretative codes as you proceed from one interview transcript to the next, until you feel you have done a thorough job of capturing the meanings offered by the text. In judging when you have reached this point, remember to keep your research question in mind – avoid spending large amounts of time refining interpretations for aspects of the data which are clearly quite tangential to it.

Stage three: defining overarching themes

At the third stage of coding, you identify a number of overarching themes that characterise key concepts in your analysis. These should be built upon the interpretative themes, but are at a higher level of abstraction than them. At this stage you can draw directly on any theoretical ideas or applied concerns that might underlie your study, so long as these are supported by the analysis

Interview extract (with highlighting)	Descriptive codes	Interpretative codes
1 So I was kind of developing this relationship along the	*Future busn. plans*	EXPECT. OF COMMON GOAL
2 lines of, that we would possibly be running a business		TRUSTING NATURE (L)
3 together, but as the weeks and months went by, um, the	*Failure to discuss (H)*	COMMN. ISSUES
4 business was actually changing hands but my		
5 involvement was never really discussed, in spite of me	*Attempt to discuss (L)*	COMMN. ISSUES
6 sort of approaching Helena and saying 'how's it getting	*Failure to discuss (H)*	
7 on? Where do you see me fitting in to this?' etc etc and,		
8 um, I guess not being a mistrustful kind of person I just	*L's self-percept: trusting*	TRUSTING NATURE (L)
9 sort of accepted any, um, excuses or explanations that		NAÏVETY (L)
10 she gave me, and it was only when my husband sort of	*Doubts about H (L's husband)*	SUSPICION
11 said to me 'hold on a minute, what's going on here?' that		NEED FOR CONFIRMATION
12 I started POSSIBLY to think about it. So that was the	*L's reluctance to doubt H*	TRUSTING NATURE (L)
13 example that I was going to give you.	*Doubts about H (L)*	SUSPICION

Figure 9.3   Example of interpretative coding stage

so far. You would normally try to restrict the number of overarching themes as far as the data will allow – between two and five is probably the norm, although you should not see this as prescriptive. Usually themes are only identified if they apply to at least a substantial minority of cases, but if it would help your overall analysis, you may on occasion choose to define a theme that only occurs in one or two cases. To do this you would need to be able to show that the theme featured strongly in these cases (or case) and that defining it contributed something important to the analysis as a whole. This could be because an issue that is a major focus for one respondent is notable by its absence in all the others, and this comparison reveals something important for the study as a whole. For example, in a study of patient experiences of diabetic renal disease, King et al. (2002) found a major theme of 'hopelessness' in just one of the 20 cases. Focusing on this one exceptional case led us to some valuable insights into the coping strategies of the rest of the participants, and what they did to ward off a sense of despair.

In the example shown in Figures 9.2 and 9.3, there are two overarching themes that draw upon the interpretative themes we have identified. Of course, in a real analysis you would never base overarching themes on such a short extract of data. The first of these is the conceptualisation of mistrust as a *betrayal of a relationship*. We see this in the way Lorna describes her expectation of an ongoing business relationship (and perhaps by implication a personal one too), and in her focus on Helena's wilful failure to respond to her attempts to communicate with her. The second theme is Lorna's portrayal of *trust as the norm*. She became mistrustful only when a significant third party (her husband) raises suspicions, and in spite of her initially naïve acceptance of Helena's 'excuses'. To help your readers to understand how your levels of coding relate to each other, it can be very helpful to present a diagram of it. If you have a large number of descriptive codes, it may be necessary to just show those that most strongly underpin the interpretative ones, though you should acknowledge that you are doing this. In a thesis or dissertation, you would normally be expected to place the full details of identified codes in an appendix. An example of a diagram relating to the mistrust study extract is shown in Figure 9.4.

Assessing the quality of qualitative analysis

In quantitative research, there are universally recognised criteria for assessing the quality of the analysis in any study. Thus *reliability* is concerned with how accurately any variable is measured, while *validity* is concerned with determining whether a particular form of measurement actually measures the variable it claims to. While there are disagreements over the best ways to assess these and other quality criteria, the use of the criteria themselves is not disputed. Things are very different in qualitative research. There is no general agreement about which criteria to use when assessing quality, or how to apply the criteria. Indeed, some scholars argue against the use of any

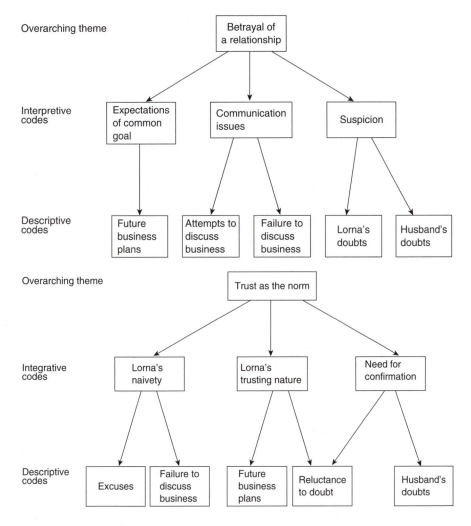

Figure 9.4   Diagram showing all three coding levels

set criteria at all. This diversity is not surprising, given the range of philo-sophical, theoretical and methodological positions informing qualitative research (see Chapter 2). For many writers, this inevitably means that we need to develop different quality criteria and quality assessment techniques for different qualitative traditions – what Johnson, Buehring, Cassell and Symon (2006) refer to as a 'contingent criteriology'.

It is possible to identify three broad positions in relation to the use of quality criteria in qualitative research. First, there are those who argue that qualitative research can and should use the same criteria as quantitative research (especially reliability and validity), though with some modification. Second, some argue that qualitative research should use a separate set of criteria from those employed in quantitative. Third, others assert that qualitative research should not advocate any general fixed criteria at all. We will consider each of these claims in turn, before looking at some of the main strategies used to put various criteria into action.

Using quality criteria from quantitative research

Qualitative researchers who take this position invariably are working within realist approaches, from which it makes sense to utilise quality criteria that address the correspondence between the 'real' world and the researcher's interpretation of it. Validity is the key concept here, and it is commonly argued that qualitative research is intrinsically well placed to ensure high validity (e.g. LeCompte and Goetz, 1982) because of the way it takes context seriously and grounds its development of concepts in close, detailed attention to the data. Reliability is more problematic, as even realist qualitative researchers acknowledge that the researcher's subjectivity shapes the research process. This means that one cannot expect that the findings produced by one researcher will simply be replicated by a second researcher following the same methodology as the first. As Murphy et al. (1998) point out, it can be useful here to distinguish between 'external' and 'internal' reliability. The former applies to the kind of replicability sought in quantitative studies, and will always be problematic for qualitative research, which emphasises the collection of data in unique natural settings. Internal reliability is defined by Murphy et al. as 'the extent to which, given a set of previously generated concepts, new researchers would match these concepts with the data in the same way as the original researchers' (1998: 176). This criterion can realistically be addressed in qualitative research, as we will show in the section below on 'Procedures for assessing quality'.

Using alternative quality criteria

Many researchers argue that qualitative research requires agreed quality criteria, but that these should be different from those of quantitative research. This view is promoted especially by those taking contextualist approaches, but is shared by some realist and relativist researchers as well. There is, however, no general agreement as to which alternative criteria to use, with variation in preferences according to disciplinary, philosophical and theoretical commitments. One of the most influential attempts to devise alternative criteria has been the work of Lincoln and Guba (1985). In this, they suggested four criteria as direct alternatives to the main criteria used in quantitative research:

- *Credibility* in place of validity: this refers to the extent to which the researcher's interpretation is endorsed by those with whom the research was conducted.
- *Transferability* in place of generalisability: this is based on the ability of the researcher to provide sufficient rich detail that a reader can assess the extent to which the conclusions drawn in one setting can transfer to another.
- *Trackable variance* in place of reliability: the conventional notion of reliability assumes a high degree of stability in research settings, such that replication is a realistic possibility. Qualitative research generally assumes that real-world settings

inevitably change, and replication is thus unachievable. Lincoln and Guba therefore argue that instead qualitative researchers need to demonstrate that they have 'taken into account the inherent instability of the phenomenon they are studying' (Murphy et al., 1998: 170). In particular, they need to try to distinguish between instability that is integral to the research context itself and that which they have introduced themselves through the research process.

- *Confirmability* in place of neutrality: qualitative research does not pretend to objectivity; rather, researchers should present sufficient detail of the process of their data collection and analysis so that a reader can see how they might reasonably have reached the conclusions they did.

There have been many criticisms levelled at this formulation, some arguing against specific criteria and some questioning the whole enterprise as inimical to philosophical positions that argue for the existence of multiple social worlds (e.g. Smith, 1984). Lincoln and Guba themselves developed a further set of alternative quality criteria that were more in tune with a relativist position, based around the notion of 'authenticity' (Guba and Lincoln, 1994). Nevertheless, their original criteria remain widely cited.

Rejecting the use of quality criteria

While Guba and Lincoln (1994) argue that even from a relativist position it is possible to develop general quality criteria for qualitative research, others take the view that any such attempt is futile. If one takes the postmodern view that there are no limits and no essential foundations to the ways in which language can construct reality, then it is illogical to suggest criteria for assessing the value of any particular version of reality. The researcher can only offer his or her account as one among many possible competing interpretations, which readers will judge from their own perspectives. This is a coherent position to take, but if qualitative researchers want their work to engage with the world outside academia it creates difficulties. Those who wish to draw on research to make decisions for policy or practice may be uncomfortable with studies that effectively deny the possibility of applying criteria to assess their quality. However, many of those taking a postmodernist stance are highly sceptical about notions of 'applying' research (Willig, 1999a). They tend to see their engagement with the wider world in terms of challenging dominant discourses and giving voice to those alternative constructions of reality that have been silenced or marginalised (Johnson et al., 2006).

Procedures for assessing quality

There exists a wide range of procedures for assessing quality in qualitative analysis. Your choice of which to use must be consistent with your philosophical and methodological position, although it is worth noting that similar procedures can sometimes be used in very different ways to reflect different stances taken by researchers. We will focus on four main approaches here: the use of independent coders and expert panels, respondent feedback, triangulation, and the provision of thick description and audit trails.

Independent coding and expert panels

It is common in thematic analysis to utilise some form of independent coding as a quality check. In the most positivistic forms of qualitative research, this might involve the statistical calculation of inter-rater reliability, of the kind used in quantitative content analysis or structured observation (Boyatzis, 1998). More often, though, this would not be deemed appropriate, as even realist qualitative researchers generally assume that the unique perspective of the individual researcher will shape the analytic process. The aim of independent coding in most cases is thus not to prove reliability but rather to help researchers to think critically about the thematic structure they are developing and the coding decisions they have made. It can highlight where analysts' assumptions and expectations might have blinkered them to alternative readings of the data, or where they may have overlooked material that could enrich their interpretation. To a large extent, then, independent coding is being used here as a way of facilitating reflexivity on the part of the analyst.

If you choose to employ independent coding in your analysis, you have three key decisions to make: when in the process you should carry it out, what you should ask your coders to do, and who should do it. Regarding the first question, the most thorough approach would be to carry out independent coding at all three stages of the analysis. If this is unrealistic within the time and resources available to you, your choice should be guided by your judgement of where the greatest threats to the quality of your analysis lie. For instance, if you did not feel confident about identifying descriptive codes, you could concentrate the independent coding on this stage. Similarly, if you were concerned that your knowledge of the topic area might skew your definition of overarching themes, you could make this the focus of the independent coding task.

On the question of what coders should do, we would argue that there are two main strategies that can be used. The first can be called a *code-defining* approach. Here, you and the coder(s) carry out the stage of analysis in question independently and then meet to compare and critically discuss the coding you have produced. In contrast, the second strategy is *code-confirming*, where you provide the transcripts you are using for the task and your coding of them, and ask the coder(s) to critically scrutinise them. The code-defining style might be seen as more rigorous because it allows less risk of the coder(s) being led by your own coding. It is also usually much more time-consuming to carry out than the *code-confirming* style. It may well make sense to use different styles at different stages, and your choice should also be influenced by who is carrying out the coding. While considering what coders should do, another decision you have to make is how much material they should be given. We would suggest that it is unlikely to be sufficient to use just a single transcript, and the more diverse your interviews are, the more material you are likely to want to provide for independent coders. If you have purposively sampled distinct groups for your study, you would normally want to include at least one transcript from each group. As a very rough rule of thumb, for a study with ten interviews you might want to use three or four transcripts at each quality check stage.

In many research projects, independent coding is carried out within the team. This is a perfectly acceptable process when using a code-defining approach; team members have the contextual knowledge of the data to enable a thorough debate about how codes should be defined and structured. We would be more hesitant about recommending a code-confirming approach for within team use, as the inclusion of external views is generally required to give such a process credibility. If you wish to use an external independent coder, you might seek a colleague with experience in thematic analysis and at least some broad familiarity with the topic area. Better still (but more time-consuming), you might convene an expert panel that includes people with detailed knowledge of aspects of your study from different perspectives. For example, in a study looking at the decisions family doctors made about referring patients to hospital, the first author gathered a panel including academics and practising family doctors to scrutinise the analytic process (King et al., 1994).

Respondent feedback

Another procedure quite commonly used to assess the quality of qualitative analysis is respondent feedback (sometimes referred to as 'member validation'). In this, the researcher takes the analysis back to the participants, to ask how well the interpretation fits their own lived experience (e.g. Jones et al., 2000; Oxtoby et al., 2002). This is seen by some writers as an ethical and/or political requirement as much as a quality issue, since it allows participants a stronger voice in how they are presented than would otherwise be the case. At the same time there are potential problems with the use of respondent feedback (Barbour, 2001; Ashworth, 2003). People may have good reasons for denying the accuracy of an interpretation that in fact they recognise as a fair picture. For instance, there may be aspects of their views or actions that are socially undesirable or that they may be concerned about others seeing (colleagues, managers, family members, and so on). Equally, participants may sometimes express agreement when they actually are not persuaded that the account is accurate – perhaps because it is flattering to them or because they do not want the researcher to feel their time has been wasted. If participants were able to look at an interpretation of what they said in an interview and judge it as right or wrong, then why would we bother interviewing them and painstakingly analysing the transcript in the first place?

We would agree with Ashworth's (2003) view that treating respondent feedback as if it could simply confirm or disconfirm an analysis is an untenable position. However, if such feedback is considered more critically – in effect as a further stage of data collection – then it can be a useful element in strengthening the quality of analysis. Should you wish to use the procedure, you need to decide whether you will return to all your participants or only a sub-sample of them, and if the latter, on what basis to select them. You will also need to produce an explanation of your analysis that is sufficiently detailed to give the participant a clear idea of what you did, but that is also comprehensible to someone who may have no prior knowledge of social scientific methodology.

Triangulation

The concept of triangulation relates to the use of multiple methods of data collection or multiple sources of data to study a particular phenomenon (Mays and Pope, 2000). There are many different types of triangulation proposed in the literature, but the distinctions drawn by Denzin (1978) remain widely cited:

- *Data triangulation*: using a variety of data sources within a single study. For example, in a study about children's responses to street crime, you might interview children, parents, youth workers and police officers.
- *Methodological triangulation*: using different methods to address the same research problem. This could mean a combination of qualitative methods (e.g. interviews and participant observation) or a mixture of qualitative and quantitative methods.
- *Investigator triangulation*: systematically comparing the data collected by different researchers, perhaps selected to ensure they vary in their relationship to the research topic. Thus you might use one researcher who is a member of the group being studied and one who is not, to compare 'insider' and 'outsider' perspectives.
- *Theory triangulation*: using different theoretical models to make sense of the same set of data.

The claim that triangulation – and especially methodological and data triangulation – enhances the validity of qualitative research is the subject of considerable dispute in the literature. Some writers see it as the best way to avoid the intrinsic limitations of individual methods (e.g. Patton, 1990), while others are sceptical about whether perspectives obtained from different methods or sources within a single study can truly be integrated (e.g. Mays and Pope, 2000). For example, if they produce conflicting accounts of a phenomenon, in what sense can they be seen to 'validate' each other? Even if we are reluctant to recommend triangulation as a way of enhancing validity, it may still be valuable as a way of making a study more comprehensive in the way it approaches its subject matter, and (in a similar way to independent coding) it can be a useful stimulant to reflexivity on the part of the researcher.

Thick description and audit trails

The term 'thick description' (which originated with Geertz, 1973) refers to the notion that qualitative researchers should provide detailed descriptions of the phenomena they study and their context. This is relevant to quality assurance as it should help a reader to judge whether the interpretation emerging from the analysis seems consistent with the description presented. Thick description can never be a guarantee of the quality of analysis on its own, since researchers, of necessity, must be selective in what they choose to present – especially in a relatively short piece such as a journal article. Nevertheless, it is a good guiding principle to try to provide as much detail about the focus of the research and its context as practically can be achieved.

Thick description ideally helps the reader to understand how researchers reached their conclusions from the data available. This can be enhanced by the inclusion of detail about the development of the analytic process itself, for example, by providing illustrations and commentary on the way in which a thematic coding structure developed over the course of the project. Such details constitute an 'audit trail' that documents the development of a researcher's thinking as their analysis progressed. We would particularly recommend the inclusion of this kind of material in postgraduate theses, where the student needs to convince an examiner that they have reflected carefully on the way they applied their analytical techniques to the data.

Writing up a thematic analysis

The most common way of organising a report on the findings of thematic analysis is to describe and discuss each of the overarching themes in turn, referring to examples from the data and using direct quotes to help characterise the theme for readers. It is not necessary to refer to every constituent code within each theme – especially the descriptive codes. Rather, you should focus on those that most strongly illustrate what the theme is covering, and which most effectively address your research question. As Braun and Clarke (2006) argue, the aim is not merely to provide a descriptive summary of the content of the theme, but rather to build a narrative that tells the reader how your findings have cast light upon the topic at hand. The choice of extracts to quote should also serve this purpose:

> Extracts need to be embedded within an analytic narrative that compellingly illustrates the story you are telling about your data, and your analytic narrative needs to go beyond description of the data, and make an *argument* in relation to your research question. (Braun and Clarke, 2006: 93, original emphasis)

Choose quotes that highlight the nature of the theme vividly, are easily understood and, where possible, give some sense of the character of the speaker – for instance, showing their use of humour, a tone of pessimism, hope or stoicism, and so on. On the whole, longer extracts achieve these goals better than very short ones, although there are sometimes brief phrases that sum up a point particularly well and are worth quoting directly. It is usual to present quotes as separate paragraphs and indent them (as we have done above), unless they are less than a line in length in which case they are included in the main text, with quotation marks.

The disadvantage of the conventional theme-by-theme presentation of findings is that it makes it difficult to gain much sense of how individual accounts are shaped. If you are particularly keen to preserve the holistic nature of accounts, an alternative approach is to present findings case by case, discussing relevant themes within each of them. This really only works when you have a small number of cases, otherwise it is likely to become repetitive – and very long. Phenomenological studies looking at four or five cases in great depth are the kind of work that might benefit from this style of presentation. A third option that can be very effective is to select a subset of interviews to present as cases, followed by a theme-by-theme analysis of the full data set.

The case examples need to be chosen on a meaningful purposive basis: for instance, they might illustrates two (or more) clear positions within the data, or represent members of distinct participant groups.

Alternative styles of thematic analysis

As we noted earlier, there are many different versions of thematic analysis used in qualitative research. In the remainder of this chapter we will present two types of analysis that differ in quite important ways from the basic version covered above, and that may be particularly valuable for certain types of research project.

Template analysis

A 'template' style of analysis was described by Crabtree and Miller (1992), and the approach has been further developed by the first author (King, 1998, 2004b). It involves the conventional move from preliminary coding close to the text to higher order themes, but differs in several respects to our basic form of thematic analysis. At the heart of the approach is the construction of a coding structure – the template – that is applied to the data and revised as necessary until it captures as full a picture of the analyst's understanding as possible. It is normal to construct an initial template on the basis of a sub-sample of the data set (e.g. six out of 20 interviews), and then apply that to code subsequent transcripts. Where material of interest in these does not fit well with any of the themes on the initial template, the template is revised, perhaps by adding a theme or redefining an existing one. The iteration of applying, revising and then reapplying the template continues until the analyst feels it is clear and thorough enough to serve as a basis for building an account of the findings. Below we outline some of the main ways in which template analysis differs from systems like the one we described earlier in this chapter.

Levels of hierarchical coding

Template analysis does not stipulate a fixed number of hierarchical coding levels. Researchers are encouraged to use as many levels as they find helpful to capture and organise the meanings they identify in the data. Those aspects that provide the richest insights into the topic addressed by the research question will generally be coded in greater depth (i.e. to more levels) than areas of more tangential relevance. Coding to four or five levels is not uncommon. Figure 9.5 shows an extract from a template used by the first author and colleagues in a study of multidisciplinary clinical supervision in primary care.

The study focused on a group of four staff in a family doctor's surgery who piloted a novel form of group supervision (the staff were a family doctor, a health visitor, a district nurse and a practice nurse). They took it in turns to bring an issue relating to their clinical practice to the group, where another member would act as facilitator to the discussion of the current supervisee's concerns. We observed and taped a number of these sessions and then interviewed the participants. The template extract shows the first four top-level themes produced from our analysis, and their subsidiary themes. As can be seen, the second two – *Group dynamics* and *Roles in the Group supervision process* – encompass a more detailed and deeper set of sub-themes (up to four levels) than the first two. This reflects the richer information relating to these issues that we extracted from the transcripts. Interestingly, in the initial version of the template, the *Group dynamics* theme was much less elaborated than it is in the final one. This change is an

---

1. Issues re. Model of supervision
    1.1   Contract
    1.2   Comparison with other approaches
    1.3   Use of 'reflexive cycle' diagram
    1.4   Training
    1.5   Familiarity with...

2. Practicalities
    2.1   Timing issues
    2.2   Length of sessions
    2.3   Location of sessions

3. Group dynamics
    3.1   Atmosphere/climate
        3.1.1   Formal/informal
        3.1.2   Tense/relaxed
        3.1.3   Focused/unfocused

    3.2   Cohesiveness
        3.2.1   Group as a whole
        3.2.2   Sub-groups
            3.2.2.1   Nurse/Doctor
            3.2.2.2   Practice-based/Practice-attached

    3.3   Issues of power & authority

4. Roles in the Group supervision process
    4.1   Supervisee's role
        4.1 1   Issues brought (what & why)
        4.1.2   Comfort with role
        4.1.3   Helpfulness (or not) of group members' contributions

    4.2.   Facilitator's role
        4.2.1   Comfort with role
        4.2.2   Style adopted (inc. adherence to model)
        4.2.3   Clarity of role

    4.3.   Group member's/supervisor's role
        4.3.1   Comfort with role
        4.3.2   Nature of interventions
            4.3.2.1   Type
            4.3.2.2   Frequency
        4.3.3   Clarity of role

Figure 9.5   Template extract from a study of multidisciplinary clinical supervision in primary care (based on King et al., 2000)

example of how the iterative process of applying and modifying the template can help researchers recognise the importance of aspects of the data that may at first have been somewhat overlooked.

Types of theme

Template analysis does not systematically differentiate between 'descriptive' and 'interpretative' coding. In part, this is because it assumes that the two can never be entirely separated – any theme must be grounded in what is actually present in the data (and so is to some extent descriptive) but at the same time it accepts that there can be no such thing as 'pure' description untouched by human interpretation. The hierarchy of themes in a template is therefore not one based on a move towards greater abstraction and interpretation as it is in the basic version of thematic analysis presented earlier. Rather, organisation is on the basis of scope, with lower-level themes representing distinct instances or manifestations of the concept identified by the higher-level theme. This does not mean that template analysis rejects any distinction between description and interpretation: rather, it treats them as more like the poles of a dimension than a dichotomy. Some themes will be more strongly interpretative than others, and on the whole analysis will tend to become more interpretative overall as the researcher proceeds and grows in understanding of the data. The key point, though, is that recognising a theme as more or less interpretative does not determine where it should be placed within a template.

Use of a priori themes

Template analysis allows the researcher to define some themes in advance of the analysis process – referred to as a priori themes. These may relate to important theoretical concepts or perspectives that have informed the design and aims of the study, or to practical concerns such as evaluation criteria that the researcher has been funded to address. Generally, though, it is recommended that researchers do not identify too many a priori themes as this may lead to a blinkered approach to analysis. Template analysis can be seen as standing in between the very 'bottom-up' approaches, such as descriptive phenomenology (Giorgi and Giorgi, 2003) and grounded theory (Corbin and Strauss, 2008), and the more 'top-down' styles of the matrix approach described in the next section of this chapter.

When to use template analysis

The template approach can be used with any size of study; indeed, the first author recently employed a version of it in a piece of autobiographical research (King, 2008). However, it is especially well suited to projects with a sample of between 10 and 25 hour-long interviews. It also works well where there are two or more distinct groups within the data set that you wish to compare. Finally, because it allows the researcher to identify some themes in advance, it is well suited to studies which have particular theoretical or applied concerns that need to be incorporated into the analysis.

Matrix approaches

The use of data matrices within qualitative analysis was pioneered by Miles and Huberman (1984, 1994). Central to the approach is the use of visual displays of the data, which typically tabulate units of analysis (such as individual participants, groups, organisations) against key concepts or issues relevant to the research questions of a study. These displays not only help the researcher to analyse the data – for instance, by facilitating comparisons across units of analysis – but also help to make the process transparent to readers. A number of different matrices may be used at different stages of a study, and there is often a process of data condensation across successive matrices. Thus a first matrix may display analysis with the individual participant as the unit of analysis, enabling comparisons between them to be carried out. In a second matrix, data may be condensed to highlight the distinctive perspective of groups of participants enabling comparisons between these – for instance, comparing organisations or demographic categories in their perspectives on the topic at hand (see King, Thomas et al., 2005, for an example of the use of this kind of condensing process). Alternatively, an initial case-by-case matrix may be followed by one that is organised around the key themes themselves in order to gain an overview of how these are patterned across the data set as a whole. An example of this kind of strategy is shown in Box 9.1.

Box 9.1   Example of stages in matrix analysis

This example comes from a study of users' experiences of a Community Gym in Halifax, West Yorkshire, UK. The gym was supported by the West Central Halifax Healthy Living Partnership (WCHHLP) with the aim of improving health and well-being in a very deprived part of the town, with a high South Asian (mostly Pakistani) immigrant population. WCHHLP funded the research (see King and Little, 2007, for a report on this study). Interviews were carried out with 13 gym users as well as three members of staff.

Level one matrix

Initially, we constructed a matrix that we completed for each individual participant. An extract from one participant (referred to pseudonymously as 'Labib') is shown below. The completed matrix extended over three pages, with eight main thematic areas defined. Four of the main thematic areas are split into subsidiary areas, including those in the extract. This is because these areas are both rich in terms of the data relating to them and of particular relevance to the aims of the research. Note that although we did not seek to index each instance relating to a particular thematic area, we have used line numbers to indicate where especially useful passages are found in the transcript, to facilitate the selection of quotes at the writing-up stage.

(Continued)

(Continued)

Pseudonym and biographical details	Benefits of using the gym			Facilitators of gym use			
	Physical health and fitness	Mental health and well-being	Social	Educational	Access	Cost	Cultural
Labib (Male, age 49, has angina and diabetes)	Significant improvement to health – seen in ability to walk much further than he could before joining gym (35–9) Gives him energy to do more (198–9) At gym, able to push himself more (226–8) – though recognises if pushing self too hard (394–6) – admits sometimes pushes a little bit more than should (439–40) Getting more fit helps him to look younger – others comment on this (286–91)	Having time for himself away from stresses of home is helpful (236–9)	Sees friends at gym. Exercising with friends (47–50) or just seeing/other users at gym motivates him (229–30, 442–4) Knows local community very well – lived here 36 years – so sure to meet someone he knows at gym (54–9)		Very close to home – important because hasn't got a car, and also time-limited by family commitments (102–11) Compares easy access – in middle of community – to difficulty in travelling to previous exercise classes at Spring Hall (378–81)	Low cost – important because he is unemployed (174–9)	Separate male and female sessions preferred by Asian users, though not bothered himself (339–41)

Level two matrix

Once the individual level-one matrices were completed for each participant, key themes within each thematic area were identified across the sample as a whole, and these were then summarised on a level-two matrix, an extract from which is shown below. This makes it easy for the researcher to recognise patterns of themes across the data set – for instance, whether certain issues tended to dominate for older rather than younger participants, or men rather than women. In the extract below, we show the level-two matrix at the point where the first five participants' data had been entered on it (including Labib's).

Benefits from using Gym

Health and fitness	Less out of breath	Akash, Habiba (implied by Labib)
	Less back pain	Akash, Malika
	Less joint pain	Akash, Malika
	General feeling of fitness	Akash, Habiba, Labib
	Re. specific illnesses	Amina
	Increased ability to do everyday things	Habiba, Labib
	Weight loss/control	Malika
	Younger appearance	Labib
	Improved mood	Akash, Habiba
Mental health and well-being	Relief of stress/tension	Habiba, Labib
	Alleviates depression	Amina
	Forgetting about health worries (inc. pain)	Malika
Educational	Learning about wider health issues	Amina, Habiba
Social	Meets friends at gym	Akash, Habiba, Labib, Malika
	Goes on own	Akash, Habiba, Labib, Malika
	Enjoys social aspect	Akash, Amina, Malika
	Social aspect not crucial to attendance	Akash, Malika
	Feeling part of community	Habiba, Labib
	Motivating effects of exercising with others	Labib

Facilitators of Gym use

Access	Convenience of location	Akash, Amina, Habiba, Labib, Malika
Cost	Affordable	Akash, Labib
Cultural	Separate men's and women's sessions	Labib
	Staff who speak own language	Malika
	Support from family	Malika

Additional matrices may also be developed to focus on specific issues highlighted in an initial, more broadly focused matrix. Nadin and Cassell (2004) provide an illustration from a study examining the nature of the 'psychological contract' between employers and employees in small businesses. Their first matrix presents a broad and detailed overview of participants' views relating to the research topic. From this, they identified the issue of 'incidents of theft' as a type of contract violation that was worthy of further examination, and developed a further matrix focused specifically on this theme.

Defining thematic areas

We use the term 'thematic area' here to refer to the concepts, issues, behaviours and so on into which the data relating to each case on this matrix are organised. Thus in the matrix extract in Box 9.1, based on the Community Gym evaluation study, we showed the thematic areas of *benefits from using the gym*, and *facilitators of gym use*. Other thematic areas in this matrix included: *joining the Gym, involvement in other physical activities*, and *drawbacks and areas for improvement*. In matrix-based approaches, these are usually defined to a considerable extent on the basis of a priori concerns – sometimes these are theoretical but more often pragmatic (reflecting the strongly applied focus of Miles and Huberman's original work). However, it is generally recommended that the researcher allows some modification to the thematic areas in the light of ongoing analysis. For instance, in the Framework Analysis approach, widely used in Health Services research (Pope et al., 2000), 'identifying the thematic framework' occurs after a 'familiarisation' phase, which ensures that the thematic structure is not purely determined by a priori issues.

Coding

The task of identifying material to enter into the cells of a matrix is essentially one of thematic coding. The precise coding techniques to be used are not stipulated. Rather, the researcher should use whichever seem well suited to the needs of the particular research project. It is worth noting that because matrix analysis tends to be used with relatively large data sets (as discussed below), and often focuses mainly on analyses across groups, sites or organisations, it is not always necessary to code every transcript on a line-by-line basis. Instead, the researcher may, after carefully reading through transcripts, choose to highlight certain sections that most strongly address the concerns of the study at hand.

Comparing matrix analysis and template analysis

There are certainly commonalities between matrix and template approaches to analysis. Both commonly make use of a priori coding categories, and both place an emphasis on the effective visual display of the analytic structure – to aid the analyst's thinking and ultimately to facilitate the presentation of the analysis to readers. At the same time, the approaches differ in significant ways. Matrix analysis is a more 'top-down' approach than template analysis: once the matrix headings are defined, there is usually relatively little modification to them in the course of the analysis. In contrast, template analysis encourages an iterative process of application and modification (as described above), such that even a priori themes are likely to be redefined, merged or deleted in the course of the analysis. A further contrast is that matrix analysis does not necessarily rely on line-by-line coding of the full transcript, while template analysis invariably does. This reflects the 'broader brush' nature of the former compared to the latter.

When to use matrix analysis

A matrix approach is useful where you have a large, complex data set, especially where the research design involves comparisons between sites, organisations or groups. (As a rough rule of thumb, we would consider a qualitative study with 30 or more hour-long interviews to be 'large'.) Studies with a very strong a priori focus invite a matrix approach – for instance, larger qualitative evaluation studies where key evaluation criteria are set in advance. Finally, the less idiographic focus of matrix analysis (compared to other thematic approaches), and the fact that line-by-line coding is not necessarily required, can make this a resource-efficient approach, well suited to situations where time and/or personnel are limited.

In some studies, the optimum analytical strategy can involve a combination of matrix and template approaches. This may be achieved by first carrying out a matrix analysis, to produce a broad picture of key issue in the data (as they relate to a study's a priori concerns) and then carrying out a more detailed reanalysis using the template approach, on elements of the data identified as being particularly rich and interesting. For example, in an ongoing study by the first author looking at the impact of involvement in allotment gardening, an initial matrix analysis was carried out, strongly driven by the evaluation criteria of the organisation that had funded the work. Subsequently, a subset of thematic areas that were of especial interest (in terms of potential contribution to the academic literature) were reanalysed in more depth, using a template style (King et al., 2007).

Conclusion

In this chapter we have provided you with sufficient information to carry out a straightforward thematic analysis of your interview transcripts, and have also described two further types of analysis (template and matrix) that could be useful to you. We strongly recommend that you read more widely around this topic – perhaps starting with our 'recommended reading' (below) – before you determine exactly how you are going to approach your analysis. A key point to bear in mind is that qualitative analysis should never slavishly follow a 'cookbook' of instructions; you should always consider the requirements of your own study, both theoretical and pragmatic, and be willing to modify aspect of the analytic process accordingly. While you are relatively new to this area, it *is* probably best to stick quite closely to the guidelines for the particular approach you choose to use, but as you gain in experience you should become more confident in modifying the analytic procedures to suit your needs. So long as you understand how your approach is grounded in the philosophical and/or theoretical stance of your research (and can justify this to others), you should increasingly be able to approach qualitative analysis in a creative way.

Recommended reading

Braun, V. and Clarke, V. (2006) Using thematic analysis in psychology. *Qualitative Research in Psychology*, 3: 77–101.

A useful discussion of thematic analysis in general, with detailed instructions for one way of carrying it out. While focusing on psychology, it is relevant to other disciplines too.

King, N. (2004b) Using templates in the thematic analysis of texts, in C. Cassell and G. Symon (eds), *Essential Guide to Qualitative Methods in Organizational Research*. London: Sage.

A thorough account of how to use the template style of analysis, based around a detailed example. See also the template analysis website at: www.hud.ac.uk/hhs/research/template_analysis/index.htm (accessed 21/08/08).

Nadin, S. and Cassell, C. (2004) Using data matrices, in C. Cassell and G. Symon (eds), *Essential Guide to Qualitative Methods in Organizational Research*. London: Sage.

A helpful overview of the ways in which data matrices can be used in analysis, with a detailed illustrative case.

TEN

Interviews in Phenomenological Research

Phenomenology is a philosophical tradition that has had an enormous influence on the development of qualitative methods in the social sciences. In the first part of this chapter we will provide an overview of phenomenological theory and its influence on social scientific research. We will then look more closely at what it entails to carry out qualitative interviews from a phenomenological perspective. We will include here interview-based methods adapted from Kelly's (1955) Personal Construct Theory (PCT) which, we argue, can be used in a phenomenological manner, as well as techniques more directly drawn from the phenomenological tradition. We will cover the following areas:

- phenomenology: key concepts
- the use of interviews in phenomenological research
- analysing phenomenological data

Phenomenology: key concepts

Development of phenomenology

Phenomenology, as it is now recognised, originates in the work of the German philosopher Edmund Husserl (1859–1938). Husserl was concerned that scientists of the time were too ready to impose their own theories on the topic they studied in a premature attempt to construct explanations. He argued that instead, science needed to try to set aside preconceptions and closely describe how phenomena appeared to human consciousness. Only through such careful description (which Husserl famously referred to as getting back 'to the things themselves!') could we build a firm foundation for scientific investigation.

To achieve his goal, Husserl developed his *phenomenological method*, central to which is the notion that the investigator needs to set aside (or 'bracket') his assumptions about the phenomenon under scrutiny and attempt to see it afresh. This process of recognising and setting aside the taken-for-granted ways of seeing the world is known in phenomenology as the *epochē*. By utilising the phenomenological method, Husserl claimed that we would be able to describe the *essence* of any particular phenomenon, stripped of the cultural and personal preconceptions through which we normally see it. This emphasis characterises a tradition that is known as *transcendental phenomenology*.

Husserl's ideas were taken forward and in some important respects modified by a succession of philosophers known as the existential phenomenologists, foremost among whom were Martin Heidegger (1889–1976), Jean-Paul Sartre (1905–80) and Maurice Merleau-Ponty (1908–61). Despite important differences between them, they shared a common concern with questions of the nature of human existence:

> ...existential phenomenology can ... be characterized by its emphasis on several key 'themes' of human existence, such as freedom and its limitations, temporality, engagement and encounter with the world and/or others, and meaning/meaninglessness. (Spinelli, 2005: 103)

The existential phenomenologists were sceptical of the extent to which we can actually set aside our preconceptions, in the way Husserl describes in his transcendental approach. They argued that our existence is intimately bound up with the world we find ourselves in: we can never entirely step outside it to see things objectively as they are. Because of this, existential phenomenologists – and social scientific researchers influenced by them – tend to be less concerned with essences than their transcendental colleagues, and more focused on describing and interpreting aspects of people's 'lifeworld'.

Even in this very brief historical overview, we have introduced a number of key terms and concepts that may well be unfamiliar to you. Phenomenology is rather prone to the use of jargon that can make it seem impenetrable to those without a strong grounding in philosophy (Spinelli, 2005), though as Ihde (1986) says, any school of thought attempting to deal with complex ideas inevitably develops its own 'tribal language' to facilitate their discussion. Before we look at the influence of phenomenology on social scientific research, we will attempt to elucidate a little further some of these central ideas, specifically: intentionality, the epochē, essence and lifeworld.

Intentionality

The notion of intentionality is central to phenomenology's understanding of the nature of human consciousness, as first expounded by Husserl (influenced by his tutor Brentano) (Moran, 2000). When phenomenologists talk about our consciousness always being 'intentionally' related to the world, what they mean is that we are always conscious of something. We see a particular object, we feel an emotion towards a particular person or situation, we contemplate a particular idea. Consciousness is never some pure, abstract, disembodied state – it always and inevitably connects us to the world we inhabit. At first, this might seem an uncontroversial point, but its implications challenge some basic assumptions behind the dominant understanding of the human mind over the last few hundred years. In this period, the natural and social sciences have predominantly taken the view espoused by Descartes in the seventeenth century that mind and body are separate 'stuff'. It follows from this that if we want to understand consciousness, we need to understand what goes on within the mind, which from the mid-twentieth century onwards has increasingly been equated with brain activity and become the province of cognitive psychologists and neuro-scientists. However, if we accept Husserl's argument regarding intentionality, we recognise that a thorough understanding of consciousness must be based on an examination of how we are engaged with the people and objects that make up our world. It cannot be achieved by just looking 'inside' the mind.

Following Husserl's position on intentionality, phenomenologists have argued that we need to attend to two aspects of our experience of any phenomenon: *what* it is we experience, and *how* we experience it. In phenomenological language, these are referred to as noema and noesis, respectively. So, for example, imagine you were watching a cat playing with a ball of wool. Your noematic focus is the content of the cat's actions that you are attending to, while your noetic focus is the meaning of the phenomenon for you and your associated feelings about it. Another person watching the same event may differ from you in both noematic and noetic focus, because of the way in which their intentionality connects them to the phenomenon. Perhaps you are in a friend's house, you are not a cat owner and you find the way in which the creature toys with the wool fascinating and the whole episode rather endearing. In contrast, your friend is focusing not on the detail of the cat's play (with which she is very familiar), but on where it is heading with the ball of wool, for fear it might knock a vase off a coffee table. She watches with a mixture of mild anxiety and irritation.

There is always a noematic and noetic aspect to any experienced phenomenon: we can never attend just to *what* is present or just to *how* it is present for us. However, as Ihde (1986) points out, in different circumstances, one or other aspect (or 'pole' in Ihde's terms) may be more prominent in our consciousness. In the cat example, you might be more focused than your friend on the detail of what the cat is doing (i.e. on the noematic pole) while your friend may be more focused on their feelings and anticipations than you are (i.e. on the noetic pole).

The epochē

The term 'epochē' refers to the essential step in the process of phenomeno-logical analysis by which you recognise and set aside your preconceptions about the phenomenon under consideration, and try to perceive it afresh. This is very different from our ordinary way of perceiving things, where we very often rely on taken-for-granted assumptions and stereotypes to influence our responses. As research in cognitive and social psychology makes clear, using such shortcuts is inevitable – there is simply too much sensation and information surrounding us for us to be able to attend to it all in close detail.

Nevertheless, when we are approaching the social world as researchers, wish-ing to understand particular phenomena in real depth, such shortcuts can seri-ously limit our endeavours. We need to set aside (or *bracket*, as many authors say) not only the commonsense understandings prevalent in our society – which phenomenologists sometimes refer to as *the natural attitude* – but also the theories produced from previous academic work in the area. For instance, if you were researching the experience of developing a chronic illness, there are a whole series of preconceptions that might blinker your attempts to examine the phenomenon. These include popular beliefs about what counts as a good or bad way of adapting to illness and social scientific theories about the consequences of such life events. The former might include the notion that stoicism is a 'better' response than self-pity. The latter could include concepts of psychological dysfunction, such as depression and anxiety, or sociological ideas about the way society defines the 'sick role'.

The notion that it is possible to entirely bracket off our preconceptions has long been criticised – especially by the existential phenomenologists – as it suggests that we can in some way step outside the world to which we are inextricably connected (through our intentionality). Nevertheless, this does not mean we should abandon the idea of the epoché altogether. It is fundamental to all phenomenological inquiry that we strive to go beyond commonsense or habitual ways of seeing things; we just need to recognise that, ultimately, there are always limits to how far we can achieve this.

Essence

The essence of any phenomenon is that which makes it what it is and not something else; it is what remains when we have stripped away all our personal and collective preconceptions about the phenomenon. This concept is closely linked to Husserl's philosophy and the transcendental tradition in phenomenological research that developed from it (Moustakas, 1994). By looking at a phenomenon across different contexts, a researcher can, through the phenomenological method, arrive at a description of its *invariant structure* – that is, those characteristics that persist across contexts. So, if we obtained descriptions from a range of participants about the experience of 'feeling surprised', we could produce an account of the invariant and essential features of this phenomenon. We will discuss the application of this approach below when we describe the methodology developed by Amadeo Giorgi and colleagues in the Duquesne School of phenomenological psychology (Giorgi, 1985; Giorgi and Giorgi, 2008).

As you may have inferred from our discussion of critiques of the epoché, the notion of essence is problematic for existential phenomenology, which tends to associate it with the transcendental school's attempts to adopt a 'God's eye' view. It therefore does not generally figure prominently in the interpretative phenomenological research tradition that has grown out of it. This will be evident in the methodological techniques of interpretative phenomenology that we highlight later in this chapter.

Lifeworld

The term 'lifeworld' (in German, *Lebenswelt*) originates with Husserl, who used it (particularly in his later work) to refer to the world of concrete experience as it is lived by people (Langdridge, 2007). This is what phenomenology should be concerned with, rather than abstractions and theoretical concepts about the nature of the world. An emphasis on the lifeworld became central to existential phenomenologists. Philosophers such as Heidegger, Sartre and Merleau-Ponty were concerned with the way we make meaning for ourselves in the world we find ourselves in, a world that ultimately does not offer clear and unambiguous meaning to us. Understanding the lived experience of the lifeworld is the main goal of most research in the interpretative phenomenological tradition, as we will see below. A key aspect of this, especially in the work of Merleau-Ponty, is the notion of 'embodiment'. We experience our lifeworld as embodied beings – not *with* our bodies, as if they were tools used by but separate from our minds (the Cartesian Dualist view), but *through* our bodies, as what Merleau-Ponty calls 'body-subjects'. This emphasis on our embodied engagement with the world is something neglected in much of social scientific research, and represents a key contribution of phenomenology.

Phenomenology and social scientific research

Phenomenology as a philosophical tradition has, from the start, stressed the need to employ its ideas in the direct exploration of the world of lived experience. As Ihde (1986: 14) says: 'Without doing phenomenology, it may be practically impossible to understand phenomenology.' As we have noted, for Husserl the project was no less than the reform of all the sciences, but not surprisingly it has been in the social sciences that the influence of phenomenology has been most strongly felt. The application of phenomenology to sociology was pioneered through the work of Alfred Schutz (Barber, 2007), some of whose best-known work deals with the lived experiences of being a 'stranger' and a 'homecomer'. Schutz's collaborator, Thomas Luckmann, went on to co-author with Peter Berger the seminal volume *The Social Construction of Reality* (Berger and Luckmann, 1967), which played a key role in the development of the social constructionist movement in social psychology (Burr, 2003) – although arguably social constructionists have tended to downplay this grounding in phenomenology, to the detriment of their field (Butt, 2004).

Phenomenology and psychology

The relationship between phenomenology and psychology is a long and complex one. Husserl himself wrestled with the problem of what a phenomenological psychology should look like, while Merleau-Ponty commented extensively on contemporary psychological issues and from 1949 to 1952 held the Chair in Psychology and Pedagogy at the Sorbonne (Matthews, 2002). In spite of this, phenomenology remained very much peripheral to the mainstream of Psychology, dominated as it was by American behaviourism. This began to change with the appearance of humanistic psychology in the 1960s, when its leading figures cited phenomenology as an important influence. However, many commentators have noted that they displayed some fundamental misunderstandings of European phenomenology – for example, in arguing for the existence of a unitary 'real' self (Spinelli, 2005) and in seeing the individual as in some ways separate from a (generally hostile) social world rather than inherently embedded within it (Butt, 2004). Rather than humanistic psychologists such as Abraham Maslow and Carl Rogers, it was Amadeo Giorgi and his colleagues at Duquesne University who really began the task of developing a phenomenological psychology that was genuinely grounded in the philosophy of Husserl and those who followed him (Giorgi, 1970). Since then, various strands of phenomenological psychology have emerged, drawing on different aspects of phenomenological thought, including Van Manen's (1990) hermeneutic approach, Smith's (1996) Interpretative Phenomenological Analysis, the Sheffield School (Ashworth, 2003) and Langdridge's (2007) Critical Narrative Analysis.

Kelly's Personal Construct Theory and phenomenology

George Kelly developed his Personal Construct Theory (PCT) as a way to understand the personal meanings of people's experiences, and how these are organised (Kelly, 1955). He did this from a psychotherapeutic concern to help people with psychological difficulties, but the theory has since been applied much more widely in psychology (Butt, 2008). Kelly is sometimes seen as part of the same broad humanistic movement as the likes of Rogers and Maslow. It is true that he shares their view of people as agents, who are able to shape their own development, in contrast to the more deterministic perspectives of psychoanalysis and behaviourism (the former seeing people as driven by their unconscious, the latter as moulded by environmental reinforcers). However, Kelly rejects the humanistic view that people have a single 'true' self, and an innate tendency to personal growth. Instead he views the person as being like a scientist, building 'theories' on the basis of experience that help them to anticipate what to expect in social situations, and to therefore act appropriately. Kelly argues that these 'theories' take the form of bipolar 'constructs' which are organised for each person in a unique construct system. Sometimes people's construct systems develop in ways that are unhelpful to their interactions with others and their feelings about themselves: it is then that various kinds of psychological difficulties can arise. For Kelly, the way that professionals can help with such difficulties is not to diagnose a particularly psychopathology, and then treat the person as a 'case' of depression, anxiety, or whatever. Rather, they should seek to examine the person's construct system, in order to identify where the client's way of making sense of the world is letting them down. Kelly and later construct theorists developed a range of original and creative methods to help the psychotherapist in this task, of which the repertory grid is the best known (Bell, 2003). Many of these techniques can also be used as research methods, as we will see later in this chapter.

In his own writing, Kelly appears rather hostile to phenomenology. However, this is probably due to his association of the term with the humanistic psychology movement and its emphasis on an innate self-actualisation drive and the uncovering of the 'true' self (Butt, 2008). As we have seen, this position is at odds with the European phenomenological tradition. Ironically, Kelly's theory has more in common with that tradition – especially the existential strand in it – than the humanistic psychologists who claimed it as an antecedent. It should be noted, though, that PCT itself has developed different emphases, which vary in the extent to which they share common ground with phenomenology. On the one hand, many writers emphasise PCT's cognitive aspects, treating constructs as entities that exist within the mind. On the other hand, there is a strong social psychological strand that focuses on construing in terms of the way people interact with their social world (Chiari and Nuzzo, 1996; Butt, 2003). It is this version of PCT that has clear parallels with phenomenology:

> *A focus on meaning-making and experience*: Kelly's view of 'the person as sci-
> entist', testing out their understanding of the world through interaction with it, is
> similar to the existential phenomenological view of the person as 'thrown' into
> the lifeworld and forced to make sense of it. In both cases, the notion of an under-
> lying 'human nature' that directs this quest, such as the drives proposed (in very
> different forms) by both psychoanalysts and humanists, is rejected.

> *Construing as action*: The social psychological reading of PCT and phenome-
> nology both argue that much of the time we act in our social world without prior
> conscious reflection. In fact, if we stopped to reflect before we did everything,
> we would hardly get anything done at all! This is not to devalue reflection – it is
> a crucial human capability – but rather to emphasise that in our active engagement
> with our social world it is the exception rather than the rule.

> *The interrelationship between personal and social construing*: Although PCT sees
> the configuration of each person's construct system as unique, this does not mean that
> personal construing is purely idiosyncratic. How we construe things personally is
> inevitably influenced by the way things are construed in our society more widely.
> This view that personal meanings are related to (though not entirely determined by)
> socially shared meanings is also held by phenomenology.

It is important not to overstate the parallels between phenomenology and PCT. There are some aspects of Kelly's theory that are problematic for any phenomenologist, such as the assumption that meanings are, of necessity, organised into bipolar constructs, or the emphasis on construing rather than perceiving the world (Ashworth, 2008). Nevertheless, many of the research techniques developed in PCT can be used in a phenomenological manner, and deserve to be more widely known by phenomenologically-oriented qualitative researchers.

Phenomenology and practice-based disciplines

As well as the development of phenomenological perspectives in sociology and psychology, phenomenology has also played an important role in many prac-tice-oriented disciplines, such as education and the health professions. Its emphasis on looking closely at lived experience in specific settings, rather than abstract theorising about 'human nature', appeals to academics and practition-ers in such disciplines, who are aware of the dangers that can follow when 'expert' professionals impose their own theories on the experiences of the people they are supposedly serving. For example, Sumsion (2002) used a single case study to explore over several years the personal meaning of being an early childhood teacher. She describes the initial enthusiasm and eventual disillusionment of her participant, eventually leading to her leaving the profession. Close attention to this one person's lived experience casts important light on issues concerning attrition in teaching. Turning to the health context, Beck (1997) carried out a phenomenological study of how nurses used humour in their everyday practice, providing insights into how they dealt with the demands of their professional role. Again, the rich detail of the phenomenological method provides a depth of understanding missing from quantitative studies that try to understand such experiences by defining people in terms of broad 'coping styles'.

The use of interviews in phenomenological research

Having provided an overview of phenomenology and its application in the social sciences, in the second part of this chapter we will look specifically at the ways in which interviews can be used in phenomenological research. We will consider key features of interviews in this context, and then examine some techniques from PCT that may be useful for phenomenological researchers. Finally, we will give a brief account of two of the main methods used to analyse phenomenological interview data: Giorgi's descriptive phenomenology (Giorgi, 1985) and Smith's Interpretative Phenomenological Analysis (IPA) (Smith, 1996).

Key features of the phenomenological interview

Interviews are widely used in phenomenological research, though they are more dominant in some traditions than others. Smith and Osborn (2008) describe semi-structured interviews as the 'exemplary' method for IPA, because of the emphasis in this approach on exploring how people interpret their experience. In descriptive phenomenology, as developed by Giorgi and the Duquesne School, alternative methods are often used to gather detailed accounts of specific experiences. These include the use of written accounts (Beck, 1997), video-recordings and the 'think aloud' method, where the participant provides a real-time verbal description of the phenomenon under investigation (e.g. Aanstoos' 1985 study of chess-players). Nevertheless, many descriptive phenomenological studies do use interviews, sometimes in combination with written accounts, as we will discuss below.

On the whole, the issue of what is (or should be) distinctive about a phenomenological interview is not explored in much depth in the methodological literature. Researchers, especially in IPA, tend to use fairly generic semi-structured interviews, although with a stronger emphasis than we might see elsewhere on the importance of gathering very detailed descriptions of particular phenomena as they are experienced. It is in data analysis, rather than collection, that the links between the philosophical ideas and research practice tend to be explicitly addressed. We would argue, however, that more thought needs to be given to how interviews can be used in a truly phenomenological manner, grounded in the philosophy. We will look at three ways in which this can be achieved: using *written descriptions* within the interview, using *imaginative variation*, and viewing the interview as an *embodied relationship*.

Using written descriptions

As noted above, there are a number of studies in the literature where researchers have collected data through a combination of written accounts and interview. For example, Morley (1998) asked participants to write about an experience of daydreaming and then explored the experience in more depth with them in interview. Bargdill (2000) followed a similar procedure in a study of the experience of 'life-boredom'. The rationale for this approach is to maximise the depth of description of a particular phenomenon experienced by a particular person – in Husserlian terms, to get to 'the things themselves'. A written account alone may require further elaboration or clarification for the researcher to feel able to produce a thorough analysis, while an interview alone may not give the participant the time and space necessary to carefully recollect the experience – they may be 'swept along' with the research agenda and their dialogue with the researcher. By enabling the participant to produce an account at their own pace, and then basing an interview on that account, it is possible to draw on the strengths of both methods. Behind this approach is an important assumption: it is not a simple matter for participants to describe their experiences in the level of detail required for a good phenomenological analysis. Much of the time, we do not stop and reflect on our experience, and when we do there are always some aspects that are to the forefront of our consciousness and some that remain as background. As researchers, if we want our participants to produce a description that goes beyond a very superficial account of the phenomenon we are interested in, we need to incorporate techniques for assisting them in this somewhat unusual process.

In practical terms there are several points you need to address if you wish to incorporate written descriptions into your interview design in a phenomenological study. First, you need to give a clear brief to your participants as to what is required of them for the written description. You need to tell people the basis on which they should choose the example to describe, and to emphasise that you want them to include whatever contextual detail they consider might help to clarify the experience for you. While not wanting to be prescriptive, it is normally best to give some kind of indication of the approximate word length required – you do not want people giving you a two-line summary, or to feel obliged to present several thousand words of autobiography (the former is much more likely to happen than the latter!). The guidance you give will need to reflect the nature of your study, but as a rough rule of thumb such accounts tend to be in the 500–2,000 word bracket.

Second, you have to think about how long to leave between the production of the written description and the interview. You need enough time to read the description carefully, and to think about the kinds of questions that it raises for your interview. However, you do not want to leave too long a gap as there are advantages in interviewing the participant while the experience in question is fresh in their mind. An interval of about a week is a reasonable target to aim for in many cases. It is usually a good idea to return a copy of the description to the participant shortly before the interview date, asking them to read through it again. We would also recommend that you take a copy for each of you to the interview itself.

Third, before you start data collection, you need to think carefully about how you are going to develop the interview questions for each participant. In most studies of this kind, there will be some general questions – or at least question areas – defined in advance that potentially relate to all participants, with subsidiary and additional questions devised from the written description for each individual interviewee. The case-specific questions can address any feature of the written account that you feel needs clarification or elaboration. They can also address areas that you might have expected to appear in the description but that did not do so. For example, in a study of the experience of starting university, you might be surprised if the participant did not mention in her written account which subject she was studying. Phenomenology recognises that what is not said about a phenomenon can be as important as what *is* said. Take care, though, not to become leading in the way you question people about apparent omissions. You do not want to give the impression that you are making any judgement of the participant because they have not mentioned something they 'should' have.

Using imaginative variation

Imaginative variation is the process of imaginatively altering aspects of a phenomenon in order to clarify which are essential to the experience of it. Husserl (1931/1960) gives the example of the perception of a table to illustrate what he meant by the concept. The reader is invited to call to mind a table and then systematically vary aspects of it in their imagination and consider whether each variation would threaten its perceived identity as a table. For instance, would it remain a table if it changed colour? If it had more, or fewer, legs? The first author has used this task as an exercise in class many times, and found that certain variations are quite commonly perceived to result in the phenomenon no longer being experienced as a table. For instance, students feel that if the object is not raised above the ground, or if it does not have a surface on which things can be put, it could not count as a table. In contrast, altering its colour, height or number of legs does not prevent it from being a table. In phenomenological terms, we would say that imaginative variation suggests that the first two features are part of the 'essential structure' of the phenomenon of a table, while the latter three are not. It is important to note that in stating this we are not claiming to have uncovered universal essential features of a table that exist outside any human experience of the phenomenon (the kind of thing Plato meant by his notion of 'ideal types' underlying imperfect human perceptions). Rather, we are seeking to obtain a fuller (or more 'adequate' to use the favoured term) description of a particular phenomenon as it presents itself to the consciousness of particular people.

Typically, imaginative variation has been used in phenomenology in the kind of thought experiment described above. Within phenomenological research in the social sciences, this means that it has come into play during the analysis of the data, in the process of recognising and setting aside presuppositions and then developing an adequate description of the phenomenon under investigation. However, the technique can also be used very effectively within the data collection stage, as part of the interview design. Interviewees can be asked to reflect on an experience of relevance to the research project, and tell the researcher how they think it would be different if certain aspects were changed. For example, a criminologist might be interested in fear of crime and perceptions of safety or danger in specific locations. In an interview, she could ask the participant to describe a setting where he felt anxious about his safety. She could then ask him to imaginatively vary the setting to make it feel more or less threatening. He might say that it would feel safer if there were better lighting, if more people were about, or if he was with a friend. Equally, he might say that if he was unfamiliar with the location, or if there were groups of youths hanging around on street corners he would feel less safe. The researcher could then encourage the participant to reflect further on these aspects of the phenomenon to get a more adequate description of this person's experience. Bevan (2007) used this kind of technique to explore patients' perceptions of receiving dialysis at satellite dialysis units (small, specialist units away from the main hospital) rather than on a ward in a large general hospital.

People may occasionally use a form of imaginative variation within an interview – for example, making comparisons between the experience at hand and other similar instances (real or hypothetical) to clarify what they saw as distinctive to the present case. However, you cannot rely on this always occurring where it would be useful, so it is worth planning where you might most fruitfully suggest the technique in the interview. The invitation to use imaginative variation can be seen as a special form of a 'prompt', as discussed earlier in Chapter 4. As with prompting to clarifying a question, you need to be sure that you are not leading the participant when you introduce imaginative variation. Thus you should encourage variations in different directions. We saw this in our example above, where the researcher asked the participant about changes that could make a setting seem more threatening and those that would make it feel safer. Our experience, and that of Bevan (2007), suggest that many participants find the use of imaginative variation in interviews an interesting exercise that they understand readily.

The interview as an embodied relationship

As we noted above, phenomenology has drawn attention to the importance of examining our bodily relationship to the world. We do not experience our bodies as objects like any other; rather, they are the subject of experience, and as such should be a central focus of any attempt to study lived experience. However, not only has mainstream positivistic social scientific research neglected this, even phenomenological research has often failed to take embodiment seriously in its research practices. The dominance of the interview as a method of data collection may have contributed to this. As Finlay (2006) points out, even phenomenological researchers can become overly focused on words (as presented in interview transcripts) to the neglect of the embodied experience of the interview participant. She argues that researchers should attend closely to their own and the participant's bodies in the interview situation. Furthermore, the relationship between interviewer and interviewee itself should be recognised as a bodily one, and the way in which each responds to the other's bodily presence and action can be revealing about the phenomenon under discussion. Finlay describes the attitude required of the researcher to draw fully on the embodied nature of the interview as one of 'reflexive, embodied empathy' (Finlay, 2005: 27).

To give an example, Finlay (2006) recounts an interview carried out with a health practitioner/academic ('Kath') on the experience of mistrust (the interview is presented in more detail in King, Finlay et al., 2008). Kath recalls a situation where her professional competence was undermined by the actions of a small group of colleagues. She makes frequent use of bodily metaphors to describe how she felt during the period when this was going on: she felt 'reduced' from her normal 'big' self, 'shaky', and insubstantial – 'a paler shade of me'. Finlay describes how, in the course of interviewing Kath, she, as interviewer, became aware of her own bodily responses mirroring those of her interviewee:

> As I was listening to Kath, it seemed that what I was feeling was, in some sense, mirroring something in her. I rode with this idea. If this was the case, one way into understanding Kath's experience was to try to understand what was happening within me – or, more specifically, within and to *my* body. With this in mind, during the interview, I shared with Kath what was happening to me. I was aware that this could have had the unfortunate result of re-directing the focus from Kath to me. However, as it happened, I don't feel that what occurred detracted from Kath's experience. Instead, I believe that my attempt to empathise seemed to help her better articulate the pain of being a big woman forced to 'reduce'. (Finlay, 2006: 26–7)

Perhaps because mainstream social science has for so long accepted the Cartesian separation of mind and body – and neglected the latter – it can be difficult at first to grasp what phenomenologists are saying about embodiment. In particular, it can be hard to recognise the implications for research practice. There is no doubt that sensitivity to bodily aspects of the interview is something that becomes easier with experience, but there are practical steps you can take even as a novice researcher to ensure that you can begin to incorporate this important element into your interviewing. These are summarised in Box 10.1.

Box 10.1   Embodiment and the interview

Here are some suggestions for how you can become more sensitive to the embodied nature of the interview, and use this to gain greater depth in phenomenological research.

- Watch as well as listen closely. Where possible take brief notes of any bodily actions that stand out as powerful or revealing, so you can connect these to the interviewee's words when you transcribe (see Chapter 4).
- Pay particular attention to what participants say about bodily aspects of the experiences they are talking about. These are often important points to probe further for more detailed description.
- Be aware of your own bodily reactions to your interaction with the interviewee, and consider these as possible cues for you to probe further – as in the example of 'Kath' described by Finlay (2006).
- As it is not always possible or appropriate to take notes during an interview, as soon as possible afterwards record anything that strikes you about the bodily presentation of the interviewee and your response to it. You might do this sitting in the car before you set off, or on the bus home, or in a nearby café. You can record your impressions in writing or on the tape or digital recorder you have used for the interview.
- Where you feel embodiment is likely to be an especially strong focus of your research, consider the possibility of video-recording interviews.

Interview techniques from Personal Construct Theory

One of the most valuable contributions of Kelly's Personal Construct Theory (PCT) is its very creative approach to exploring how people make sense of their world. While its methods in the main developed in the context of clinical work, most are readily transferable to research settings. In this section we will focus on how certain techniques derived from PCT can be used in qualitative interviews from a broadly phenomenological perspective. We will concentrate on three techniques: the repertory (or 'rep') grid, the Pictor technique and the Salmon Line.

The repertory grid technique

The rep grid is without question the most well-known method developed in PCT. It is widely used in both clinical and research work, in just about every area of application. We will only provide a brief overview of it here, both because there is already a voluminous literature available elsewhere and because it is the least phenomenological in character of the examples we are discussing. A thorough examination of the field of repertory grid methods is provided by Fransella, Bell and Bannister (2003). For a more introductory account, see Jankowicz (2003).

The repertory grid technique was developed by Kelly to investigate the ways in which individuals made sense of their world – particularly their social world. As we have seen, Kelly argues that we do this in the form of a system of interconnecting bipolar constructs, which (while drawing on socially available constructions) are unique to each person. Rep grids are used to systematically elicit constructs from participants, and to analyse how they are related to each other. There are many different variants of the method, but in the classic form suggested by Kelly, the researcher asks the participant to carry out a series of triadic comparisons to identify their constructs. This involves them in bringing to mind three people and suggesting ways in which one of them differs from the other two. Thus a participant might choose to start with her father, her best friend and her boss, and state that her father and best friend treat her respectfully while her boss is condescending to her. 'Respectful $\Rightarrow$ Condescending' would then be noted as one of the participant's constructs. The triadic comparison is repeated many times, with different triads, until the participant is struggling to identify any further constructs. The elicited constructs are now placed on a grid, with the extreme poles of each anchoring each end of a dimension, and participants are asked to indicate where they see themselves on each. Depending on the aims of a research project, they may also be asked to compare themselves in different situations (e.g. 'me at work' vs 'me at home'), themselves with others, or to contrast actual and anticipated conditions (e.g. 'how I see myself now' vs 'how I imagine myself in five years'). Grids may be analysed qualitatively, using forms of thematic analysis (e.g. Cassell and Walsh, 2004), or statistically, for which purpose several dedicated statistical packages have been developed. They may also be used to help inform subsequent, more open-ended interviews. Box 10.2 presents an example of a qualitative interview-based study using repertory grids.

Box 10.2   Example of a repertory grid interview study

Background

This study, carried out by the first author and Viv Burr, set out to examine how the meanings women associate with footwear might provide a way of exploring aspects of identity. There is a considerable amount of research that illustrates how the consumer choices we make can reveal significant aspects of how we see ourselves and others, and it was clear through everyday observation that shoes have a particularly strong attraction for many women (several female colleagues used the word 'passion' to describe their relationship to shoes). In informal conversations, what struck us was that women did not just talk about how a pair of shoes looked and what they might 'go with', but frequently considered what social scientists would call identity issues: 'Am I the kind of woman who could "carry off" wearing these shoes?' 'How would other people see me if I wore that pair in this sort of setting?' 'I couldn't wear those boots – they're just not me!' This seemed a very appropriate topic for a Personal Contruct Theory PCT study, using repertory grid-based interviews. It was evident that women's constructs surrounding footwear were highly personal and at the same time drew on socially-shared construing. Equally, women sometimes struggled to explain the meanings they construed – exactly what was it that made them so sure a particular shoe 'wasn't me', for example. The repertory grid is a very effective tool for helping interview participants to consider their own meaning-making.

Method

As this was a small-scale exploratory study, we restricted our sample to four women. We selected them opportunistically through personal networks, and on the basis of informal discussion about the proposed study identified and recruited two women who expressed a strong interest in shoes and two who said they saw them as just functional objects.

The first step in our study was to gather a large, varied pool of images of women's footwear. From these we purposively selected a sample of 33, based on including a variety of styles within a number of main categories of types of women's footwear: flat shoes, high heels, sandals and boots (ankle, knee and thigh length). At the start of each interview we presented these images and asked the participant to choose 12–15 of them, including some they liked, some they disliked and some they had no strong feelings about. Following the traditional 'triadic' method in PCP, we picked three images arbitrarily, and asked them to say how two of them were similar and both differed from third. The only briefing we gave was that we wanted them to concentrate on what the images meant to them rather than just on physical features. We then brought in new images to help them make further comparisons, enabling them to add to and elaborate on the emerging constructs.

Once this process had produced a good range of constructs we drew up the grid, as shown overleaf. For each construct the participant was asked to define the two poles and state which was their preferred pole. The preferred pole is placed on the left side of the grid. We then asked them to choose from all the images their three favourites and the three they liked the least. These were listed at the head of the columns between the two sets of construct poles; for each shoe on each construct the participant now had to indicate whether they saw it as located towards the preferred (marked '1') or non-preferred (marked '0') pole. The completed grid was then used to help the participant reflect further on questions of identity that had arisen. The entire interview process was tape-recorded.

Example grid

This grid was produced in the interview with 'Lucy', who was one of the women who initially expressed a lack of interest in shoes, beyond the purely practical. The six images she chose for the grid were as follows:

Liked
12 Very high heeled red shiny knee-length lace-up boot.
10 Flat baseball boot
30 High heeled plain black ankle boot

(Continued)

(Continued)

Disliked
15 High heeled red court shoe with black lace trim
17 High heeled pink satin mule with red satin rose trim
8 High heeled baby pink fluffy mule

	Shoe image code					
Preferred pole (1)	Favourites			Most disliked			Non-preferred pole (0)
	12	10	30	15	17	8	
Comfortable	0	1	0	0	0	0	Uncomfortable
Confident feminine	1	1	1	0	0	0	Helpless feminine
Safety	0	1	1	0	0	0	Fun
Toned down sexual	0	1	1	0	0	0	Overtly sexual
Informal	1	1	0	0	0	1	Formal
Not making statement	0	1	1	0	0	0	Making statement

We will give one example where we feel that the repertory grid method allowed insights into the way Lucy construed her identity that might not have been achieved with a more conventional semi-structured interview. It can be seen that the three disliked shoes are all placed at the non-preferred poles of all the constructs (with one exception for shoe 8). However, Lucy places two of her three favourite shoes at the non-preferred poles of several constructs – indeed, example 12 is only at the preferred pole for two of the six constructs. This finding prompted further discussion with Lucy as to why she favoured a shoe (or actually in this case a boot) that she perceives as having attributes that she generally avoids in her footwear? What became clear from the interview was that in thinking about shoes she would like to wear, there was a strong disjuncture for Lucy between what she saw as her 'actual' and 'wished-for' identity. She felt she was not the sort of person who could carry off presenting herself as 'fun', 'overtly sexual' and 'making a statement' – but at least in some circumstances would quite like to be able to do so. Even in her 'wished-for' identity, though, it was crucial that her appearance carried a message of 'confident' rather than 'helpless' femininity. She strongly felt the red high-heeled boots conveyed this, described them as having a 'rock chick' look that she could identify with. In contrast, looking 'girly' and 'helpless' was completely alien to her. Note that this is the one construct for which all Lucy's favourite shoes are at the preferred pole and all her most disliked shoes are at the non-preferred pole.

In many studies, the process is taken a further step. Another grid is produced with the bipolar constructs as rows, and participants are asked to rank or rate a series of elements on each of the constructs. Elements are often individual people but they can also be groups or types of people ('your family', 'your work team') or aspects of the self ('your ideal self', 'how you are at work', 'how you are with your children'). The selection of elements will be guided by the aims of a particular research project. The ratings or rankings can then be analysed to examine how constructs relate to each other within one person's grid and also to look for patterns across many grids. This kind of analysis is commonly carried out using statistical techniques such as factor analysis and cluster analysis.

It is evident from the above that the repertory grid technique diverges from phenomenological principles in some substantive ways. It is strongly based on the assumption that we organise our meanings in the form of bipolar constructs, which phenomenological researchers would not accept as an a priori assumption. The common use of multivariate statistics to identify patterns across large volumes of grid data is also not compatible with phenomenology's concern with personal experience. It should be noted, though, that many advocates of PCT are aware of the danger that the availability of sophisticated statistical techniques for analysing grids can distract from a focus on the way in which people make sense of their world, which is at the heart of Kelly's theory (Bannister, 1985; Cassell and Walsh, 2004). In spite of these divergences, the repertory grid – if used with a good grasp of its underlying theory – is a versatile and efficient technique for exploring personal meanings that does at least share common ground with phenomenological research.

The Pictor technique

Underlying many of the methods used in PCT is the assumption that our ways of construing are not always easily available to conscious reflection – we cannot just look 'inside' ourselves and observe our own construct systems. Rather, it is by helping the person to become aware of their construing in the context of specific aspects of everyday life that the researcher or clinician can build a fuller picture of how they engage with their world. In the classic rep grid method, as we have seen, this is achieved by the use of triadic comparisons. Another approach is to ask the participant to produce some kind of visual representation of how they view themselves and their social world. There are numerous such visual techniques that have been developed in PCT (see Denicolo, n.d., for an overview; and Denicolo and Pope, 2001, for more detailed accounts of several examples). In the next section we discuss one of these, the Salmon Line, but first we will describe a more recent addition – the Pictor technique.

Pictor was developed as a research tool by the first author and colleagues at Huddersfield University specifically to explore experiences and understandings of interprofessional working in a community healthcare context. It is applicable, though, to any setting that involves complex working relationships focused on a particular case or project. Pictor developed from a method employed in PCT-based family therapy, to enable the therapist to help clients articulate how they construe their relationships with each other (Hargreaves, 1979). It was first used in a research setting by Angela Ross, in her doctoral study of collaborative working between social workers and community nurses (Ross, 2005; Ross et al., 2005). Subsequently, we have used it in a project examining roles and relationships among different types of community nurse in the context of caring for terminally ill patients and their families (King, Melvin and Ashby, 2008).

The Pictor technique uses a participant-generated graphical representation of a specific case of collaborative working in order to encourage reflection on, and discussion of, role, identity and relationship issues. The first step in the process is to ask the participant to bring to mind a case of collaborative working that they remember clearly. This will often be a recent case, but it does not have to be if there is an older example that they recall especially strongly. They are then provided with a large blank sheet of paper – such as a sheet from an A1-size flipchart pad – and a stack of arrow-shaped 'Post-It' notes (originally arrow shapes cut from thin card were used, but the 'Post-Its' are preferable if you can find them, for reasons that will become apparent). The participant is asked to write on the arrows an identifier for every person they can think of who had some involvement in the case (e.g. their initials, role title or a pseudonym). They must include themselves, but otherwise they may include whoever and as many people as they want. Participants are not prevented from including groups of people on a single arrow (e.g. 'District Nursing Team') – and in projects at Huddersfield we have had cases where those included are not restricted to *homo sapiens* – 'pets' and 'the weather' have featured, for instance.

Before participants start writing names on the arrows, the remainder of the task is explained to them. They are asked to place the arrows on the sheet of paper in a manner that helps them conceptualise the case as a whole, and in particular the nature of relationships among those involved in the case. They are told they may choose to lay the arrows out to represent qualities of relationships. For instance, proximity on the paper may be used to suggest how closely people worked together, and the direction of the arrows may indicate whether people were moving towards the same or different goals. However, it is stressed that there is absolutely no requirement that they use them in such a manner, and that they can do whatever they find most helpful to represent the case. To allay any suspicions the participant might have, the researcher should make it absolutely clear that the exercise is not a psychological test or assessment.

Once all these instructions have been given, and the participant has had a chance to ask any questions they wish to, the researcher leaves them alone for 10–15 minutes to carry out the task. On returning to the room, the researcher checks that the participant has completed the task, and if not, asks them whether they would like to be left alone again until it is done. Once the chart is ready, the researcher draws around each arrow to make a permanent record of it. The chart then serves as the basis for an interview examining in-depth their perceptions of their involvement in the case. The researcher will probe about why particular people are included where they are and how the participant has used the arrows to indicate the nature of relationships. The participant may add additional arrows if more people involved in the case come to mind, and they may move arrows to indicate changes in the dynamics of the case over time (the researcher would then draw around the relevant arrows and note that they had been moved).

If the Pictor technique is being used within a traditional PCT framework, the interview would focus on eliciting bipolar constructs and exploring how they relate to each other. However, at Huddersfield we have used it in a more phenomenologically-oriented manner, without assuming that people's understandings are organised in such a form. The interview proceeds rather like the standard semi-structured type, but with the chart acting as the source of questions and probes. To use the technique effectively it is important that questioning is strongly anchored to the chart; more abstract or general questions should flow from responses elicited from discussion of material included on the chart. Box 10.3 shows an example of a Pictor case from the Huddersfield community nurses study, including the chart, an extract from the interview, and a summary of key findings from it.

Box 10.3   Example of the use of the Pictor technique

Taken from a research project examining community nursing relationships, roles and identities in community palliative care, funded by Macmillan Cancer Support.

Pictor chart: Wynn Pearson, Community Matron, Goldborough

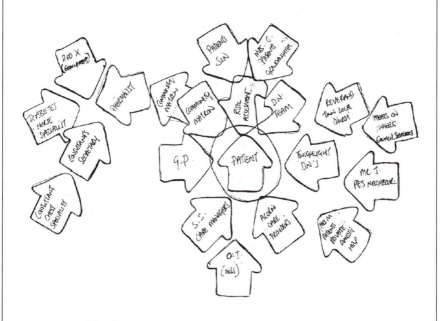

(Continued)

(Continued)

Interview extract

Wynn: I picked her (i.e. the patient) up when I started my new role back in October last year and it was quite clear she'd had a couple of hospital admissions prior to my picking her up and then her condition deteriorated so it became quite clear she'd be somebody that would be palliative.

Interviewer: How did you get her – how did you get the referral?

Wynn: I got the referral from the GP.

Interviewer: And you've pointed him (i.e. his arrow) towards you, no towards the patient, in this outer circle.

Wynn: Yes, I've done that because he – 'he' was a 'she' actually – she is such a lovely GP and she did such a lot of home visits.

Case summary

Margaret was a woman in her late 70s with Chronic Obstructive Pulmonary Disease (COPD) and diabetes who had been on Wynn's caseload for several months. When she took Margaret on, she was already receiving a care package from social services, including Home Carers from a private agency, and Occupational Therapy input. Soon her condition began deteriorating and it became necessary for Wynn to involve other agencies – especially as the patient lived on her own and was adamant that she did not want to go into hospital or a hospice. Wynn made numerous joint visits with the GP, and brought in the district nursing team along with the 'twilight' team, who provide nursing support for the early evening period. She also liaised with a range of other agencies, including the acute sector, pharmacists and social services. As Margaret's health worsened, Wynn was required to carry out a risk assessment, to enable the involvement of social care staff to continue.

Wynn's work with this patient also involved interaction with her family and friends. Her son and his daughter were in regular contact with her by telephone. They lived a long way away, and Wynn describes them as 'extremely caring' but also commented that 'they didn't drop everything and come down, so it's a bit of a strange relationship'. Wynn realised that Margaret was concealing the severity of her illness from her family, and persuaded her to be more open with them so that proper arrangements could be set up for communication between all parties in case of an emergency. In supporting the patient, Wynn was able to rely on the help of Brian, a neighbour who, although over 80 himself, proved very reliable in checking up on Margaret every day. Another old friend, Jenny (who had previously been employed for many years by Margaret as a cleaner), also called in regularly. The local vicar from the church where Margaret attended a luncheon club visited once; Wynn describes him as 'a very nice chap'.

In the end, after several falls, Margaret was admitted to hospital with heart failure. She died within 48 hours. Although Wynn and the other agencies had not been able to keep her at home until the very end, she was pleased that they had managed to prevent admission for as long as they did. Wynn attended the funeral and the family expressed gratitude for meeting Margaret's wishes as well as possible.

On her Pictor chart, Wynn placed what she referred to as an 'inner' and an 'outer circle' of those directly involved in helping and supporting the patient – the distinction indicating the regularity and closeness of involvement. She used two over-lapping arrows to show herself both closely supporting the patient, and reaching out to a separate cluster of agencies whose input she needed to coordinate but who did not directly contact the patient: the pharmacist, equipment hire service, diabetic spe-cialist nurse, and Consultant chest specialist (accessed via his secretary). The circle she chose to draw around the 'patient' arrow emphasises Margaret as the centre of all this activity.

Data produced from Pictor interviews may be analysed using whichever thematic approach is most appropriate to your study. If you are taking a phenomenological approach, the kind of idiographic analysis used in Interpretative Phenomenological Analysis could be used, as could template analysis. For a larger-scale evaluation study, a matrix approach might be most suitable (see below for IPA and Chapter 9 for a detailed discussion of types of thematic analysis). Whatever method you choose, it is important that you attend closely to how the arrows are used (and what participants say about their use) as well as what they say more directly about the subject matter under investigation. Thus in the example used in Box 10.3, the participant describes how her placement of the GP's arrow indicated her positive view of this person's involvement with the placement. Elsewhere in the interview she explains how the groupings on the chart of an inner circle, an outer circle and a small grouping set away from the rest reflect aspects of her experience of how different people were engaged with her in the case. Given the necessity to pay close attention to the way a chart is used, we would recommend that you have it in front of you alongside the interview transcript while you are carrying out your analysis.

One final word of warning about the interpretation of Pictor data is necessary. It can be very tempting – especially for a researcher with a background in more positivistic research – to try to draw conclusions from patterns in the charts themselves, without reference to the interview material. For instance, if one group of participants consistently used more arrows than another, you might be tempted to conclude that the former had wider or more complex patterns of relationships than the latter. To make such an assumption is problematic because it treats the charts as if they were something akin to a psychological test score, revealing some stable, internal characteristics of the persons producing them. But the charts are actually stimuli for reflection in the interview, produced for a particular purpose in a particular context – they do not constitute 'the data' in and of themselves. Patterns across cases should certainly attract your attention, and should be investigated in your analysis of the interview data. They may turn out to indicate meaningful and important differences within your sample – or they may not. It is only through a full analysis of the data that you can come to a conclusion.

The Salmon Line

Personal change is a key concern of PCT, and many of its clinical methods are concerned with helping people to consider how they might alter unhelpful ways of seeing themselves and their world in order to act differently in future. As change is a key element of many research studies, such methods are of great potential value to researchers. The 'Salmon Line' was developed by Phil Salmon to elicit personal constructs and help people reflect on how their construing could change (Salmon, 1994, 2003). The technique involves presenting participants with a straight line marked on a large piece of paper (or on a whiteboard or similar). The two poles of a bipolar construct are then written at either end of the line. Participants are then asked to put elements on the line, in positions corresponding to how each is seen in relation to the construct. As with repertory grids, the elements will usually be individual people, but can also represent dyads or groups of people, or different versions of the self (e.g. 'how I am now', 'how I would like to be'). Participants can then be interviewed, using the elements' positions on the line as the starting point for questioning.

Salmon first used the line in the context of educational research. As part of a project examining collaborative models of learning, Salmon and Claire (1984) compared Design Technology teachers' and their pupils' understandings of what constituted ability in the subject. The teachers placed their pupils on a Salmon Line running from 'very low ability' to 'greatest possible ability' at the subject. They were then questioned about how they explained the different rankings, what less able pupils could do to move 'up' the line, and so on. Pupils then carried out a similar task, placing themselves on the line in relation to a selection of their classmates. Comparisons of the two groups showed that they had very different understandings of the basis of ability and the possibility of change. The teachers focused on individual creativity and imagination, which they saw as potentially available to everyone. In contrast, the pupils focused on technical skill and in particular the quality of the final artefacts produced in class. They tended to see ability as largely inborn, and accepted stereotypical views of boys' innate superiority to girls (Salmon, 2003).

The Salmon Line is a flexible tool that can be used in any number of settings. It can also be used effectively in combination with other interview-based techniques. Angela Ross used it in combination with a version of the Pictor technique to look at how district nurses and social workers understood each other's roles in collaborative working (Ross, 2005; Ross et al., 2005). Participants first produced a Pictor chart illustrating their perceptions of different professionals' roles in a particular community health case, and discussed this in a related interview. They were then given a Salmon Line with the poles 'poor team working' and 'good team working' marked on it, and asked to place markers for each person included on the Pictor chart on the line in a position to represent how effectively they worked with that person. These placements were then discussed further, and in particular participants were asked to consider what would need to change in order for specific working relationships to move further towards the positive pole of the line. An example of a Salmon Line from this study is shown in Box 10.4.

Box 10.4   Example of a Salmon Line

The case used here was provided by Maxine, a district nurse (senior community nurse with team leadership responsibilities). It involved a patient with complex and serious health problems, including multiple sclerosis and diabetes, who was receiving support from a wide range of health and social care agencies. Maxine identified the construct 'Poor team working ⇒ Good team working' as a key one in her experience of this case. The interviewer asked her to write down the two pole descriptions at either end of a line on a large sheet of paper representing the construct. Then she placed markers on the line to represent each of the professionals she had contact with in the case, and how she saw them in relation to the construct.

The resultant diagram served as a stimulus for further discussion: the interviewer questioned Maxine about why she placed each person where she did, what led to one being further up (or down) the Salmon Line than another, and finally what she thought could be done to move some of those at the 'poor' end of the construct towards the 'good' end. You can see that she perceived the podiatrist to have demonstrated the best team-working because she shared a 'common perspective' with her and because the podiatrist was always quick to follow up in response to patient needs. The hospital wards showed the poorest team working because Maxine perceived them to lack any understanding of how community teams functioned. For further details of this study, see Ross et al. (2005).

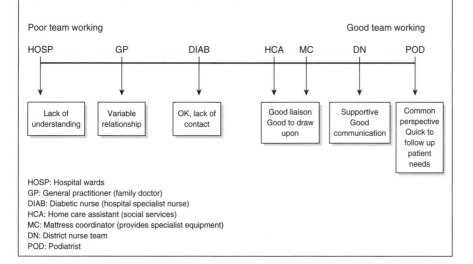

HOSP: Hospital wards
GP: General practitioner (family doctor)
DIAB: Diabetic nurse (hospital specialist nurse)
HCA: Home care assistant (social services)
MC: Mattress coordinator (provides specialist equipment)
DN: District nurse team
POD: Podiatrist

In keeping with Umoquit et al.'s (2008) recent findings, the use of graphical methods to stimulate reflection on lived experience – such as the Salmon Line and Pictor – has proved to be both effective in terms of data quality and popular with participants. These techniques derived from PCT can readily be incorporated into phenomenological interviews to help deepen understanding of certain aspects of participants' perceptions and experiences.

Analysing phenomenological data

In the final section of this chapter we will look at how data produced from phenomenological interviews may be analysed. We will focus here on two of the best-known and most widely used techniques, which illustrate some of the key distinctions between descriptive and interpretative approaches: Giorgi's method (Giorgi, 1985; Giorgi and Giorgi, 2008) and Smith's Interpretative Phenomenological Analysis (IPA) (Smith, 1996; Smith and Osborn, 2008). We recognise that there are many other variants of phenomenological analysis, and refer you to Langdridge (2007) for wide coverage of many of them.

Giorgi's descriptive method

The method of analysis developed by Giorgi and colleagues, principally at Duquesne University, USA, draws closely on Husserl's philosophy. It seeks to provide the analyst with a method to describe the essential features of any given phenomenon experienced by research participants. It progresses in four stages to produce what it refers to as a 'structural description' of the phenomenon in question.

Stage one: reading through the transcript
Because phenomenological analysis should be holistic, it is vital that you read through a transcript in full at least once before carrying out any further analytic steps. Throughout the subsequent process, the analysis of specific aspects of the data must always be carried out in the context of an awareness of the participant's whole account.

Stage two: defining meaning units
Here, the entire text of the transcript is divided into 'meaning units', defined to indicate every point at which the researcher identifies a transition in meaning in the account. Giorgi emphasises that this is a pragmatic step, aiming to help the researcher in the transformation of the data and production of a structural description. As such, it does not matter that two analysts might define units somewhat differently; what *is* important is that the definition is based on apparent meaning rather than any attempt to apply an 'objective' grammatical rule to the task (e.g. defining units in terms of clauses, sentences or paragraphs). While striving to avoid imposing any theoretical ideas on the

task of defining units, it is appropriate for you to be particularly sensitive to issues broadly relevant to your discipline. So, a psychologist might define units somewhat differently from a sociologist working with the same material. Similarly, the phenomenon that the research is seeking to elucidate may legitimately guide your process of meaning unit definition. Box 10.5 shows an extract from an interview (on the experience of seeing a ghost), divided into meaning units.

Box 10.5   Example of division into meaning units

This extract is from an interview carried out by the first author with a woman in her 50s (given the pseudonym 'Frances') on her experience of seeing a ghost in her childhood. Double slashes (//) indicate where meaning units have been distinguished.

Frances: Yeah, my mother was definitely in the house. // It was early morning so I don't know whether my Dad had left for work or not, // my recollection is that I went down to breakfast and my mother was there, and my brother – who's younger than me – // um, I've got two older sisters who would have been at secondary school at that time and so would have left earlier. // I certainly don't remember them being around, // but it's like a long time ago and I remember the incident, that's what sticks in my mind, rather than...// I was trying to think who was around. // But that's my recollection, that my mother and my younger brother were downstairs in the house, but that I think the others had gone to work or to school. // So I was upstairs // and as far as I recall [p] I would, the um...// It was an old house we lived in and it was a strange SHAPE, so the er bathroom was too small to have a washbasin in so there was a washbasin that was sort of just a bit cordoned off from the rest of my parents' bedroom, // so I would have been along there anyway // we'd all have been along there at various stages to get washed in the morning. // So my recollection is that it was fairly routine for me to be brushing my hair in their bedroom, in front of their dressing table mirror, rather than anywhere else. //

Nigel: Right, so this is like part of your, would be part of your normal *schoolday routine?*

Frances: [talking over] *schoolday routine,* getting up type of thing. // Um and my recollection is that I was brushing my hair, // and for some reason, um [p] I turned sort of just like if this was the mirror there, I turned towards that direction...[indicates direction]

Nigel: To your right?

(Continued)

(Continued)

Frances: To my right. // Um, no idea particularly why, and I guess if I hadn't seen anything [*laughing tone to voice*] I wouldn't even have recollected having done that, probably just a movement that I happened to make. // And that was when I saw this // – whatever it was. I mean it was only a part of a person, // I recall that it sort of faded away from the sort of chest upwards [Nigel: yeah] and from sort of lower body downwards. And from one side, // so all I saw was this part of what looked like some kind of a dark jacket, // I don't recall sort of the details of it. //

Stage three: transformation

Once the meaning units are defined, they go through one or more stages of transformation, through which the researcher tries to assess what each unit might suggest about the nature of the phenomenon under investigation. This involves considering each unit in the context of the transcript as a whole and summarising what it reveals about the phenomenon. In doing this, you try to move away from the specific instance captured in the transcript towards a more general account. As Giorgi and Giorgi (2008: 44) put it, the aim is 'to go from the concrete lived situation as an example of something and clarify what it is an example of'. While the analysis at this stage will be shaped by the parameters of the research project as a whole, it must not be influenced by particular theoretical concerns.

To aid the process of abstraction from the specific example, it is normal to write the transformed units in the third person (though note that some researchers write the meaning units in the third person at stage two). During the transformation, some meaning units may prove to offer nothing to the understanding of the phenomenon, and others may need to be combined to enable a fruitful understanding to be achieved. You should progress cautiously in transforming the data, aware of the danger that you might allow your own assumptions to lead you to making judgements about meanings that are not fully grounded in the text itself. For this reason, there are often two or more stages of transformation, as the analysis moves to a more general, abstract account. As far as the practicalities of carrying out the analysis go, it is common for meaning units to be placed in a column on a table, with transformations written in parallel to them in a further column. Tables 10.1 and 10.2 show two stages of transformation to the meaning units from the interview extract shown in Box 10.5.

Stage four: structural descriptions

The final stage of the analysis is to write a structural description of the phenomenon that has been studied. The structural description is usually a fairly short, condensed account of what is, in Giorgi's term, 'typically essential' to

Table 10.1   First transformation of meaning units

	Meaning units	First transformation
1	Yeah, my mother was definitely in the house.	F recalls that her mother and younger brother were in the house. She reasons that her dad and older sisters would already have left at the time of the incident – and certainly doesn't recollect their presence.
2	It was early morning so I don't know whether my Dad had left for work or not,	
3	my recollection is that I went down to breakfast and my mother was there, and my brother – who's younger than me –	
4	um, I've got two older sisters who would have been at secondary school at that time and so would have left earlier.	
5	I certainly don't remember them being around	
6	but it's like a long time ago and I remember the incident, that's what sticks in my mind, rather than…	F recalls the incident of seeing the apparition clearly – more so than the surrounding circumstances; she states that it was a long time ago.
7	I was trying to think who was around.	F repeats her recollections of who was present in the house at the time.
8	But that's my recollection, that my mother and my younger brother were downstairs in the house, but that I think the others had gone to work or to school.	
9	So I was upstairs	F states she was upstairs.
10	and as far as I recall [p] I would, the um…	F describes the layout of the upstairs of the house, to explain why there was a washbasin in her parents' room instead of the bathroom.
11	It was an old house we lived in and it was a strange SHAPE, so the er bath-room was too small to have a wash-basin in so there was a washbasin that was sort of just a bit cordoned off from the rest of my parents' bedroom,	
12	so I would have been along there anyway	She presents it as 'normal' for her to be in her parents' room at this time, empha-sising this by stating that all the family would have used the washbasin in a morning. It was likewise normal for her to brush her hair in the room. She describes these actions as part of her regular schoolday routine rather than a specific recollection of the incident itself.
13	we'd all have been along there at vari-ous stages to get washed in the morning.	
14	So my recollection is that it was fairly routine for me to be brushing my hair in their bedroom, in front of their dressing table mirror, rather than anywhere else.	
15	[talking over] schoolday routine, getting up type of thing.	

(Continued)

Table 10.1   (Continued)

	Meaning units	First transformation
16	Um and my recollection is that I was brushing my hair,	She now specifically recollects the run-up to the incident; brushing her hair and turning away from the dressing table mirror to look to the right, for a reason she cannot recall. She physically demonstrates this – suggesting the clarity of her memory.
17	and for some reason, um [p] I turned sort of just like if this was the mirror there, I turned towards that direction… [indicates direction] N. To your right? F. To my right.	[included in cell above]
18	Um, no idea particularly why, and I guess if I hadn't seen anything [laughing tone to voice] I wouldn't even have recollected having done that, probably just a movement that I happened to make.	She is only able to recollect this sequence of actions so clearly – she suggests – because it was immediately followed by her seeing the apparition.
19	And that was when I saw this	
20	– whatever it was. I mean it was only a part of a person	She describes seeing part of a person – one side of the mid-part of the body. The missing parts she describes as fading away.
21	I recall that it sort of faded away from the sort of chest upwards [N. yeah] and from sort of lower body downwards. And from one side,	
22	so all I saw was this part of what looked like some kind of a dark jacket,	She recalls the apparition to be wearing a dark jacket, but not any detail of it.
23	I don't recall sort of the details of it.	

the phenomenon – put simply, what makes it *this* thing and not something else. Giorgi recommends that researchers strive to produce a single structural description across all cases in a project, but also makes it clear that should there not be sufficient commonality to allow this, more than one can be written. It generally becomes easier to produce a structural description the more cases you have to work with, because the greater variation in the phenomenon makes it clearer which aspects appear essential. However, it is possible (though difficult) to write a structural description for a single case.

The task of producing the structural description involves carefully reading through all the final transformations of the data, searching for commonalities that may suggest essential features. In line with Giorgi's advice, you should start with the goal of developing a single description. However, if there are aspects

Table 10.2 Second transformation of the data

	First transformation	Second transformation
1	F recalls that her mother and younger brother were in the house. She reasons that her dad and older sisters would already have left at the time of the incident – and certainly doesn't recollect their presence.	F's recollection of the apparition incident itself is vivid and detailed. Her memories of the surrounding circumstances vary in clarity. Some features she can recall quite clearly, while others she largely deduces from general recollections of family life routines at that time.
2		
3		
4		
5		
6	F recalls the incident of seeing the apparition clearly – more so than the surrounding circumstances; she states that it was a long time ago.	
7	F repeats her recollections of who was present in the house at the time.	
8		
9	F states she was upstairs.	
10	F describes the layout of the upstairs of the house, to explain why there was a washbasin in her parents' room instead of the bathroom.	
11		
12	She presents it as 'normal' for her to be in her parents' room at this time, emphasising this by stating that all the family would have used the washbasin in a morning. It was likewise normal for her to brush her hair in the room. She describes these actions as part of her regular schoolday routine rather than a specific recollection of the incident	
13		
14		
15		
16	She now specifically recollects the run-up to the incident; brushing her hair and turning away from the dressing table mirror to look to the right, for a reason she cannot recall. She physically demonstrates this – suggesting the clarity of her memory.	F recalls her actions immediately leading up to the apparition experience in detail – not because they were unusual but because of the powerful impact of the incident itself.
17	[included in cell above]	
18	She is only able to recollect this sequence of actions so clearly – she suggests – because it was immediately followed by her seeing the apparition.	
19		
20	She describes seeing part of a person – one side of the mid-part of the body. The missing parts she describes as fading away.	The startling feature of the apparition was that it was of only part of a person. The clothing it wore also made a strong impression on her.
21		
22	She recalls the apparition to be wearing a dark jacket, but not any detail of it.	
23		

that seem centrally important to the phenomenon in some cases but absent in others, two (or more) descriptions may need to be written. A structural description from the interview on 'seeing a ghost' is shown in Box 10.6.

**Box 10.6   Structural description
of experience of seeing a ghost**

Frances has a vivid and detailed image of her experience of actually seeing a ghost. The most striking aspect of this is the fact that it was not an apparition of a complete human figure but rather of part of a person. The apparition appears as an interruption to the familiar routine of a schoolday morning. It is suddenly just there, and equally suddenly disappears. Straight after the sighting, Frances feels a sense of disjuncture between her outward actions (conveying normalcy) and her inner thoughts and feelings that are dominated by the experience. In her recollection of this part of the experience she is preoccupied with the latter; she only recalls awareness of the detail of her physical surroundings at the point where she tells another person about what she has seen.

Strengths and weaknesses of the method

Giorgi's method is well supported with both methodological texts and published empirical examples to help the inexperienced researcher understand what it entails. Perhaps its greatest strength is its strong grounding in phenomenological philosophy. If followed closely, it undoubtedly facilitates a truly phenomenological orientation to the data. As an example, take Giorgi's insistence that the entire text is divided into meaning units and that the contribution of each unit to an understanding of the phenomenon is carefully considered. This part of the process reflects the phenomenological concept of *horizontalisation*, the notion that to break free of the 'natural attitude', we must start by rejecting any notion that some aspects of the phenomenon may be more important than others. We can contrast this to thematic approaches where invariably the analyst makes a judgement that some parts of the transcript data are not of interest – and are therefore not coded – at a fairly early stage in the process.

On the negative side, Giorgi's method is very time-consuming to carry out in full, and where a researcher does not have a strong theoretical interest in phenomenology *per se*, this might outweigh its strengths in terms of philosophical foundations. Also, despite the availability of published material, as noted above, it can be difficult for a newcomer to grasp what is meant in practice by the various stages – especially 'transformation' – without guidance from an experienced colleague.

Of course, Giorgi's philosophical foundations may themselves be seen as a limitation by those who feel themselves more aligned to an interpretative form of phenomenology. Such critics would argue that Giorgi's method, and others like it, fail to give proper consideration to the role of the interviewer in co-creating the account with the interviewee. Similarly, Giorgi's approach may be seen as too ready to accept that the researcher can stand aside from their own assumptions in analysing the data.

Interpretative analytical approaches have developed to address these points, and we will now turn to the most widely used of these: Smith's Interpretative Phenomenological Analysis (IPA).

Interpretative Phenomenological Analysis

Smith argues that IPA is based on a two-stage interpretation of textual (and almost always interview-based) data. First, in providing their account of the phenomenon in question, the participant is interpreting their actual lived experience for the interviewer. Second, the researcher when analysing the data is trying to interpret the participant's own interpretation. This position, which is often referred to as a 'double hermeneutic', makes explicit that the researcher can never entirely step outside their own position in producing their analysis – a view congruent with the critiques of Husserl offered by existential phenomenologists. However, unlike social constructionism (see Chapters 2 and 11), IPA does assume that what people say in an interview to some extent reflects their actual lived experience, although not in a simple and transparent fashion (Smith and Osborn, 2008). IPA (like Giorgi's descriptive method) was developed in psychology, but can be used in any disciplinary context where the researcher is concerned with understanding personal experience. IPA studies have addressed a very wide range of topics, although the method has become particularly prominent in health contexts, examining such phenomena as understandings of anorexia nervosa (Jarman et al., 1997), the experience of back pain (Smith and Osborn, 2007), and the meanings of bodily changes in pregnancy (Johnson et al., 2004).

In contrast to Giorgi's descriptive phenomenology, IPA employs a thematic style of analysis. It does not seek to be entirely prescriptive about the procedures to be followed, but generally the analysis of a single transcript follows four steps: *familiarisation with the data, identifying themes, clustering themes* and *constructing a summary table*. Except in single-case studies, a further stage is *integrating themes* across all cases once subsequent transcripts have been analysed. Note that almost invariably in IPA the first transcript is analysed in full before the researcher moves on to further transcripts.

Familiarisation with the data

As with most qualitative methods, you should begin by familiarising yourself with the data. This means reading and re-reading the transcript carefully, and noting anything that strikes you as potentially relevant to the research topic. It is conventional in IPA for such notes to be made in the left-hand margin of the transcript (margins should be set wide – around 4 cm or so – and the whole transcript double-spaced to allow plenty of room for annotation).

There are no stipulations as to what should be included in these preliminary notes. They may be paraphrases of key points made by the interviewee, possible connections you observe between different parts of the interview, queries for you to return to later as your understanding of the interview increases, and so on. It is best to keep any interpretations you are making clearly provisional; if you jump to very definite conclusions at this early stage they may blinker your further analysis.

Identifying themes

Once you have completed the first stage, you should begin to more formally define themes that characterise key aspects of the participant's experience of the phenomenon. (See Chapter 9 for a fuller discussion of what we mean by 'themes'.) Read through the transcript and your notes in the left-hand margin, and consider what light (if any) is thrown upon the nature of the participant's experience. Where you feel there is something significant and relevant there, write a short phrase that encapsulates the theme in the adjacent right-hand margin. These themes are usually defined at a somewhat more abstract level than your initial notes, and may reflect broad theoretical concerns within your discipline, but should not include concepts associated with a particular theory. For instance, if a participant said that they found it hard to make new friends, it might be appropriate to define a theme of 'relationship formation difficulties', but it would be wrong to invoke the concept 'attachment problems' because it ties your analysis specifically to attachment theory. Box 10.7 shows the first two stages of an IPA analysis of the interview on seeing a ghost that we used to illustrate Giorgi's method. As can be seen, preliminary notes are made in the right-hand margin of the transcript and emergent themes identified in the left.

Box 10.7   Example of notes and emerging themes for IPA

Preliminary notes		Emerging themes
Quite long reflection on what she remembers and why – some aspects more certain than others	Frances: Yeah, my mother was definitely in the house. It was early morning so I don't know whether my Dad had left for work or not, my recollection is that I went down to breakfast and my mother was there, and my brother – who's younger than me – um, I've got two older sisters who would have been at secondary school at that time and so would have left earlier.	Considers quality of own memories
		Shared routine
Everyday family routine		

Preliminary notes		Emerging themes
'The incident' stronger in memory than other surrounding details	I certainly don't remember them being around, but it's like a long time ago and I remember the incident, that's what sticks in my mind, rather than... I was trying to think who was around. But that's my recollection, that my mother and my younger brother were downstairs in the house, but that I think the others had gone to work or to school. So I was upstairs and as far as I recall [p] I would, the um... It was an old house we lived in and it was a strange SHAPE, so the er bathroom was too small to have a washbasin in so there was a washbasin that was sort of just a bit cordoned off from the rest of my parents' bedroom, so I would have been along there anyway we'd all have been along there at various stages to get washed in the morning. So my recollection is that it was fairly routine for me to be brushing my hair in their bedroom, in front of their dressing table mirror, rather than anywhere else.	Incident recalled vividly
		Contextual details less vivid
Locates herself		
		Defines location
Describes house – old, strange shape – explains layout of room where apparition is seen		
		Describes setting
		Qualities of setting – old, strange shape
Routine for her to be brushing hair here		
Confirms it as a routine schoolday		Routine morning activities – own and shared
Describes own precise movements prior to apparition		
Not sure why she turned to right	*Nigel*: Right, so this is like part of your, would be part of your normal *schoolday routine*? *Frances*: [talking over] *schoolday routine*, getting up type of thing. Um and my recollection is that I was brushing my hair, and for some reason, um [p] I turned sort of just like if this was the mirror there, I turned towards that direction...[*indicates direction*]	Own actions prior to ghost experience.
Probably only recalls this because then immediately saw the apparition		

(Continued)

(Continued)

Preliminary themes		Emerging notes
Precise point where saw apparition – suggests uncertainty re what it was	*Nigel*: To your right?	
Only part of person	*Frances*: To my right. Um, no idea particularly why, and I guess if I hadn't seen anything [*laughing tone to voice*] I wouldn't even have recollected having done that, probably just a movement that I happened to make. And that was when I saw this – whatever it was. I mean it was only a part of a person, I recall that it sort of faded away from the sort of chest upwards [*Nigel*: yeah] and from sort of lower body downwards. And from one side, so all I saw was this part of what looked like some kind of a dark jacket, I don't recall sort of the details of it.	Reflects on own memory process
Recalls what it wore, though not in detail		Incident recalled vividly
		Anomaly in routine
		Physical description of apparition
		Unusual quality – partial person
		Clothing
		Limits to recollection

Clustering themes and producing a summary table

Identifying a comprehensive set of themes that covers everything you feel is important in the transcript may well require you to work through the preliminary annotations several times, refining your definitions as your understanding of the account deepens. Once you feel you have achieved this, you should compile a list of all the themes you have defined, and look for meaningful clusters of themes that address related issues. As you do this, you will often find that some of the themes you initially proposed overlap with each other to such an extent that it makes little sense to retain them as discrete entities. You may then merge them, using whichever definition seems most helpful or a new definition that embraces them both (or them all, if you are merging three or more themes). Each cluster of themes is then given a suitable title that summarises the commonalities among its constituent themes, and as a final step in the single case analysis, the clusters – now referred to as 'superordinate themes' – are organised on a table in a coherent order that can be used to help structure your write-up of the findings. You should provide page and line references to the original transcript to show where examples of each themes may be found. At this last stage you should still be critically considering the themes you have included. You may decide that some further redefinition is required, or that some themes can be dropped entirely because they add little to the goal of producing a full and rich understanding of the topic. Box 10.8 shows the thematic clusters for the interview on seeing a ghost, while Box 10.9 presents the final table of themes relating to this interview extract.

Box 10.8   Clustering themes in IPA: analysis of interview on seeing a ghost

Here the list of emergent themes (in the right-hand margin in Box 10.7) is organised into clusters that seem to meaningfully belong together.

Considers quality of own memories
Incident recalled vividly, contextual details less vivid
Reflects on own memory process
Incident recalled vividly
Limits to recollection

Defines location
Describes setting
Qualities of setting – old, strange shape

Routine morning activities – personal and shared
Anomaly in routine

Own actions prior to ghost experience
Physical description of apparition
Unusual quality – partial person
Clothing

Box 10.9   Tabulating themes in IPA: analysis of interview on seeing a ghost

The clusters from Box 10.8 are now provided with titles, defining superordinate themes. Some of the subordinate themes are now redefined to improve the clarity of the analysis in the light of further reflection by the analyst.

(Continued)

(Continued)

Participant's reflections on own memory process
Considering quality of own memories
Incident recalled vividly, contextual details less vivid
Limits to recollection

The setting of the experience
Defining own location
Describing setting
Qualities of setting – old, strangely shaped house

Apparition experience as disruption to the ordinary
Routine morning activities – personal and shared
Sudden anomaly in routine

Intregrating themes across cases

IPA studies may involve just a single case (e.g. Eatough and Smith, 2006), but more often they involve multiple cases, with around 6–10 participants being typical. For these studies, the final stage of analysis is to integrate themes across the data set as a whole. Researchers may analyse each interview transcript individually, following the process described above, and only then begin to look for commonalities across cases. Or they may take at least some of the themes defined in the first case as a starting point to analysing the following transcripts – a procedure similar to that used in template analysis (King, 2004b; see also Chapter 9). Either way, the final task involves looking closely at the tables of themes identified in each individual case and grouping these together on what is known as the 'Master table' for the study as a whole. Again, during this process you might become aware of limitations in your earlier analysis and need to go back and work further on some of those themes.

Strengths and weaknesses of the method

The growing popularity of IPA over the past decade can be attributed in part to the clear procedures it offers for those interested in exploring personal lived experience in depth. It is sparing in its use of the kind of specialist philosophical terms that can make other phenomenological methods rather opaque for those unfamiliar with the underpinning philosophy. Furthermore, there are many good methodological texts describing the method and examples of empirical work available in the literature. Another strength for some researchers is that it presents itself as complementary to other traditions in psychology, rather than as standing in overt opposition to them. This contrasts with the discursive approaches (examined further in Chapter 11) that emerged as a strong critique of mainstream social psychology. With a growing interest in many disciplines in multi-method research based on a pragmatic recognition of the differing contributions of different methods, IPA has much to offer. Finally, within the range of phenomenological methods, IPA offers scope for reflexive consideration of the role of the researcher in the interpretative process, and is therefore attractive to those who feel this is not adequately addressed in descriptive approaches.

In many respects, the strengths and weaknesses of IPA are the inverse of those we highlighted for Giorgi's method. Thus, while the latter is very strongly grounded in its philosophical roots, for many critics IPA's connection with phenomenological thought is rather loose. The strongest criticisms have been levelled at the way IPA claims to be dealing with 'cognition' – the way people think about themselves and their experience – because this appears to reinstate the dualistic separation of mind and body that phenomenology rejects. In addition, although IPA encourages reflexivity, as noted, as of yet little detailed consideration has been presented as to how this is to be achieved within the procedures offered by the method.

Conclusion

In this chapter we have sought to demonstrate that to make effective use of phenomenological methods, you need to grasp the main tenets of the philosophy that underpins them. It is not enough to simply ask a few open-ended questions about the topic you are interested in. Phenomenology makes some distinctive claims about the nature of lived experience and what we as researchers can know about it, and these feed into the ways in which phenomenological inquiry is carried out. Techniques such as imaginative variation and reflexive attention to embodiment can add real depth to phenomenological interviews, and some of the innovative methods devised in Personal Construct Theory can be incorporated into a phenomenological study in very fruitful ways.

We have emphasised that phenomenology is not a monolithic tradition – there are a range of different strands of thought within it that have different implications for research practice. If you are planning a phenomenological study, you need to at least recognise the broad distinction between descriptive and interpretative approaches, as your position in relation to these may influence aspects of interview technique as well as the kind of analysis you carry out. For instance, including written descriptions as part of the interview process is especially useful in descriptive phenomenology, while a strong emphasis on reflexivity is required in interpretative approaches in order to attend to the co-construction of meaning between interviewer and interviewee.

We have warned before of the danger of taking a 'cookbook' approach to qualitative research, in which methodological guidelines are followed in an inflexible fashion. This applies very strongly to phenomenological research, where the task is to obtain something as close as possible to another person's way of perceiving the world. To do this, the way you design and carry out interviews, and the way you analyse the transcripts, must respond to the particularities of each encounter between interviewer and interviewee. The methods we have discussed in this chapter should be seen as a starting point for achieving this goal, drawing on collective wisdom of many other researchers and writers in the field. As you increase your understanding of phenomenology, you should become more confident in adapting them to the needs of your own research.

Recommended reading

Finlay, L. (2006) The body's disclosure in phenomenological research. *Qualitative Research in Psychology*, 3 (1): 19–30.
An interesting account of how to utilise an awareness of embodiment within the context of a qualitative research interview.

Giorgi, A. and Giorgi, B. (2008) Phenomenology, in J.A. Smith (ed.), *Qualitative Psychology: A Practical Guide to Research Methods* (2nd edition). London: Sage.
A clear explanation of Giorgi's descriptive phenomenological method.

Langdridge, D. (2007) *Phenomenological Psychology: Theory, Research and Method.* Harlow: Pearson.
A very good introduction to key concepts in phenomenology, and the most wide-ranging presentation of different phenomenological methods currently available in a single volume.

Smith, J.A. and Osborn, M. (2008) Interpretative phenomenological analysis, in J.A. Smith (ed.), *Qualitative Psychology: A Practical Guide to Research Methods* (2nd edition). London: Sage.
An accessible, practical guide to using this popular form of phenomenological analysis.

Spinelli, E. (2005) *The Interpreted World: An Introduction to Phenomenological Psychology* (2nd edition). London: Sage.
Much less coverage of research methods than the Langdridge book, but a lively and informative introduction to the theory that underpins them.

ELEVEN

Interviews and Narrative

Narrative theorising has its roots in literary studies but is increasingly assuming considerable recognition in the social sciences. Possibly, this recognition is long overdue as narration, the telling of stories, is a 'basic human activity' (McLeod, 1997: 29) with examples going back to biblical times and contemporary usage evident in novels, TV and even gossip. The fundamental significance of narrative in relation to qualitative interviewing is made explicit by Mishler (1986), who explains that narration is how people express their understandings of events and experiences. The point he makes is that when engaged in conversation with one another we automatically tell stories, and thus the qualitative interview is a site of endless possibilities. While such ideas appear patently understandable, a note of caution should be offered. The field of narrative inquiry in the social sciences is broad and complex, spanning the study of sociolinguistics, identity, social action, culture and aesthetics. It is therefore all too easy to become overwhelmed with the abundance of paths you might take when embracing narrative ideas. For this reason, alongside giving practical information on narrative interviewing, we spend considerable time in this chapter engaging with theoretical debates that offer different ways of understanding both human experience and the qualitative interview process.

- experience and narrative knowing
- discourse and narrative
- narrative configuration
- modes of narrative interviewing
- models of narrative analysis

Experience and narrative knowing

Sitting firmly within the interpretivist tradition, narrative has been characterised as a 'way of knowing' concerned with how we make sense of our lives (Reissman, 1993; Hatch and Wisniewski, 1995). Jerome Bruner's (1986, 1990) work has, without doubt, been influential in shaping the assimilation of narrative ideas into the social sciences. He distinguished between two types of knowing: *paradigmatic knowing* and *narrative knowing*. Paradigmatic knowing is rooted in scientific, positivist modes of thought, representing the world through abstract propositional knowledge based upon categorisation and classification. Conversely, narrative knowing is a fundamental means through which people come to understand themselves, organising interpretations of the world in storied form (Murray, 2003).

Bruner's view is that both paradigmatic and narrative ways of knowing are essential features of the human capacity to make sense of the world. Yet, in attempting to be scientific, social scientists have concentrated on paradigmatic, propositional knowledge with narrative knowing occupying a marginal space. Indeed, until quite recently narrative knowing had been dismissed as subjective, vague, immaterial and somehow lacking in legitimacy. Sarbin (1986: 8) and others (Polkinghorne, 1995; Freeman, 1997; Mishler, 1999) have brought about a transformation, showing how 'human beings think, perceive, imagine and make moral choices according to narrative structures'. Narrative, says Sarbin, is 'an organizing principle for human action' that enables people to impose some sort of structure on their everyday experiences. The obvious explanation for why we tell stories is therefore that we understand, describe and bring order to the disorder of everyday experience using narrative. Without the ability to narrate, it would be difficult to comprehend how we could secure a sense of continuity and familiarity in our daily lives.

Life as lived, life as told

The notion of narration invokes a degree of concern for social researchers around the authenticity of an account. To what extent is the narrative being told a 'truthful' account of events and experiences? Narrative and its relationship with actual experience can be explored in more depth if we consider *life as lived* and *life as told*. Narrative accounts might simply represent actual experience, recreating and reproducing events and experiences as they occurred; thus they portray life as lived. Alternatively, when we take a more 'constructivist' position we become aware of how retelling or reflection on events brings about a change. Constructivism, as Burr (2003: 19) makes clear, sees the person 'as actively engaged in the creation of their own phenomenal world'. Take, for example, meeting a friend for coffee. They ask how your day is going. Do you engage in telling exact events as they occurred? Of course not. Even if we could remember the unfolding action as it occurred, who would be interested in such a telling? The 'story' of your day is life as told, being narrated in a way that transforms life as lived into a meaningful and interesting account (version) of you and your experiences. This version of events is not necessarily accurate in a realist sense. Rather, we have edited our lives in ways that make sense to us, have value, possibly enhancing our understandings of who we are.

Polkinghorne (1996: 82) explains that 'narrative knowing is one of the mental activities that structures and orders elements of experience so that they appear in awareness as meaningful and related'. The point being made is that as human beings we are always actively engaged in creating meaningful and related stories. Evidence for this can be found in very early research. Michotte (1943/1963) asked participants to describe the movements of small triangles on a screen. What he inadvertently discovered was that participants could not resist humanising the triangles and telling stories about them, for example: 'It is as if A's approach frightened B and B ran away'. Thus we narratively organise even the most inane interactions and facets of our lives. While life as lived is incessant, confusing and ambiguous, narrative knowing is an artful structuring of these experiences, enabling us to make meaningful connections. The challenge for the narrative interviewer is to encourage and enable such connections to come into view. As we will see later in this chapter, there are variations around why and how this is achieved.

Discourse and narrative

In our society we give meaning to events by describing them with words. Without language our communication would be minimal and we wouldn't be able to share knowledge or develop collective ways of seeing/construct-ing the world. Indeed, our knowledge never objectively reflects the external reality; it is always a creation (a construction) that is brought into being through language. When we engage in narration we are using language to con-struct and represent events and experiences. Therefore, narrative approaches can be situated within a more general shift towards language-based research, often referred to as *textual* or *discursive* approaches. Discursive, language-based approaches are broadly rooted within social constructionism briefly discussed in Chapter 2. As might be expected, social constructionism oper-ates with what is referred to as a 'linguistic ontology', exploring the ways in which language is actively involved in the construction of reality. Discourses are sets of statements that bring phenomena into view. For example, the term 'Size 0' not only denotes clothing size, it is a phrase that is now used to refer to a set of wider concerns around eating behaviour. The term has successfully brought into view a set of discourses which are often focused upon refuting the emphasis on slender and thin bodies as the expected norm. Thus, knowledge and understanding are seen as socially produced through talk, with reality inevitably constituted through shared discursive resources. By this, we mean sets of statements, ways of talking that are available in our world.

Within this textual, social constructionist domain the stories we tell, the ways we narrate our lives, are infused with the power and knowledge made available by existing discourses. Taking up the previous example of the 'Size 0' discourse, a young woman who is extremely thin might feel it necessary to narrate her life in a particular way resisting being characterised as 'anorexic'. The young woman is fully aware of the discourses that construct being overly thin as dangerous and highly suspect and therefore she mobilises alternative discourses of sporting activity and healthy eating to avoid being located within more negative discourses. However, we have earlier implied that life as told has a constructivist rather than constructionist ontological quality. Of use here is the following distinction made by Gergen and Gergen (1991: 79):

...a constructivist approach tends to lead inward. For, if there is no exit from personal subjectivity, then we find individuals looking back at themselves. ... In contrast, a social constructionist view invites the investigator outward – into the fuller realm of shared language.

When making this observation Gergen and Gergen were engaged in a debate about reflexivity, but the explanation has relevance in relation to narration. While it is possible to take a constructivist position, concentrating on how people internally create their world, this might neglect the influence of wider cultural and historical meanings that exist out in the social world (such as the Size 0). With the inclusion of a textually based appreciation of narrative knowing, the narrator is positioned within a wider cultural context where certain ways of telling and understandings prevail. These are challenging ideas and it is possible to gain an understanding of the narrative study of lives without delving too much into the complexities of textual based approaches. But, in our view, this omission would narrow the field of possibilities both in terms of knowledge generation and developing methodological justification for narrative interviewing. Therefore, we try to offer a necessarily selective passageway into the often taxing yet stimulating world of linguistics and discursive methodologies. In doing so we strive to show how narratives are themselves 'accumulating constructions' (Andrews et al., 2000) formulated through language.

Structuralism and poststructuralism

The argument for both structuralism and poststructuralism is that we can know nothing except through the mediation of language and, accordingly, language should be the central focus when studying the world. Beginning with structuralism, the structural linguist Ferdinand de Saussure (1857–1913) explained language as a system of 'signs' with a particular structure and specific rules of operation. Taking on board such ideas requires an acceptance that meaning is to be found within the structure of a whole language system rather than in the analysis of individual words. The structure of language, and its referential system, is what circumscribes our world, rather than a pre-existent or essential reality (see Burr, 2003, for a comprehensive explanation). In this theoretical arena, individuals are shaped by sociological, psychological and linguistic structures over which they have no control. The structure of language precedes us; it is what divides up our experience.

Taking these complex ideas further, structuralism introduces the idea of the 'subject' rather than the more familiar idea of the individual. The term 'subject' helps us to think of human reality as a construction, being the product of signifying systems that are both culturally specific and generally unconscious. The conventional conceptualisation of the 'inner' stable and agentive self is found to be no more than part of the existing structures that constitute our world. The self, like all other things, is signified and culturally constructed. Structuralism then leads us to see everything as 'textual', being constituted through signs and structured conventions. One of the first methods of narrative analysis, which we return to later, was structural – developed by William Labov and colleagues (Labov and Waletsky, 1967).

Michel Foucault (1926–84), often referred to as a poststructuralist, agreed that language and society were shaped by rule-governed systems, but he disagreed with the structuralists in very fundamental ways. Foucault did not subscribe to the view that there were definite underlying structures. For him, the meanings purveyed through language are not fixed, but rather are open to question, temporary and ever-changing. Fundamental to this analysis is the view that discourse and power are ultimately inseparable, with discursive meanings being continually negotiated and realised in complex power relations. For Foucault, power is not confined to obvious institutions or individuals and not only acts to hierarchically repress, but is dispersed across many discursive locations. For example, children are often portrayed as lacking in power. However, within their own social locations they are able to mobilise certain discursive resources. What parent has not succumbed to children who successfully utilised the powerful discourse of guilt when being asked to buy yet another 'must have' item? Also consider how parenting was once set within a discourse of discipline and control whereas contemporary parenting is now located within a discourse of equality, opportunity and mutual respect. Therefore, while discursive practices act to legitimate and uphold particular worldviews, these are always open to question and can change over time.

Poststructuralism, then, is opposed to a realist ideology that suggests signifying systems are stable and unproblematic representations of the world. Instead, language plays an active role in the meaning-making process, with negotiation, contradiction and conflict inevitably occurring. Tensions around the impact of dominant discourses (versions of reality) can be seen throughout the breadth of social life, with race, gender, education and age, for example, all discursively constructed. It would be hard to overstate the importance of language as a resource with which we bring into being particular versions of reality. Therefore, when we narratively present versions of events we mobilise and draw upon familiar but constantly shifting discursive, cultural resources. Thus the narrative study of lives is part of this critical language-based approach in the social sciences, having implications not only for qualitative interviewing but also for how we understand human experience.

The narrated self

In accordance with a textual appreciation of life, Brockmeier and Carbaugh (2001) tell us that with narrative, concerns are moved from the internal work-ings of the mind to the 'discursive arena'. While this change in emphasis might exist, it should not foreshadow the many tensions and variants that prevail in the field. Poststructural conceptions of text, and the potential for textually based approaches to represent people's actual lives, have been widely ques-tioned. Reducing the individual to a language-based construction appears offensive, failing to comply with our sense of reflexive agency (our belief that we are in control of our lives). Nikolas Rose (1998) considers this issue, exploring how we seek to account for the self in terms of narrative – the stories we tell one another and ourselves. Drawing upon Gergen and Gergen (1988), he explains how we have available culturally-provided stories, or social constructions, about lives and how they unfold. It is through these narratives that we make ourselves intelligible with coherent and unified identities.

Even so, having suggested that the self is made and maintained in a discursive arena, there are those who offer a more internalised, agentive, reflexive account. Here, the story metaphor has taken on a sometimes disarmingly simple but nonetheless powerful meaning in relation to identity and selfhood. McAdams (1985) tells of how an individual's life story has the power to tie together past, present and future, providing a sense of coherence and sameness across situations. In this account, then, self-identity is conceived as an internalised life story that evolves and develops across the life course. It is through the process of actively putting together aspects of our lives into story form that we become fully aware of our lives. Indeed, the life story is seen as a central facet of who people know themselves to be. The life story can take many forms, being factual, metaphorical, poetic or told in other creative ways. Hence, it is important to ensure that the story being told in the narrative interview is in the form, shape and style most comfortable for the person doing the telling. The importance of this lies in appreciating that life story narratives, if enabled to flow from the teller, include how the individual has come to see and understand the fundamental nature of their whole experience.

Nevertheless, these ideas can be premised on quite complex theoretical ideas. Drawing on psychodynamic notions, McAdams focuses on the mental and emotional life that lies behind the story that is being told. He suggests that particular motivational forces and structures underpin personal stories with tensions between *agency* and *communion*. Agency refers to being autonomous and in control, to being powerful and active, while communion acknowledges a striving to develop close relationships – to be part of something more. For McAdams, the personal story expresses the position adopted by the person on this agency–communion dimension. The point to note in relation to the narrated self is that the story is emergent from the person. While possibly being subject to basic motivational forces, they are nevertheless the active creator of the story that is being told.

These are profound ideas where we are asked to believe that it is through narratives that we define ourselves, being reactive and/or active agents in the describing and redescribing of our lives. Thus within the narrative domain the self can be described in a range of ways: as the product of signifying practices, a narrative construction and a reflexive life story. With this ontology (or ontologies) there is a necessity to methodologically appreciate the epistemological status of data generated in qualitative narrative interviews. Crossley (2007) suggests a 'chain of connection' between language and the experiencing 'self', where how a person thinks and experiences the world can be assumed to be associated with what they say or write. Thus, as Crossley argues, it can be claimed that narrative approaches are founded upon a realist epistemology as there is a direct relationship between what people say and how they subjectively feel, construct and make sense of their lives. Possibly this is so, but maybe a categorical realist view is too confident, having established the constructive and powerful quality of language and narrative. A compromise would be a *critical realist* position which recognises the complexity of language and reality but nonetheless acknowledges a 'relationship' between how people narrate their world and their experiences (Hollway and Jefferson, 2000).

Narrative configuration

One of the most fundamental ways in which narrative inquiry differs from other qualitative approaches is the emphasis placed on 'narrative configuration'. In mobilising this phrase, we adopt Polkinghorne's (1995: 5) usage, referring to 'the process by which happenings are drawn together and integrated into a temporally organised whole'. Fundamental to the process of organising and making sense of experiences is a 'thematic thread' which is more ordinarily referred to as a *plot*. Mattingly (2002) makes the point that 'life as lived', referred to in a previous section, lacks plot. The intergrating activity of bringing things together into an organised whole that takes on narrative meaning is called *emplotment*. In the example referred to earlier, where you met a friend for coffee, the act of editing your day into an organised telling is evidence of emplotment, as is the storying of geometric shapes in Michotte's research.

Plots often have a moral perspective, making causal connections where motives and consequences become condensed into a particular reading of events. Hence, Ricœur (1984: 41) points out the essential differentiation between narration that is merely successive, one thing after another, and narration that implies one thing because of another. Taking this further, we often emplot our stories in line with dramaturgical conventions – *romance, tragedy, comedy, satire* – which are easily recognisable by our audience. Plots often configure events into a story with a beginning, middle and an end, but *temporality* (the passing of time) can also be experienced/emplotted in many ways. For example, time can be emplotted as capable of reversing itself (as if we were back at the beginning), as repetitive (events repeating themselves), as circular (we've come full circle), as fragmented (things not fitting together) and as linear (moving forward). Indeed, linearity can be quite pervasive, invoking understandings of events taking place in a sequential order that lends itself to modernist notions of progress and working towards the attainment of new understandings. It is hard but we should not expect or assume linearity in storytelling nor should we suppose that when linearity is used it is always optimistically configured. Hence, an appreciation of emplotment as a sense-making process recognises the importance of ensuring that emplotment and temporal orderings flow from the interviewee. Allowing participants to show how they are making connections, emplotting and bringing order to their experience is a primary goal for the narrative interview.

Modes of narrative interviewing

Often generating narrative data is explained only briefly, with the theoretical background and analysis explained more comprehensively. This frequently leaves the researcher in uncharted territory, relying on tried-and-tested methods that may not necessarily be productive. Traditional good practice around developing rapport, carefully worded questioning and sensitivity to the interview context are often seen to hold the potential to facilitate people's stories. These may have the required outcome; indeed, experts in the field (Mishler, 1986; Riessman, 1993) have emphasised how interviewees are likely to naturally provide narratives in the interview situation. Nevertheless, it can be risky to assume that this will automatically happen; even experienced researchers describe occasions where their attempts to facilitate narrative accounts failed (Hollway and Jefferson, 2000; Chase, 2003). Far better to take an informed approach, acknowledging that narrative data may be generated more effectively if certain strategies are adopted. The distinctive ontological features of narrative, and their implications for human experience and meaning-making, lead us to suggest some basic pointers for narrative interviews:

- ensure that the focus of the interview remains on eliciting narratives/stories,
- provide people with time and space to make their own connections, imposing order in ways that make sense for them, and
- acknowledge the constructive nature of language and its importance in the making of narrative.

Adding to these basic pointers is Mishler's (1986) useful advice explaining that interviewing practices that empower the interviewee are more likely to facilitate the telling of stories with people speaking in their own 'voices'. For example, people need to feel that their experiences and ways of making connections can be candidly expressed and are of primary importance to our work. If the interview is to live up to such expectations, the narrative interviewer needs to be able to interact with the interviewee as a storyteller rather than someone who merely reports or answers specific questions.

We can make distinctions between generating different kinds of narratives. The narrative interview can concentrate on limited topics, therefore, eliciting narratives that are situationally motivated, such as explaining or giving an account of a certain event, situation or experience. Alternatively, the focus might be on eliciting life stories. Therefore, to accommodate the breadth of approaches available we present different strategies for narrative interviewing but these are by no means exhaustive. We specifically draw upon Free Association Narrative Interviewing (FANI) (Hollway and Jefferson, 2000), Biographic-Narrative-Interpretative Method (BNIM) (Wengraf, 2001) and McAdams' (1985, 1993) Life Story Interview to show some of the fundamental aspects of what is an incredibly diverse field of inquiry.

Free Association Narrative Interviewing

The Free Association Narrative Interviewing (FANI) method, developed by Hollway and Jefferson (2000), suggests four principles when developing questions designed to enable the interviewee to structure their own narrative account:

- Use open-ended not closed questions – the more open the better.
- Elicit stories – turning questions about given topics into storytelling invitations.
- Avoid 'why' questions as these may detract from the interviewee's own meaning-making frame.
- Follow up using interviewee's ordering and phrasing, aiming to retain the focus on their lives and their telling.

Hollway and Jefferson's research had a specific focus – engaging participants in conversations that aimed to explore the fear of crime. Following a detailed analysis of pilot interviews, they revised their interview questions to make them more open (see Box 11.1). The questions aimed to elicit concrete stories, inviting the interviewee to talk about their personal experiences. Looking back, they considered the first question to be 'insufficiently narrativised' because it remained too general, rather than requiring the interviewee to be specific about times and situations.

Box 11.1   First interview questions developed by Hollway and Jefferson (2000) aimed at eliciting narratives

1   Can you tell me about how crime has impacted on your life since you've been living here?
2   Can you tell me about unsafe situations in your life since you've been living here?
3   Can you think of something that you've read, seen or heard about recently that makes you fearful? Anything (not necessarily about crime).
4   Can you tell me about risky situations in your life since you've been living here?
5   Can you tell me about times in your life recently when you've been anxious?
6   Can you tell me about earlier times in your life when you've been anxious?
7   Can you tell me what it was like moving to this area?

Similar to Hollway and Jefferson, others advocate paying attention to situations or episodes that appear to be relevant to the focus of the research when engaged in narrative interviewing. Flick (1998) explains how in his research the interviews began with the interviewer explaining to participants that they would be asked to recount situations in which they have had certain experiences that relate to the question of the study. This preamble then prepares the interviewee, making them aware that recounting/telling stories is actively called for rather than merely tolerated. The interview questions are prepared in ways that offer 'narrative incentives', for example:

- If you look back, what was your first encounter with ... (insert the specific issues relevant to the research)? Could you please recount that situation for me?
- Could you please recount how yesterday went, and where and when you encountered ... (insert the specific issues relevant to the research)?

Flick (1998: 106–9) distinguishes between the 'narrative interview' and the 'episodic interview'. In making this distinction, he suggests that the narrative interview is mainly used in the context of biographical research, with the participant being asked to present the history of an area of interest. Episodic knowledge is linked to concrete situations and circumstances. The episode-based interview is not aiming to generate a single overall narrative but rather a number of bounded narratives are elicited. Episodic knowledge, relating to actual experience, is seen as invaluable in the research process. Moreover, the work by Flick, and Hollway and Jefferson, does clearly show how situation/event-based questioning inevitably offers a route to a meaningful appreciation of how people understand their lives through narration.

Life story interviews – variations on 'guided' questioning

The narrative study of lives can often focus on having people tell their life stories. We have already explored the idea of the 'narrated self' and how the self can be creatively storied. On the surface, the idea of a life story appears almost self-explanatory. Yet, there is passionate debate around what the terms *life story* and *life history* might imply, and different vocabularies have been developed in what has in the past been a marginalised area within academic thought and process. Goodson (1992: 6) explains that the life story is 'the story we tell about our life' and life history is 'the life story located within its historical context'. These are helpful distinctions as they make explicit how the life story is an active telling, but this can be placed within a broader cultural and historical context. There are a number of approaches to life story interviews that aim to elicit narrative accounts of people's lives. Atkinson (1998: 33) suggests that the researcher's primary role is to be a 'guide for the journey' and that this is not a journey for one but for two – the interviewee and interviewer. It is the guide's job to know what questions to ask, how to ask them and when. Therefore, in the following two sections, drawing on the work of Wengraf and McAdams, we give specific examples of how this might be achieved.

Biographic-Narrative-Interpretative Method

The Biographic-Narrative-Interpretative Method (BNIM) was developed by a group of researchers at the University of East London (see Chamberlayne et al., 2000). Wengraf (2001: 119) explains how BNIM, here aimed at gathering life stories, uses open-ended narrative interviews rather than a more conventional semi-structured approach. One of the defining features of BNIM is that the interviewer relinquishes control, aiming to allow the narrative to fully flow from the interviewee. We can only offer a very brief outline of Wengraf's work on BNIM, but we aim to show the potential of this narrative interviewing method. The BNIM posits three distinct sub-sessions, each with a specific approach to asking questions:

Sub-session 1: The interviewer initially asks a single question designed to elicit the full narrative. Once this question is asked, there should be no interruptions or helpful prompts. What follows is the exact wording suggested by Wengraf:

> I would like you to tell me your life story, all the events and experiences which were important for you.
> Start wherever you like. Please take the time you need.
> I'll listen first, I won't interrupt, I'll just take some notes for afterwards.

The interviewer is required to note down topics covered in the narration as these will be used later. The life story narration can last five or ten minutes or even hours. Once completed, there is a break (15 minutes or longer) where the interviewer can review the notes and prepare questions for the next interview sub-session.

Sub-session 2: The next sub-session aims to draw out further elaboration on the narrative already told. Importantly, only topics raised in the previous sub-session can be used and questions must be 'narrative-pointed'. There is a distinction made between questions 'pointed' at narratives, and ones that 'allow' narratives, with the latter being easily created (e.g. 'tell me more about...'). The 'narrative-pointed' questions suggested by Wengraf in Box 11.2 are closed in that they aim to encourage only responses in relation to the topic requested. Interviewees are nevertheless free to respond in ways that make sense for them, being unhindered by any substantive elaborations introduced by the interviewer. For this reason the interviewer must remain focused, developing skills that are supportive and non-directional.

Box 11.2   'Narrative-pointed' questions from Topic-notes (Wengraf, 2001: 126)

Topics in the order mentioned and in the terms uses by the interviewee		Plausible questions which only 'allow for' a narrative response but don't point very strongly to one, or indeed 'point elsewhere'	Questions 'pointed' at narrative
Father		Can you tell me more about your father? What do you think/ feel about your father?	Can you remember any event involving your father?
Mother	'angry when I was small'	What was it like?	Can you remember a situation when you were small and she was angry?
	'hit me when I wouldn't go to school'	Did you feel she was justified at the time? How did you/do you explain her behaviour? Why do you think that happened? What do you think was the result of that?	You said she hit you when you wouldn't go to school. Can you remember how that came about? Can you tell me in more detail how that happened?
Always feeling stupid		What was it like, to always feel stupid? What do you mean by 'feeling stupid'?	Can you remember any occasion on which you felt stupid?
Being in the countryside		What was good about the countryside? What sort of countryside was it like?	Can you remember anything particular that happened, any incident or occasion, while you were in the countryside?

Sub-session 3: This sub-session should always be a separate interview undertaken after a preliminary analysis of sub-sessions 1 and 2. It is important that the interviewee is aware of this time lapse and the reasons for this particular scheduling. The aim is to structure the interview so that it addresses the concerns of the interviewer. Questioning is not restricted to only narrative-pointed questions, although these may be included. Questions from the preliminary analysis, theoretical and practical points that may have arisen, are covered in this session, although, as Wengraf says, many of these concerns may have been covered in sub-sessions 1 and 2.

We have only presented a concise account of the BNIM approach and if you intend to use this method do ensure that you read Wengraf's (2001) elaborated outline. Nevertheless, it is clear that Wengraf's non-directional, unstructured guidance requires a great deal of interviewer self-discipline and may appear almost too reliant on the interviewee. The content and structure are all expected to flow from the first sub-session and this may raise concerns about interviewee engagement, the building of rapport, and so on. This should not necessarily deter you from adopting this approach, as giving people the space to express themselves can prove to be a revelation.

McAdams' Life Story Interview

McAdams (1985, 1993: 252) offers a more directive and structured approach to life story/autobiographical interviewing, where the interviewer is 'leading people through a series of questions about their life stories' (Box 11.3). We present only the first two sections of his interview schedule, aiming to provide a sense of this very structured approach to life story interviewing. However, we should point out that McAdams is very flexible in his approach and suggests adapting and extending questions to suit the particular interview situation. Nevertheless, rather than a somewhat brief initial generative question, as seen in BNIM earlier, the opening question is highly elaborated, offering a distinct narrative structure. Interviewees are asked to structure their life story as if it were a book, with distinct chapters, identified at the start of the interview, thus providing a general outline. The person being interviewed may decide to structure their life chapters chronologically, with the earlier chapters being about childhood, moving on to the teenage years, young adulthood, adulthood. Other people may structure their chapters according to themes, for example relationships. The interviewer can ask for elaborations, but they should be careful not to organise the table of contents for the storyteller. The second section of the interview asks the interviewee to describe in great detail eight key events (nuclear episodes) in their story. They are asked to describe conversations, where they were, who was there, what they did and what they were thinking and feeling at the time. McAdams suggests that using these key events produces rich descriptive accounts that are invaluable in understanding what motivates people, giving insight into personality and identity.

Box 11.3   McAdams' life story chapters and eight key events (nuclear episodes)

I would like you to begin by thinking about your life as if it were a book. Each part of your life composes a chapter in the book. Certainly, the book is unfinished at this point; still, it probably already contains a few interesting and well-defined chapters. Please divide your life into its major chapters as you like, but I would suggest dividing it into a least two or three chapters and at most about seven or eight. Think of this as a general table of contents for your book. Give each chapter a name and describe the overall contents of each chapter. Discuss briefly what makes for a transition from one chapter to the next. This first part of the interview can expand forever, but I would urge you to keep it relatively brief, say, within 30 or 45 minutes. Therefore, you don't want to tell me 'the whole story' here. Just give me a sense of the story's outline – the major chapters in your life.

The second part of the interview involves exploring the role of key events that capture critical moments in a person's life, McAdams describes these as nuclear episodes.

1   Peak experience: A high point in the life story; the most wonderful moment in your life.
2   Nadir experience: A low point in the life story; the worst moment in your life.
3   Turning point: An episode wherein you underwent a significant change in your understanding of yourself. It is not important that you comprehended the turning point as a turning point when it happened. What is important is that now, in retrospect, you see the event as a turning point, or at minimum as symbolizing a significant change in your life.
4   Earliest memory: One of the earliest memories you have of an event that is complete with setting, scene and characters, feelings and thoughts. This does not have to seem like an especially important memory. Its one virtue is that it is early.
5   An important childhood memory: Any memory from your childhood, positive or negative, that stands out today.
6   An important adolescent memory: Any memory from your teenage years that stands out today. Again, it can be either positive or negative.
7   An important adult memory: A memory, positive or negative that stands out from age 21 onward.
8   Other important memory: One other particular event from your past that stands out. It may be from long ago or recent times. It may be positive or negative.

(McAdams, 1993: 256)

Co-construction and performance

Whether adopting concrete situational questioning, evident in FANI, one generative question suggested by Wengraf, or taking a more structured approach, similar to McAdams, it is impossible to avoid researcher involvement in the *co-construction* of narratives. The narrative is always directed towards an audience whose role, moral understandings and status must be taken into account when the story is being told. The life story interview is intimate, highly reflexive often with a deeply confidential atmosphere. This may suggest a heightened personal commitment to the narrator's story and to their self-presentation. The consequence may be that the narrator appears throughout as 'the kind of person I feel obliged to be'. For example, we might omit less positive aspects of our life story in order to continue to portray ourselves as the hero of our tale, we might emphasise the more distressing areas of our lives if we experience this as receiving support and sympathy from the interviewer. This positioning of the storyteller, in relation to the audience, is seen as a *performance*. Within the narrative performance the interviewee has licence to create an account but their performance is always subject to the evaluation of the audience. Yet, it is important to remember that like all performance events, personal narratives are structured by the culture in which they operate.

Models of narrative analysis

Throughout this book we have tried to emphasise how theory and research practice are interconnected. The approach taken to data analysis will therefore reflect variations in overall methodological approach. Narrative research, looking at an entire life story, will adopt a different mode of analysis from research focusing on much briefer and more specific/episodic stories. However, Murray (2003) offers some sound advice, explaining that narrative analysis is not a passive process. Indeed, we would suggest that no qualitative analysis is passive. Hence, within this 'active' process the researcher is required to be aware of what theoretical assumptions guide the analysis and to 'play' with the account. Murray discusses two broad phases in the analysis of narrative accounts – the first is descriptive and the second interpretative. The first phase concentrates on becoming familiar with structure and content. Here we might use narrative configuration in relation to key elements. For example, is there a discernible beginning, middle and end? How is the narrative emplotted and is there evidence of a particular kind of temporal ordering? Once a detailed appreciation of content and structure has been captured, the second step would be to draw in broader theoretical literature to interpret the story. While this is helpful as a generic overview, it is important to note that there are various models of narrative analysis, offering a range of approaches (Cortazzi, 1993; Mishler, 1995; Riessman, 2005). In the final part of this chapter we briefly present different approaches to narrative analysis that reflect a diverse understanding of language and its impact within the field of narrative inquiry.

Content and thematic analysis

Certain forms of narrative analysis focus on the content: 'what' is said rather than how the story unfolds. Elliott (2005) explains how this can include a detailed examination of the content of a single biographical life story where the content in many respects speaks for itself. Thus a person's account can reveal personal values and feelings but also provide access to the social and cultural world that people inhabit. By focusing on content, we can begin to look for common experiences or elements within one interview or across several interviews. Notably, there is an uncomplicated but often unacknowledged philosophy of language underpinning such a content-driven, thematic approach to narrative analysis. Language is seen as a resource, offering a direct route to meaning. Similar to the thematic approach outlined in our earlier chapter on analysis, narrative data is searched and types of narrative that have common thematic elements are identified. For example, Wilson's (1999) interviews with African Americans who grew up in the 1950s yielded 'nostalgic narratives'. Interview data was searched for expressions of nostalgia for the 1950s. The analysis showed that while the data revealed remembered pain, and difficulties associated with segregation and exclusion, there were also pleasant nostalgic narratives:

> It was a carefree time, it was a time of early marriage, babies. ... People had time to make homemade chicken soup. People had time to listen, people had time to care. (Wilson, 1999: 313)

There is acceptance in the analysis of contradiction, ambivalence and how meanings change over time. Yet, there is a belief that what was said in the research interview, in relation to nostalgic narratives, is what was felt and experienced when looking back at those times. Indeed, Riessman (2005: 3) says, when taking a thematic approach to the analysis of narratives: 'Language is viewed as a resource not a topic of investigation.' Thus, when grouped into such thematic categories, we might assume that everyone means the same thing when talking in this way. As such, this approach is not necessarily exploring the constructive aspects of language but it is useful for theorising across a number of cases/interviews, possibly leading to useful typologies.

Structural analysis

A structural analysis focuses on the 'way' the story is told, seeking to define the structural components of a narrative and formulate an analysis based on these components. There are several ways to undertake a structural analysis and this could involve examining the narrative for literary structure such as plot, temporal ordering and characters in the story. Labov and Waletzky's (Labov and Waletzky; 1967; Labov, 1972) sociolinguistic model of analysis is the best known. This approach enables consideration of how the narrative is structured and how different elements within a story might function. Two social functions of narrative are proposed: the 'referential' and the 'evaluative' function. The *referential* function is to give the audience information, with the narrator recapturing the experience in the same order as it occurred. However, Labov (1972) maintains that this rarely happens. Rather, people evaluate events and therefore the *evaluative* function communicates the meaning of the narrative to the audience, establishing why the story is being told. This approach adopts the clause as the unit of analysis, asking the fundamental question: 'How can we relate the sequence of clauses in the narrative to the sequence of events inferred from the narrative?' Labov and Waletzky (1967: 20) describe fully formed oral narratives of personal experience as having six elements (see also Cortazzi, 1993):

- the abstract: summary or point of a story
- orientation: details of time, persons, place
- complicating action: what happened then? gives the event sequence, often with a crisis or turning point
- evaluation: highlights the point of the narrative, why the story is being told
- result/resolution: describes the outcome
- coda: returns to the present bringing the story to an end

While not all stories contain each of these elements, and the sequence may vary, this analytical approach makes visible the effect that language structure can have on the making of narratives. Indeed, Riessman (1993) suggests that starting with an analysis of structure avoids reading simply for content.

Box 11.4 shows an extract from a narrative interview with a man who is talking about his treatment for drug misuse. Using this structured approach, the evaluation elements convey an appreciation of how the participant is understanding, making sense of and conveying not only the event but also his involvement in coercive treatment. The abstract gives a general statement about what had occurred, with the orientation outlining the setting. The complicated action describes in sequence how Joe (another man in treatment) was able to avoid acupuncture and the way in which he was allowed to 'do something else'. This is essentially the content of the narrative. The evaluation, why the story is being told, is implicit in the line 'But it's not doing anything for me'. This 'reveals the attitude of the narrator towards the narrative by emphasizing the relative importance of some narrative units as opposed to others' (Labov and Waletzky, 1967: 37). The resolution is particularly interesting in terms of understanding how he is making sense of treatment. Even though he had 'told em', he is still expected to comply and the further evaluation explaining his annoyance highlights the point of the narrative. The coda marks the close of the narrative. In this example, the participant finishes by saying 'That's why I remember it'. Even this small section of narrative data is revealing when subjected to a line-by-line structural analysis. We are able to appreciate some underlying events but also how the speaker experienced these events.

Box 11.4 Using Labov and Waletzky's structural model of narrative analysis

Extract from a marrative interview with a man on a coercive treatment programme for drug misuse.

A   The other day joe managed to get out of stuff.

O   We were having acupuncture done,

Ca   and um … he turned round to em (treatment providers) and says 'oh well I'm not

Ca   really getting anything out of this, it's not really benefiting me I'm not gonna let

Ca   them do it'.

Ca   So they says to him 'Oh well just do something else then'.

E   But it's not doing anything for me.

R   I've told em this but I've still got to comply with it, an I expect to comply with it.

E   It really annoyed me that, him not doing acupuncture the other day.

1C   That's why I remember it.

Key: A = abstract; O = orientation; Ca = complicating action; E = evaluation;
    R = resolution; C = coda

Structural narrative analysis is undertaken on conversational narratives, focusing on the function of a clause in the overall narrative and involving very detailed analysis of small sections of qualitative data. Arguably, with this approach, the more holistic sense of an interview is lost. Narratives are decontextualised and historical and interactional facets of life are generally not included within this approach to analysis. Still, Labov (2001) shows this type of analysis being used with data from testimonies in the Truth and Reconciliation Hearings that took place in South Africa. Evident in his analysis is the way in which a structural analysis reveals how speakers can transform reality by techniques more subtle and effective than lying. This work shows the potential inherent in attending to narrative structure in order to understand better the transformative character of conversational narratives.

Analysis and identity

Bamberg (2004: 223) says that '[i]n sum, narratives, irrespective of whether they deal with one's life or an episode or event in the life of someone else, always *reveal* the speakers' identity'. Yet interestingly, Elliott (2005) says that despite the potential for qualitative research to explore the reflexive maintenance of identity, there exist only a few empirical studies that fully embrace the narrative construction of identity. While in relative terms this might be the case, acclaimed research is available showing the insightful, therapeutic and emancipatory potential of such work (e.g. Frank, 1997; Riessman, 2000; Livesey, 2002).

McAdams (1993) suggests that we construct identity in a similar way to how a storyteller composes a story. Speaking from a constructivist position, McAdams puts forward principal elements that can be used to structure an analysis focused on identity and life story, personal narratives: *narrative tone*, *imagery* and *theme*. *Narrative tone* is seen to be the most pervasive feature of personal narratives and is conveyed in both the content of the story and the manner in which it is told. Although not explicitly defined by McAdams, tone is suggested to imply a person's feelings towards something, this being conveyed in both the content and the manner in which the story is told. Accordingly, an optimistic story can be identified as such because good things happen, or it may be optimistic because even though bad things happen the person constructs themselves as remaining hopeful. A pessimistic story may be characterised in this way because a series of misfortunes are narrated. Alternatively, it may be pessimistic because good things are set within a negative light. While McAdams locates his understanding of narrative tone within early childhood and attachment relationships, this does not preclude using narrative tone in a more generic sense. Hence, personal narratives can be searched for narrative tone, aiming to grasp how someone is constructing their lives and experience.

Personal narratives use *imagery* to construct identity, including symbols, objects and metaphors that are dependent upon the cultural and historical context we experience. For example, the imagery of self-fulfilment and success in our society is exemplified in a well-paid job that brings with it certain objects: a large house, an expensive car, holidays. Imagery around family – good father, mother, son, daughter – can also infuse the personal narratives we tell. Moreover, exploring imagery and theoretically considering how such images might be both made and maintained in the dominant discourses of society goes beyond a thematic or structural analysis. Here language can be seen to actively impact on the associations and perspectives people have on their lives – who they believe themselves to be. Nevertheless, drawing upon a constructivist viewpoint, McAdams (1993) explains that *theme* is a recurrent pattern of human intention. He argues that power and love are two of the most important themes in personal narratives. Therefore, when analysing personal narratives, the researcher should be sensitive to motivational themes, aiming to make evident what drives the teller to story their lives in a particular way and how this is important.

Conclusion

With only a brief exploration into the area of narrative interviewing and narrative analysis it becomes obvious that there are diverse, yet often overlapping, approaches. The field of narrative inquiry is exciting and constantly expanding, opening up new forms of understanding and ways of talking about human experience. Narrative interviewing privileges subjectivity and the position of the narrator, while at the same time offering an appreciation of the social world from which narrations are drawn. The role of language is a central facet of narrative interviewing and we have therefore spent time discussing textual understandings of social reality and subjectivity. We have also purposively chosen to identify specific narrative interviewing approaches, moving from situational/episodic interviewing to then cover both an unstructured and structured approach to life story interviewing. In doing this, we aimed to show the breadth of methods that can be used when drawing on narrative interviewing. It is, however, important to note that there are many other possibilities. Perhaps this breadth is what makes the field of narrative inquiry both attractive and daunting.

Recommended reading

Chase, S.E. (2003) Taking narrative seriously: consequences for method and theory in interview studies, in Y.S. Lincoln and N.K. Denzin (eds), *Turning Points in Qualitative Research*. New York: Altamira Press.
This is an extremely engaging chapter that shares the challenges encountered when aiming to generate narrative data.

Czarniawska, B. (2004) *Narratives in Social Science Research*. London: Sage.
This is a comprehensive book that includes a wealth of theoretical and practical information for those intending to use narrative interviewing.

Polkinghorne, D.E. (1995) Narrative configuration in qualitative analysis, in J. Amos Hatch and R. Wisniewski (eds), *Life History and Narrative*. London: The Falmer Press. pp. 5–24.
In this chapter Polkinghorne provides a comprehensive overview of the different aspects of narrative configuration in relation to qualitative research.

Riessman, C. (2005) Narrative analysis, in N. Kelly, C. Horrocks, K. Milnes, B. Roberts and D. Robinson (eds), *Narrative, Memory and Everyday Life*. Huddersfield: University of Huddersfield Press.
In this short chapter Riessman provides a brief and highly accessible general outline of different approaches to narrative analysis.

References

Aanstoos, C. (1985) The structure of thinking in chess, in A. Giorgi (ed.), *Phenomenology and Psychological Research*. Pittsburgh, PA: Duquesne University Press.

Alvesson, M. and Sköldberg, K. (2000) *Reflexive Methodology: New Vistas for Qualitative Research*. London: Sage.

Andrews, M., Day Sclater, S., Squire, C. and Treacher, A. (2000) *Lines of Narrative: Psychosocial Perspectives*. London: Routledge.

Ashworth, P. (1993) Participant agreement in the justification of qualitative findings. *Journal of Phenomenological Psychology*, 24 (1): 3–16.

Ashworth, P. (2003) An approach to phenomenological psychology: the contingencies of the lifeworld. *Journal of Phenomenological Psychology*, 34 (2): 145–56.

Ashworth, P. (2008) Conceptual foundations of qualitative psychology, in J.A. Smith (ed.), *Qualitative Psychology: A Practical Guide to Research Methods* (2nd edition). London: Sage.

Atkinson, R. (1998) *The Life Story Interview*. London: Sage.

Axelrod, M.D. (1979) 10 essentials for good qualitative research, in J.B. Higginbotham and K.K. Cox (eds), *Focus Group Interviews: A Reader*. Chicago: American Marketing Association.

Bamberg, M. (2004) Narrative discourse and identities, in J.C. Meister, T. Kindt, W. Schernus and M. Stein (eds), *Narratology beyond Literary Criticism*. Berlin and New York: Walter de Gruyter. pp. 213–37.

Banister, P., Burman, E., Parker, I., Taylor, M. and Tindall, C. (1994) *Qualitative Methods in Psychology: A Resarch Guide*. Buckingham: Open University Press.

Bannister, D. (1985) Introduction, in N. Beail (ed.), *Repertory Grid Techniques and Personal Constructs: Applications in Clinical and Educational Settings*. London: Croom Helm.

Barber, M. (2007) Alfred Schutz, in E.N. Zalta (ed.), *The Stanford Encyclopedia of Philosophy* (Summer 2007 Edition). Available at: www.plato.stanford.edu/archives/sum2007/entries/schutz/ (accessed 04/12/09).

Barbour, R.S. (2001) Checklists for improving rigour in qualitative research: a case of the tail wagging the dog? *British Medical Journal*, 322: 1115–17.

Barbour, R.S. (2007) *Doing Focus Groups*. London: Sage.

Bargdill, R.W. (2000) The study of life boredom. *Journal of Phenomenological Psychology*, 31 (2): 188–219.

Beck, C.T. (1997) Humour in nursing practice: a phenomenological study. *International Journal of Nursing Studies*, 34 (5): 346–52.

Bell, R.C. (2003) The repertory grid technique, in F. Fransella (ed.), *International Handbook of Personal Construct Psychology*. Chichester: Wiley.

Berg, B.L. (2001) *Qualitative Research Methods for the Social Sciences* (4th edition), London: Allyn and Bacon.

Berger, P. and Luckmann, T. (1967) *The Social Construction of Reality*. Harmondsworth: Penguin.

Bevan, M.T. (2007) Experiencing dialysis: a descriptive phenomenological study of nurses and patients in dialysis satellite units. Unpublished PhD thesis, University of Huddersfield. Available at: www.eprints.hud.ac.uk/963/ (accessed 04/12/09).

Bhaskar, R. (1991) *Philosophy and the Idea of Freedom*. Oxford: Blackwell.

Billig, M. (1991) *Ideology and Opinions*. London: Sage.

Birch, M. and Miller, T. (2002) Encouraging participation: ethics and responsibilities, in M. Mauther, M. Birch, J. Jessop and T. Miller, *Ethics in Qualitative Research*. London: Sage. pp. 91–106.

Blaikie, N. (1993) *Approaches to Social Enquiry*. Cambridge: Polity Press.

Blumer, H. (1969) *Symbolic Interactionism: Perspective and Method*. Berkeley, CA: University of California Press.

Bogardus, E. (1926) The group interview. *Journal of Applied Sociology*, 10: 372–82.

Bowker, N. and Tuffin, K. (2004) Using the online medium for discursive research about people with disabilities. *Social Science Computer Review*, 22 (2): 228–41.

Boyatzis, R.E. (1998) *Transforming Qualitative Information: Thematic Analysis and Code Development*. Thousand Oaks, CA: Sage.

Braun, V. and Clarke, V. (2006) Using thematic analysis in psychology. *Qualitative Research in Psychology*, 3: 77–101.

Breakwell, G.M. (1990) *Interviewing: Problems in Practice*. London: Routledge.

Briggs, C.L. (2002) Interviewing, power/knowledge, and social inequality, in J.F. Gubrium and J.A. Holstein (eds), *Handbook of Interview Research: Context and Methods*. Thousand Oaks, CA: Sage.

British Educational Research Association (BERA) (2004) *Revised Ethical Guidelines for Educational Research*. Available at: www.bera.ac.uk/publications/pdfs/ ETHICAL.PDF (accessed 04/12/09).

British Sociological Association (2002 updated 2004) *Statement of Ethical Practice for the British Sociological Association*. Available at: www.britsoc.co.uk/equality/Statement Practice.htm (accessed 04/12/09).

British Psychological Society (2006) *Code of Ethics and Conduct*. Leicester: British Psychological Society.

British Psychological Society (2008) *Report of the Working Party on Conducting Research on the Internet: Guidelines for Ethical Practice in Psychological Research Online*. Leicester: British Psychological Society.

Brockmeier, J. and Carbaugh, D. (2001) Introduction, in J. Brockmeier and D. Carbaugh (eds), *Narrative and Identity: Studies in Autobiography, Self and Culture*. Amsterdam and Philadelphia: John Benjamins Publishing Co. pp. 1–22.

Brown, T. and Jones, L. (2001) *Action Research and Postmodernism: Congruence and Critique*. Buckingham: Open University Press.

Bruce, V. (1995) The role of the face in face-to-face communication: implications for video telephony, in S.J. Emmott (ed.), *Information Superhighways: Multi-media Users and Futures*. London: Academic Press.

Bruner, J.S. (1986) *Actual Minds, Possible Worlds*. Cambridge, MA: Harvard University Press.

Bruner, J.S. (1990) *Acts of Meaning*. Cambridge, MA: Harvard University Press.

Burr, V. (1995) *Social Constructionism*. London: Routledge.

Burr, V. (2003) *Social Constructionism* (2nd edition). London: Routledge.

Butt, T.W. (2003) The phenomenological context of PCP, in F. Fransella (ed.), *International Handbook of Personal Construct Psychology*. Chichester: Wiley.

Butt, T.W. (2004) *Understanding People*. Basingstoke: Palgrave Macmillan.

Butt, T.W. (2008) *George Kelly*. Basingstoke: Palgrave Macmillan.

Cassell, C. and Walsh, S. (2004) Repertory grids, in C. Cassell and G. Symon (eds), *Essential Guide to Qualitative Methods in Organizational Research*. London: Sage.

Chalmers, A.F. (1999) *What is This Thing Called Science?* (3rd edition). Milton Keynes: Open University Press.

Chamberlayne, P., Bornat, J. and Wengraf, T. (2000) *The Turn to Biographical Methods in Social Science*. London: Routledge.

Chase, S.E. (2003) Taking narrative seriously: consequences for method and theory in interview studies, in Y.S. Lincoln and N.K. Denzin (eds), *Turning Points in Qualitative Research*. New York: Altamira Press. pp. 273–96.

Chiari, G. and Nuzzo, M.L. (1996) Psychological constructivisms: a metatheoretical differentiation. *Journal of Constructivist Psychology*, 9: 163–84.

Christians, C.G. (2003) Ethics and politics in qualitative research, in N. Denzin and Y. Lincoln (eds), *The Landscape of Qualitative Research: Theories and Issues*. London: Sage. pp. 208–43.

Clarke, J. and Cochrane, A. (1998) The social construction of social problems, in E. Saraga (ed.), *Embodying the Social: Constructions of Difference*. London: Routledge.

Code, L. (1991) *What Can She Know? Feminist Theory and the Construction of Knowledge*. Ithaca, NY: Cornell University Press.

Coffey, A. and Atkinson, P. (1996) *Making Sense of Qualitative Data Analysis: Complementary Strategies*. Thousand Oaks, CA: Sage.

Cook, C., Heath, F. and Thomson, R.L. (2000) A meta-analysis of response rates in web- or internet-based surveys. *Educational and Psychological Measurement*, 60: 821–36.

Coote, A. and Lenhaglan, J. (1997) *Citizens' Juries: From Theory to Practice*. London: Institute of Public Policy Research.

Corbin, J. and Strauss, A. (2008) *Basics of Qualitative Research: Techniques and Procedures for Developing Grounded Theory*. (3rd edition). Thousand Oaks: Sage.

Cortazzi, M. (1993) *Narrative Analysis*. London: Falmer Press.

Crabtree, B.F. and Miller, W.L. (1992) A template approach to text analysis: developing and using codebooks, in B.F. Crabtree and W.L. Miller (eds), *Doing Qualitative Research*. Newbury Park, CA: Sage.

Crossley, M. (2007) Narrative analysis, in E. Lyons and A. Coyle (eds), *Analysing Qualitative Data in Psychology*. London: Sage. pp. 131–44.

Crotty, M. (1998) *The Foundations of Social Research*. London: Sage.

Czarniawska, B. (2004) *Narratives in Social Science Research*. London: Sage.

Daaleman, T.P., Cobb, A.K. and Frey, B.B. (2001) Spirituality and well-being: an exploratory study of the patient perspective. *Social Science and Medicine*, 53 (1): 1503–11.

Denicolo, P.M. (n.d.) Pictorial ways of eliciting constructs, in J. Scheer and B. Walker (eds), *The Internet Encyclopaedia of Personal Construct Psychology*. Available at: www. pcp-net.org/encyclopaedia/pictorial.html (accessed 06.08.08).

Denicolo, P.M. and Pope, M.L. (2001) *Transformative Professional Practice: Personal Construct Approaches to Education and Research*. London: Whurr Publishers.

Denzin, N.K. (1978) *The Research Act: A Theoretical Introduction to Sociological Methods*. New York: McGraw-Hill.

Denzin, N.K. (1997) *Interpretative Ethnography*. Thousand Oaks, CA: Sage.

Denzin, N.K. (2002) Social work in the seventh moment. *Qualitative Social Work*, 1 (1): 25–38.

Denzin, N.K. and Lincoln, Y. (eds) (1994) *Handbook of Qualitative Research*. Thousand Oaks, CA: Sage.

Derks, D., Fischer, A.H. and Bos, A.E.R. (2008) The role of emotion in computer-mediated communication: a review. *Computers in Human Behaviour*, 24: 766–85.

Doucet, A. and Mauthner, N. (2002) Knowing responsibly: linking ethics, research practice and epistemology, in M. Mauthner, M. Birch, J. Jessop and T. Miller (eds), *Ethics in Qualitative Research*. London: Sage. pp. 123–45.

Eatough, V. and Smith, J.A. (2006) 'I feel like a scrambled egg in my head': an idiographic case study of meaning making and anger using interpretative phenomenological analysis. *Psychology and Psychotherapy*, 79: 115–35.

Economic Social Research Council (2008), *Research Ethics Framework (REF)*. Swindon: ESRC.

Edwards, R. and Mauthner, M. (2002) Ethics and feminist research: theory and practice, in M. Mauthner, M. Birch, J. Jessop and T. Miller (eds), *Ethics in Qualitative Research*. London: Sage. pp. 14–31.

Egan, J., Chenowith, L. and McAuliffe, D. (2006) E-mail facilitated qualitative interviews with traumatic brain injury survivors: a new and accessible method. *Brain Injury*, 20 (12): 1283–94.

Elliott, J. (2005) *Using Narrative in Social Research: Qualitative and Quantitative Approaches*. London: Sage.

Ellis, C., Kiesinger, C. and Tillmann-Healy, L. (1997) Interactive interviewing: talking about emotional experiences, in R. Hertz (ed.), *Reflexivity and Voice.* Thousand Oaks, CA: Sage. pp. 119–49.

Ess, C. (2002) Ethical decision-making and internet research: recommendations from the AoIR Ethics Working Committee. Association of Internet Researchers (AoIR). Available at: www.aoir.org/reports/ethics.pdf (accessed 11/01/09).

Fern, E.F. (2001) *Advanced Focus Group Research.* London: Sage.

Feyerabend, P. (1993) *Against Method* (3rd edition). London: Verso.

Finlay, L. (2002) Negotiating the swamp: the opportunity and challenge of reflexivity in research practice. *Qualitative Research*, 2 (2): 209–30.

Finlay, L. (2003) The reflexive journey: mapping multiple routes, in L. Finlay and B. Gough (eds), *Reflexivity: A Practical Guide for Researchers in Health and Social Sciences.* Oxford: Blackwell Publishing. pp. 3–22.

Finlay, L. (2005) Reflexive embodied empathy: a phenomenology of participant–researcher intersubjectivity. *Methods Issue: The Humanistic Psychologist*, 33 (4): 271–92.

Finlay, L. (2006) The body's disclosure in phenomenological research. *Qualitative Research in Psychology*, 3 (1): 19–30.

Finlay, L. and Gough, B. (eds) (2003) *Reflexivity: A Practical Guide for Researchers in Health and Social Sciences.* Oxford: Blackwell Publishing.

Flick, U. (1998) *An Introduction to Qualitative Research.* London: Sage.

Frank, A.W. (1997) *The Wounded Storyteller: Body, Illness and Ethics.* London: University of Chicago Press.

Frank, A.W. (2003) Survivorship as craft and conviction: reflections on research in progress. *Qualitative Health Research*, 13 (2): 247–55.

Fransella, F., Bannister, D. and Bell, R. (2003) *A Manual of Repertory Grid Technique* (2nd edition). Chichester: Wiley.

Freeman, M. (1997) Why narrative? Hermeneutics, historical understanding, and the significance of stories. *Journal of Narrative and Life History*, 7: 169–76.

Frey, J.H. and Fontana, A. (1993) The group interview in social research, in D.L. Morgan (ed.), *Successful Focus Groups.* London: Sage. pp. 20–34.

Frith, H. (2000) Focusing on sex: using focus groups in sex research. *Sexualities*, 3 (3): 275–97.

Geertz, C. (1973) *The Interpretation of Cultures.* New York: Basic Books.

Gergen, K.J. and Gergen, M.M. (1988) Narrative and the self as relationship, in L. Berkowitz (ed.), *Advances in Experimental and Social Psychology* (Vol. 21). New York: Academic Press. pp. 17–56.

Gergen, K.J. and Gergen, M.M. (1991) Toward reflexive methodologies, in F. Steier (ed.), *Research and Reflexivity.* London: Sage. pp. 76–95.

Gerson, K. and Horowitz, R. (2002) Observation and interviewing: options and choices in qualitative research, in T. May (ed.), *Qualitative Research in Action.* London: Sage.

Gill, R. (1995) Relativism, reflexivity and politics: interrogating discourse analysis from a feminist perspective, in S. Wilkinson and C. Kitzinger (eds), *Feminism and Discourse: Psychological Perspectives.* London: Sage. pp. 18–44.

Gilligan, C. (1982) *In a Different Voice.* Cambridge, MA: Harvard University Press.

Giorgi, A. (1970) *Psychology as a Human Science.* New York: Harper & Row.

Giorgi, A. (1985) *Phenomenology and Psychological Research.* Pittsburgh, PA: Duquesne University Press.

Giorgi, A. and Giorgi, B. (2003) Phenomenology, in J. Smith (ed.), *Qualitative Psychology: A Practical Guide to Research Methods.* London: Sage.

Giorgi, A. and Giorgi, B. (2008) Phenomenology, in J.A. Smith (ed.), *Qualitative Psychology: A Practical Guide to Research Methods* (2nd edition). London: Sage.

Golafshani, N. (2003) Understanding reliability and validity in qualitative research. *The Qualitative Report*, 8 (4): 597–607.

Goodson, I. (1992) Studying teachers' lives: an emergent field of inquiry, in I. Goodson (ed.), *Studying Teachers' Lives.* London: Routledge. pp. 1–17.

Gough, B. (2003) Deconstructing reflexivity, in L. Finlay and B. Gough (eds), *Reflexivity: A Practical Guide for Researchers in Health and Social Sciences.* Oxford: Blackwell Publishing. pp. 21–36.

Grinyer, A. (2002) The anonymity of research participants: assumptions, ethics and practicalities. *Social Research Update*, Issue 36, Department of Sociology, University of Surrey.

Guba, E.G. and Lincoln, Y.S. (1989) *Fourth Generation Evaluation.* Newbury Park, CA: Sage.

Guba, E.G. and Lincoln, Y.S. (1994) Competing paradigms in qualitative research, in N.K. Denzin and Y.S. Lincoln (eds), *Handbook of Qualitative Research.* Thousand Oaks, CA: Sage.

Guba, E.G. and Lincoln, Y.S. (2005) Paradigmatic controversies, contradictions and emerging confluences, in N.K. Denzin and Y.S. Lincoln (eds), *The Sage Handbook of Qualitative Research.* London: Sage. pp. 295–319.

Gubrium, J.F. and Holstein, J.A. (eds) (2002) *Handbook of Interview Research: Context and Method.* Thousand Oaks, CA: Sage.

Gubrium, J.F. and Holstein, J.A. (eds) (2003a) *Postmodern Interviewing.* London: Sage.

Gubrium, J.F. and Holstein, J.A. (2003b) From the individual interview to the interview society, in J.F. Gubrium and J.A. Holstein (eds), *Postmodern Interviewing.* London: Sage.

Hall, S. (2001) Foucault: power, knowledge and discourse, in M. Wetherell, S. Taylor and S.J. Yates (eds), *Discourse Theory and Practice: A Reader.* London: Sage.

Hargreaves, C.P. (1979) Social networks and interpersonal constructs, in P. Stringer and D. Bannister (eds), *Constructs of Sociality and Individuality.* London: Academic Press. pp. 153–75.

Hartley, J. (2004) Case study research, in C. Cassell and G. Symon (eds), *Essential Guide to Qualitative Methods in Organizational Research.* London: Sage.

Hatch, J.A. and Wisniewski, R. (1995) *Life History and Narrative.* London: Falmer Press.

Heath, C. (1997) The analysis of activities in face-to-face interaction using video, in D. Silverman (ed.), *Qualitative Research: Theory, Method and Practice.* London: Sage.

Hennink, M. and Diamond, I. (2000) Using focus groups in social research, in A. Memon and R. Bull (eds), *Handbook of the Psychology of Interviewing.* Chichester: Wiley. pp. 113–44.

Heron, J. (1996) *Co-operative Inquiry: Research into the Human Condition.* London: Sage.

Heron, J. and Reason, P. (2001) The practice of cooperative inquiry: research 'with' rather than 'on' people, in P. Reason and H. Bradbury (eds), *Handbook of Action Research: Participative Inquiry and Practice.* London: Sage. pp. 144–54.

Herzog, A.R., Rodgers, W.L. and Kulka, R.A. (1983) Interviewing older adults: a comparison of telephone and face-to-face modalities. *Public Opinion Quarterly*, 47: 405–18.

Hewson, C. (2007) Gathering data on the internet: qualitative approaches and possibilities for mixed methods research, in A. Joinson, K. McKenna, T. Postmes and U. Reips (eds), *The Oxford Handbook of Internet Psychology.* Oxford: Oxford University Press.

Holge-Hazelton, B. (2002) The internet: a new field for qualitative inquiry? *Forum: Qualitative Social Research*, 3 (2), Art. 15, www.qualitative-research.net/index.php/fqs/article/view/854 (accessed 01/11/08).

Holliday, A. (2002) *Doing and Writing Qualitative Research.* London: Sage.

Hollway, W. and Jefferson, T. (2000) *Doing Qualitative Research Differently: Free Association, Narrative and the Interview Method.* London: Sage.

Homan, R. (1991) *The Ethics of Social Research.* London: Longman.

Howitt, D. and Cramer, D. (2005) *Introduction to Research Methods in Psychology.* Harlow: Pearson.

Hunt, N. and McHale, S. (2005) Reported experiences of persons with alopecia areata. *Journal of Loss and Trauma*, 10: 33–50.

Hunt, N. and McHale, S. (2007) A practical guide to the e-mail interview. *Qualitative Health Research*, 17 (10): 1415–21.

Husserl, E. (1931; trans. 1960) *Cartesian Meditations: An Introduction to Phenomenology.* The Hague: Martinus Nijhoff.

Ihde, D. (1986) *Experimental Phenomenology*. Albany, NY: State University of New York Press.

Illingworth, N. (2001) The internet matters: exploring the use of the internet as a research tool. *Sociological Research Online*, 6 (2). Available at: www.socresonline.uk/6/2/illingworth.html (accessed 06/10/08).

Ingham, R., Vanwesenbeeck, I. and Kirkland, D. (2000) Interviewing on sensitive topics, in A. Memon and R. Bull (eds), *Handbook of the Psychology of Interviewing*. Chichester: Wiley. pp. 145–64.

Jaeger, E.M. and Rosnow, R.L. (1988) Contextualism and its implications for psychological inquiry. *British Journal of Psychology*, 79: 63–75.

James, N. and Busher, H. (2007) Ethical issues in online educational research: protecting privacy, establishing authenticity in email interviewing. *International Journal of Research and Method in Education*, 30 (1): 101–13.

Jankowicz, A.D. (2003) *The Easy Guide to Repertory Grids*. Chichester: Wiley.

Jarman, M., Smith, J.A. and Walsh, S. (1997) The psychological battle for control: a qualitative study of healthcare professionals' understandings of the treatment of anorexia nervosa. *Journal of Community and Applied Social Psychology*, 7: 137–52.

Jefferson, G. (1984) Transcription notation, in J. Atkinson and J. Heritage (eds), *Structures of Social Interaction*. New York: Cambridge University Press.

Johnson, P., Buehring, A., Cassell, C. and Symon, G. (2006) Evaluating qualitative management research: towards a contingent criteriology. *International Journal of Management Reviews*, 8 (3): 131–56.

Johnson, S., Burrows, A. and Williamson, I. (2004) 'Does my bump look big in this?' The meaning of bodily changes for first-time mothers-to-be. *Journal of Health Psychology*, 9 (3): 361–74.

Joinson, A.N. (2001) Self-disclosure in computer-mediated communication: the role of self-awareness and visual anonymity. *European Journal of Social Psychology*, 31: 177–92.

Joinson, A.N. (2005) Internet behaviour and the design of virtual methods, in C. Hine (ed.), *Virtual Methods: Issues in Social Research on the Internet*. Oxford: Berg.

Jones, S., Tanner, H. and Treadaway, M. (2000) Raising standards in mathematics through effective classroom practice. *Teaching Mathematics and its Applications*, 19 (3): 125–34.

Jordan, B. (2004) *Sex, Money and Power: The Transformation of Collective Life*. Cambridge: Polity Press.

Josselson, R. (ed.) (1996) *Ethics and Process in the Narrative Study of Lives*. Thousand Oaks, CA: Sage.

Kazmer, M.M. and Xie, B. (2008) Qualitative interviewing in internet studies: playing with the media, playing with the method. *Information, Communication and Society*, 11 (2): 257–78.

Kelly, G.A. (1955) *The Psychology of Personal Constructs*. New York: W.W. Norton.

Kiesler, S. and Sproull, L. (1992) Group decision-making and communication technology. *Organizational Behavior and Human Decision Processes*, 52 (1): 96–123.

King, N. (1998) Template analysis, in G. Symon and C. Cassell (eds), *Qualitative Methods and Analysis in Organizational Research*. London: Sage.

King, N. (2004a) Interviews, in C. Cassell and G. Symon (eds), *Essential Guide to Qualitative Methods in Organizational Research*. London: Sage.

King, N. (2004b) Using templates in the thematic analysis of texts, in C. Cassell and G. Symon (eds), *Essential Guide to Qualitative Methods in Organizational Research*. London: Sage.

King, N. (2008) What will hatch? A constructivist autobiographical account of writing poetry. *Journal of Constructivist Psychology*, 21 (4): 274–87.

King, N., Bailey, J. and Newton, P. (1994) Analysing general practitioners' referral decisions: I. Developing an analytical framework. *Family Practice*, 11: 3–8.

King, N., Carroll, C., Newton, P. and Dornan, T. (2002) 'You can't cure it so you have to endure it': the experience of adaptation to diabetic renal disease. *Qualitative Health Research*, 12 (3): 329–46.

King, N., Finlay, L., Ashworth, P., Smith, J., Langdridge, D. and Butt, T. (2008) 'Can't really trust that, so what can I trust?': a polyvocal, qualitative analysis of the psychology of mistrust. *Qualitative Research in Psychology*, 5 (2): 80–102.

King, N. and Little, A. (2007) *West Central Halifax Healthy Living Partnership, Healthy Living Gym: Qualitative Evaluation Report*. Centre for Applied Psychological Research, University of Huddersfield.

King, N., Melvin, J. and Ashby, J. (2008) *Community Nursing Roles and the Gold Standards Framework for Community Palliative Care*. Report to Macmillan Cancer Support from the Centre for Applied Psychological Research, School of Human and Health Sciences, University of Huddersfield.

King, N., Mirza, M. and Bates, E. (2007) *Paddock Pathways to Health Allotment Project: Qualitative Evaluation Report*. Centre for Applied Psychological Research, School of Human and Health Sciences, University of Huddersfield.

King, N. Roche, T. and Frost, C.D. (2000) Diverse identities, common purpose: Multi-disciplinary clinical supervision in primary care, in *Proceedings of the British Psychological Society Occupational Psychology Conference*. Brighton, 5–7 January. pp. 199–204.

King, N., Thomas, K. and Bell, D. (2003) An out-of-hours protocol for community palliative care: practitioners' perspectives. *International Journal of Palliative Nursing*, 9 (7): 277–82.

King, N. Thomas, K. Martin, N. Bell, D. and Farrell, S. (2005) 'Now nobody falls through the net': Practitioners' perspectives on the Gold Standards Framework for community palliative care. *Palliative Medicine*, 19 (8): 619–27.

Kissling, E.A. (1996) Bleeding out loud: communication about menstruation. *Feminism and Psychology*, 6: 481–504.

Kitzinger, J. (1994) The methodology of focus groups: the importance of interaction between research participants. *Sociology of Health and Illness*, 16 (1): 105–21.

Kivits, J. (2005) Online interviewing and the research relationship, in C. Hine (ed.), *Virtual Methods: Issues in Social Research on the Internet*. Oxford: Berg.

Krueger, R. (1994) *Focus Groups: A Practical Guide for Applied Research*. Thousand Oaks, CA: Sage.

Krueger, R. and Casey, M.A. (2000) *Focus Groups: A Practical Guide for Applied Research* (3rd edition). Thousand Oaks, CA: Sage.

Kvale, S. (1996) *InterViews: An Introduction to Qualitative Research Methods*. London: Sage.

Labov, W. (1972) *Sociolinguistic Patterns*. Philadelphia, PA: University of Pennsylvania Press.

Labov, W. (2001) *Uncovering the Event Structure of Narrative*. Georgetown, VA: Georgetown University Round Table, Georgetown University Press.

Labov, W. and Waletzky, J. (1967) Narrative analysis, in J. Helm (ed.), *Essays on the Verbal and Visual Arts*. Seattle, WA: University of Washington Press. pp. 12–44.

Lacohée, H. and Anderson, B. (2001) Interacting with the telephone, in R. Kraut and A. Mon (eds), *Home Use of Information and Communications Technology*. Special Issue of the *International Journal of Human–Computer Studies*, 54 (5): 665–99.

Langdridge, D. (2004) *Introduction to Research Methods and Data Analysis in Psychology*. Harlow: Pearson Education.

Langdridge, D. (2007) *Phenomenological Psychology: Theory, Research and Method*. Harlow: Pearson Education.

Layder, D. (1998) The reality of social domains: implications for theory and method, in T. May and M. Williams (eds), *Knowing the Social World*. Buckingham: Open University Press. pp. 87–102.

LeCompte, M. and Goetz, J.P. (1982) Problems of reliability and validity in ethnographic research. *Review of Education Research*, 52: 31–60.

Lewis, A. (1992) Group child interviews as a research tool. *British Educational Research Journal*, 18 (4): 413–21.

Lincoln, Y.S. (2004) Trustworthiness criteria, in M. Lewis-Beck, A. Bryman and T. Futing Liao (eds), *Encyclopedia of Research Methods for the Social Sciences*. Thousand Oaks, CA: Sage.

Lincoln, Y.S. and Guba, E.G. (1985) *Naturalistic Inquiry*. Newbury Park, CA: Sage.

Ling, R. (2000) Direct and mediated interaction in the maintenance of social relationships, in A. Sloane and F. van Rijn (eds), *Home Informatics and Telematics: Information, Technology and Society*. Boston, MA: Kluwer.

Livesey, L. (2002) Telling it like it is: understanding adult women's life-long disclosures of childhood sexual abuse, in C. Horrocks, K. Milnes, B. Roberts and D. Robinson (eds), *Narrative, Memory and Life Transitions*. Huddersfield: University of Huddersfield Press. pp. 53–64.

Lyons, E. and Coyle, A. (2007) Appendix 2: Reporting qualitative research, in E. Lyons and A. Coyle, *Analysing Qualitative Data in Psychology*. London: Sage.

Madill, A., Jordan, A. and Shirley, C. (2000) Objectivity and reliability in qualitative analysis: realist, contextualist and radical constructionist epistemologies. *British Journal of Psychology*, 91: 1–20.

Mair, M. (1989) *Between Psychology and Psychotherapy: A Poetics of Experience*. London: Routledge.

Mann, C. and Stewart, F. (2002) Internet interviewing, in J.F. Gubrium and J.A. Holstein (eds), *Handbook of Interview Research: Context and Methods*. Thousand Oaks, CA: Sage.

Markham, A.N. (2004) Internet communication as a tool for qualitative research, in D. Silverman (ed.), *Qualitative Research: Theory, Method and Practice* (2nd edition). London: Sage.

Marshall, C. and Rossman, G.B. (2006) *Designing Qualitative Research* (4th edition). London: Sage.

Mason, J. (1996) *Qualitative Researching*. Thousand Oaks, CA: Sage.

Matthews, E. (2002) *The Philosophy of Merleau-Ponty*. Chesham: Acumen.

Matthews, J. and Cramer, E.P. (2008) Using technology to enhance qualitative research with hidden populations. *The Qualitative Report*, 13 (2): 301–15.

Mattingly, C. (2002) *Healing Dramas and Clinical Plots: The Narrative Structure of Experience*. Cambridge: Cambridge University Press.

Mauthner, M., Birch, M., Jessop J. and Miller, T. (eds) (2002) *Ethics in Qualitative Research*. London: Sage.

May, T. (ed.) (2002) *Qualitative Research in Action*. London: Sage.

Mays, N. and Pope, C. (2000) Assessing quality in qualitative research. *British Medical Journal*, 320: 50–2.

McAdams, D.P. (1985) *Power, Intimacy, and the Life Story: Personological Inquiries into Identity*. New York: Guilford Press.

McAdams, D.P. (1993) *The Stories We Live By: Personal Myths and the Making of the Self*. London: Guilford Press.

McAuliffe, D. (2003) Challenging methodological traditions: research by e-mail. *The Qualitative Report*, 8 (1): 57–69.

McKenna, P.A. and Todd, D.M. (1997) Longitudinal untilization of mental health services: a time-line method, nine retrospective accounts, and a preliminary conceptualization. *Psychotherapy Research*, 7: 383–96.

McKie, L. (2002) Engagement and evaluation in qualitative enquiry, in T. May (ed.), *Qualitative Research in Action*. London: Sage.

McLeod, J. (1997) *Narrative and Psychotherapy*. London: Sage.

McLeod, J. (2001) *Qualitative Research in Counselling and Psychotherapy*. London: Sage.

Meho, L.I. (2006) E-mail interviewing in qualitative research: a methodological discussion. *Journal of the American Society for Information Science and Technology*, 57 (10): 1284–95.

Merton, R.K., Fiske, M. and Kendall, P.L. (1956) *The Focussed Interview: A Report of the Bureau of Applied Social Research*. New York: Columbia University Press.

Michotte, A. (1943/1963) *The Perception of Causality*. Trans. T.R. Miles and E. Miles. London: Methuen.

Miles, M.B. and Huberman, A.M. (1984) *Qualitative Data Analysis: A Sourcebook of New Methods*. Beverly Hills, CA: Sage.

Miles, M.B. and Huberman, A.M. (1994) *Qualitative Data Analysis: An Expanded Sourcebook*. Thousand Oaks, CA: Sage.

Miller, T. (1998) Shifting layers of professional, lay and personal narratives, in J. Ribbens and R. Edwards (eds), *Feminist Dilemmas in Qualitative Research: Public Knowledge and Private Lives*. London: Sage. pp. 58–71.

Mishler, E.G. (1986) *Research Interviewing: Context and Narrative*. Cambridge, MA: Harvard University Press.

Mishler, E.G. (1995) Models of narrative analysis: a typology. *Journal of Narrative and Life History*, 5 (2): 87–123.

Mishler, E.G. (1999) *Storylines: Craftartists' Narratives of Identity*. Cambridge, MA: Harvard University Press.

Moran, D. (2000) *Introduction to Phenomenology*. London: Routledge.

Morgan, D. (1988) *Focus Groups as Qualitative Research*. London: Sage.

Morgan, D. (1997) *Focus Groups as Qualitative Research* (2nd edition). London: Sage.

Morley, J. (1998) The private theater: a phenomenological investigation of daydreaming. *Journal of Phenomenological Psychology*, 29 (1): 116–35.

Moustakas, C. (1994) *Phenomenological Research Methods*. London: Sage.

Murphy, E., Dingwall, R., Greatbatch, D., Parker, S. and Watson, P. (1998) Qualitative research methods in health technology assessment: a review of the literature. *Health Technology Assessment*, 12: 16.

Murray, M. (2003) Narrative psychology, in J.A. Smith (ed.), *Qualitative Psychology: A Practical Guide to Research Methods*. London: Sage. pp. 111–32.

Murray, M. (2008) Narrative psychology, in J.A. Smith (ed.), *Qualitative Psychology: A Practical Guide to Research Methods* (2nd edition). London: Sage.

Nadin, S. and Cassell, C. (2004) Using data matrices, in C. Cassell and G. Symon (eds), *Essential Guide to Qualitative Methods in Organizational Research*. London: Sage.

Nicolson, P. (2003) Reflexivity, 'bias' and the in-depth interview: developing shared meanings, in L. Finlay and B. Gough (eds), *Reflexivity: A Practical Guide for Researchers in Health and Social Sciences*. Oxford: Blackwell Publishing.

Oakley, A. (1981) Interviewing women: a contradiction in terms, in H. Roberts (ed.), *Doing Feminist Research*. London: Routledge and Kegan Paul.

Opdenakker, R. (2006) Advantages and disadvantages of four interview techniques in qualitative research. *Forum: Qualitative Social Research*, 7 (11), Art. 11, www.qualitative-research.net/index.php/fqs/article/view/175/391.

Oxtoby, B., McGuiness, T. and Morgan, R. (2002) Developing organisational change capability. *European Management Journal*, 20 (3): 310–20.

Parker, I. (1999) Critical reflexive humanism and critical constructionist psychology, in D.J. Nightingale and J. Cromby (eds), *Social Constructionist Psychology: A Critical Analysis of Theory and Practice*. Buckingham: Open University Press. pp. 23–36.

Patton, M.Q. (1990) *Qualitative Evaluation and Research Methods* (2nd edition). Newbury Park, CA: Sage.

Payne, S. (2007) Grounded theory, in E. Lyons and A. Coyle (eds), *Analysing Qualitative Data in Psychology*. London: Sage. pp. 65–86.

Pidgeon, N. and Henwood, K. (1997) Using grounded theory in psychological research, in N. Hayes (ed.), *Doing Qualitative Analysis in Psychology*. Hove: Psychology Press.

Poland, B.D. (2002) Transcription quality, in J.F. Gubrium and J.A. Holstein (eds), *Handbook of Interview Research: Context and Method*. Thousand Oaks, CA: Sage.

Polkinghorne, D.E. (1995) Narrative configuration in qualitative analysis, in J. Amos Hatch and R. Wisniewski (eds), *Life History and Narrative*. London: The Falmer Press. pp. 5–24.

Polkinghorne, D.E. (1996) Narrative knowing and the study of lives, in J.E. Birren, G.M. Kenyon, J. Ruth, J.J.F. Schroots and T. Svensson (eds), *Aging and Biography: Explorations in Adult Development*. New York: Springer. pp. 77–98.

Pope, C., Ziebland, S. and Mays, N. (2000) Qualitative research in healthcare: analysing qualitative data. *British Medical Journal*, 320: 114–16.

Porter, E. (1999) *Feminist Perspectives on Ethics*. Harlow: Person Education.

Pretto, G. and Pocknee, C. (2008) *Online project collaboration ... We Still Have a Long Way To Go*. Melbourne: Australasian Society for Computers in Learning in Tertiary Education (ascilite).

Ramazonoğlu, C., with Holland, J. (2002) *Feminist Methodology: Challenges and Choices*. London: Sage.

Ramos, M.C. (1989) Some ethical implications of qualitative research. *Research in Nursing and Health*, 12: 57–63.

Reason, P. (2003) Cooperative inquiry, in J.A. Smith (ed.), *Qualitiative Psychology: A Practical Guide to Research Methods*. London: Sage. pp. 205–31.

Reason, P. and Bradbury, H. (2001) Preface, in P. Reason and H. Bradbury (eds), *Handbook of Action Research: Participative Inquiry and Practice*. London: Sage. pp. 1–14.

Reicher, S. (2000) Against methodolatry: some comments on Elliott, Fisher and Rennie. *British Journal of Clinical Psychology*, 39: 1–6.

Reinharz, S. (1997) Who am I? The need for a variety of selves in the field, in R. Hertz (ed.), *Reflexivity and Voice*. Thousand Oaks, CA: Sage.

Rice, R.E. and Love, G. (1987) Electronic emotion: socioemotional content in a computer-mediated network. *Communication Research*, 14 (2): 85–108.

Riessman, C.K. (1993) *Narrative Analysis*. Newbury Park, CA: Sage.

Riessman, C.K. (2000) 'Even if we don't have children [we] can live': stigma and infertility in South India, in C. Mattingly and L. Garro (eds), *Narratives and the Cultural Construction of Illness and Healing*. Berkeley, CA: University of California Press. pp. 128–52.

Riessman, C.K. (2004) A thrice-told tale: new readings of an old story, in. B. Hurwitz, T. Greenhalgh and V. Skultans (eds), *Narrative Research in Health and Illness*. Malden, MA: Blackwell. pp. 309–24.

Riessman, C.K. (2005) Narrative analysis, in N. Kelly, C. Horrocks, K. Milnes, B. Roberts and D. Robinson (eds), *Narrative, Memory and Everyday Life*. Huddersfeild: University of Huddersfield, Press. pp. 1–8.

Ricœur, P. (1984) *Time and Narrative* (Vol. 1). Trans. K. McLaughlin and D. Pellauer. Chicago: University of Chicago Press.

Robson, C. (2002) *Real World Research* (2nd edition). Oxford: Blackwell.

Rorty, R. (1979) *Philosophy and the Mirror of Nature*. Princeton, NJ: Princeton University Press.

Rose, N. (1998) *Inventing Our Selves: Psychology, Power and Personhood*. Cambridge: Cambridge University Press.

Rosenblatt, P.C. (2000) Ethics in qualitative interviewing in grieving families, in A. Memon and R. Bull (eds), *Handbook of the Psychology of Interviewing*. Chichester: Wiley. pp. 197–212.

Ross, A. (2005) Professional identities, inter-professional relationships and collaborative working: an investigation using a constructivist phenomenological approach. Unpublished PhD thesis, University of Huddersfield.

Ross, A., King, N. and Firth, J. (2005) Interprofessional relationships and collaborative working: encouraging reflective practice. *Online Journal of Issues in Nursing*, 10 (1), Art. 3, www.nursingworld.org/ojin/topic26/tpc26_3.htm (accessed 04/12/09).

Rubin, H.J. and Rubin, I.S. (1995) *Qualitative Interviewing: The Art of Hearing Data*. Thousand Oaks, CA: Sage.

Salmon, P. (1994) Grids are all very well, but.... *European Personal Construct Association Newsletter*.

Salmon, P. (2003) A psychology for teachers, in F. Fransella (ed.), *International Handbook of Personal Construct Psychology*. Chichester: Wiley.

Salmon, P. and Claire, H. (1984) *Classroom Collaboration*. London: Routledge and Kegan Paul.

Sarbin, T.R. (ed.) (1986) *Narrative Psychology: The Storied Nature of Human Conduct*. New York: Praeger.

Schütz, A. (1962) *Collected Papers* (Vol. 1). Den Haag: Martin Nijhoff. Cited in U. Flick (1998) *An Introduction to Qualitative Research*. London: Sage.

Scott, D. and Morrison, M. (2006) *Key Ideas in Educational Research*. London: Continuum International Publishing Group.

Seale, C. (1999) *The Quality of Qualitative Research*. London: Sage.

Shaw, I. (1999) *Introducing Qualitative Methods: Qualitative Evaluation*. London: Sage.

Shotter, J. (1993) *Conversational Realities*. London: Sage.

Shuy, R. (2002) In-person versus telephone interviewing, in J.F. Gubrium and J.A. Holstein (eds), *Handbook of Interview Research: Context and Method*. Thousand Oaks, CA: Sage.

Silverman, D. (1993) *Interpreting Qualitative Data: Methods for Analysing Talk, Text and Interaction*. London: Sage.

Simons, H. (1984) Negotiating conditions for independent evaluations, in C. Adelman (ed.), *The Politics and Ethics of Evaluation*. London: Croom Helm. pp. 56–68.

Smith, G. and Wales, C. (2000) Citizen juries and deliberative democracy. *Political Studies*, 48: 51–65.

Smith, J. (1984) The problem of criteria for judging interpretative inquiry. *Educational Evaluation and Policy Analysis*, 6: 379–91.

Smith, J.A. (1996) Beyond the divide between cognition and discourse: using interpretative phenomenology in health psychology. *Psychology and Health*, 11: 261–71.

Smith, J.A. and Osborn, M. (2007) Pain as an assault on the self: an interpretative phenomenological analysis. *Psychology and Health*, 22: 517–24.

Smith, J.A. and Osborn, M. (2008) Interpretative phenomenological analysis, in J.A. Smith (ed.), *Qualitative Psychology: A Practical Guide to Research Methods* (2nd edition). London: Sage.

Smoreda, Z. and Licoppe, C. (2000) Gender-specific use of the domestic telephone. *Social Psychology Quarterly*, 63 (3): 238–52.

Spinelli, E. (2005) *The Interpreted World: An Introduction to Phenomenological Psychology* (2nd edition). London: Sage.

Steier, F. (ed.) (1991) *Research and Reflexivity*. London: Sage.

Stewart, D.W., Shamdasani, P.N. and Rook, D.W. (2007) *Focus Groups: Theory and Practice*. London: Sage.

Stewart, K. and Williams, M. (2005) Researching online populations: the use of online focus groups for social research. *Qualitative Research*, 5 (4): 395–416.

Stieger, S. and Göritz, A.S. (2006) Using instant messaging for internet-based interviews. *CyberPsychology and Behavior*, 9 (5): 552–9.

Strike, K. (1972) Explaining and understanding: the impact of science on our concept of man, in L.G. Thomas (ed.), *Philosophical Redirection of Educational Research: The Seventy-first Yearbook of the National Society for the Study of Education*. Chicago: University of Chicago Press.

Sumsion, J. (2002) Re-reading metaphors as cultural texts: a case study of early childhood teacher attrition. *The Australian Educational Researcher*, 30 (3): 67–87.

Taylor, C. (1991) *The Ethics of Authenticity*. Cambridge, MA: Harvard University Press.

Tuffin, K. (2005) *Understanding Critical Social Psychology*. London: Sage.

Umoquit, M.J., Dobrow, M.J., Lemieux-Charles, L., Ritvo, P.G., Urbach, D.R. and Wodchis, W. (2008) The efficiency and effectiveness of utilizing diagrams in interviews: an assessment of participatory diagramming and graphic elicitation. *BMC Medical Research Methodology*, 8 (53), Available at: www.biomedcentral.com/1471-2288/8/53 (accessed 22/08/08).

Van Manen, M. (1990) *Researching Lived Experience: Human Science for an Action-centred Pedagogy*. Albany, NY: SUNY Press.

Voida, A., Mynatt, E.D., Erickson, T. and Kellogg, W.A. (2004) Interviewing over instant messaging. *Extended Abstracts of CHI 2004 Conference on Human Factors in Computing Systems, Vienna, Austria*, 1344–47. New York: ACM.

Wakeford, T., Murtuja, J. and Bryant, P. (2004) *Using Democratic Spaces to Promote Social Justice in Northern Towns*. University of Newcastle: Institute of Policy and Practice (IPP).

Walters, G. (2006) A meta-analysis of the gene-crime relationship. *Criminology*, 30 (4): 595–614.

Warren, C.A.B. (2002) Qualitative interviewing, in J.F. Gubrium and J.A. Holstein (eds), *Handbook of Interview Research: Context and Method*. Thousand Oaks, CA: Sage.

Waskul, D. and Douglass, M. (1996) Considering the electronic participant: some polemical observations on the ethics of online research. *The Information Society*, 12 (2): 129–39.

Wengraf, T. (2001) *Qualitative Research Interviewing: Biographic Narrative and Semi-Structured Method*. London: Sage.

Wilkinson, S. (1988) The role of reflexivity in feminist psychology. *Women's Studies International Forum*, 11: 493–502.

Wilkinson, S. (2003) Focus groups, in J.A. Smith (ed.), *Qualitative Psychology: A Practical Guide to Research Methods*. London: Sage. pp. 184–204.

Wilkinson, S. (2004) Focus group research, in D. Silverman (ed.), *Qualitative Research: Theory, Mind and Practice*. London: Sage. pp. 177–99.

Williams, M. (1998) The social world as knowable, in T. May and M. Williams (eds), *Knowing the Social World*. Buckingham: Open University Press.

Williams, M. (2002) Generalization in interpretative research, in T. May (ed.), *Qualitative Research in Action*. London: Sage.

Willig, C. (ed.) (1999a) *Applied Discourse Analysis: Social and Psychological Interventions*. Buckingham: Open University Press.

Willig, C. (1999b) Conclusions: opportunities and limitations of 'applied discourse analysis', in C. Willig (ed.), *Applied Discourse Analysis: Social and Psychological Interventions*. Buckingham: Open University Press. pp. 145–60.

Willig, C. (2001) *Introducing Qualitative Research in Psychology*. Buckingham: Open University Press.

Willig, C. (2008) *Introducing Qualitative Research in Psychology: Adventures in Theory and Method* (2nd edition). Buckingham: Open University Press.

Wilson, J.L. (1999) Nostalgic narratives: an exploration of black nostalgia for the 1950s. *Narrative Inquiry*, 9 (2): 303–25.

Wilson, K. and Roe, B. (1998) Interviewing older people by telephone following initial contact by postal survey. *Journal of Advanced Nursing*, 27: 575–81.

Worth, A. and Tierney, A. (1993) Conducting research interviews with elderly people by telephone. *Journal of Advanced Nursing*, 18: 1077–84.

Index

This index is in word-by-word order. Page references in *italics* indicate boxes, those in **bold** indicate tables, and those in ***bold italics*** indicate figures.